Globalization and Insecurity

GLOBALIZATION AND INSECURITY

Political, Economic and Physical Challenges

Edited by

Barbara Harriss-White

palgrave

First published 2002 by
PALGRAVE
Houndmills, Basingstoke, Hampshire RG21 6XS and
175 Fifth Avenue, New York, N. Y. 10010
Companies and representatives throughout the world

PALGRAVE is the new global academic imprint of
St. Martin's Press LLC Scholarly and Reference Division and
Palgrave Publishers Ltd (formerly Macmillan Press Ltd).

ISBN 0–333–96354–7 hardback

This book is printed on paper suitable for recycling and
made from fully managed and sustained forest sources.

A catalogue record for this book is available
from the British Library.

Library of Congress Cataloging-in-Publication Data

Globalization and insecurity: political, economic, and physical challenges/
edited by Barbara Harriss-White.
     p. cm.
   Includes bibliographical references and index.
   ISBN 0–333–96354–7
   1. Globalization. 2. Security, International. I. Harriss-White, Barbara,
1946–

JZ1318.G577 2001
327–dc21

                                                    2001034807

10   9   8   7   6   5   4   3   2   1

11   10   09   08   07   06   05   04   03   02

Printed and bound in Great Britain by
Antony Rowe Ltd, Chippenham, Wiltshire

Dedicated to the memory of Gordon White, 1942–98

Contents

List of Tables

Acknowledgements

This book is the outcome of the 1999 Wolfson College (Oxford) lecture series, 'Globalization and Insecurity'. I am very grateful to all the lecturers, including Professor David Held (whose lecture 'Regulating Globalization? The Reinvention of Politics', has been published in *International Sociology*, vol 15, no. 2, 2000) for their participation, to Professors Gosta Esping-Andersen and Colin Leys for supplementing this project later on and further to Colin Leys for his useful suggestions for editing. Zed Press has kindly given permission to include Wolfgang Sachs' chapter from his *Planet Dialectics* and Verso is publishing *Market-driven Politics*, from chapter 1 of which some of Colin Leys' contribution to this volume is drawn. I wish to record my thanks to the Academic Policy Committee for Wolfson College's intellectual and financial support, to Wolfson's then President, Sir David Smith, for chairing the series and to Jan Scriven for her help in its organization. Thanks also to Kaveri Harriss and her team of student readers, to Ailsa Thom and to Maria Moreno, who helped prepare the typescript with their customary goodwill, and to Jo North at Palgrave.

Notes on the Contributors

Samir Amin is Professor of Economics and Director of the Third World Forum's Africa Office in Dakar, Senegal.

Ian Brownlie CBE, QC, FBA is Emeritus Chichele Professor of Public International Law, Oxford University; a Member of the English Bar; and a Member of the International Law Commission of the United Nations.

Robin Cohen is Professor of Sociology at the University of Warwick, UK, and Dean of Humanities at Cape Town University, South Africa.

Gosta Esping-Andersen is Professor of Political Science at the Universidad Pompeu Fabra, Barcelona, Spain.

Valpy FitzGerald is a Professorial Fellow of St Antony's College and Director of the Finance and Trade Policy Research Centre at Queen Elizabeth House, Oxford University, UK.

Barbara Harriss-White is Professor of Development Studies at Queen Elizabeth House, and a Fellow of Wolfson College, Oxford University, UK.

John Kay FBA is a Fellow of St John's College, Oxford; founder of London Economics; ex-Director of the Said Business School, Oxford University; and a freelance consultant and writer on business.

Colin Leys is Emeritus Professor of Politics at Queens University, Kingston, Canada and co-editor of the *Socialist Register*.

Wolfgang Sachs is a Senior Research Fellow at the Wuppertal Institute for Climate, Environment and Energy and Chair of Greenpeace in Germany.

Susan Willett is Director of the Cost of Disarmament Programme at the United Nations Institute for Disarmament Research in Geneva, Switzerland.

1

Globalization, Insecurities and Responses: an Introductory Essay

Barbara Harriss-White

Defining terms and scope

The word 'globalization' is not received English. Until recently, if it was typed into word processors, it was challenged by the spellcheck software which has itself been part of the vanguard of this process. The word is both overused and underspecified.

By globalization is generally meant the worldwide integration of markets. This is a process requiring the integration of national economies and the 'loss of nationality' of firms, products and managers.[1] It is a process enormously aided by the revolution in telecommunications and the elimination of informational lags and delays. Since the Uruguay Round of the General Agreement on Tariffs and Trade which ended in 1993, the markets for most legal goods have been formally integrated, with the notable exceptions of agricultural products and oil. Yet there are distinctive differences in the extent of global integration. Financial flows have become global, as have the very meagre trickles of development aid. Services are still sticky, since deregulation requires changes in the regulatory system of each country. Law, accountancy and management consultancy firms are globalizing rapidly in response to the variety in the regulative environments faced by manufacturing and finance capital. Labour, of course, is highly selectively globalized. What Ignacio Ramonet has called the 'planetary cosmocracy' moves with greatest freedom not only as workers but also, as consumers of the physical and cultural world, as tourists. For the most part labour is completely unfree to move, confronting ever *rising* barriers to economic – let alone forced – migration.

Orthodox evaluations of globalization tend to be positive. They stress the value of the integration of diverse economies into one, the vastly

1

expanding productive capacity of globalized agriculture and industry and the increasing well-being that flows from it, the prospect of eradicating poverty, the creation of new kinds of commodities, new economies of signs and symbols,[2] new kinds of regions, the liberating capacity of communications technology to condense time and space, new forms of emancipating international relations, new politics of identity and rights, and last but not least, under the theory of democratic peace,[3] the twinned globalization of democracy and capital. By making war both unlikely and unprofitable, it is argued, our era of globalization is capable of bringing an end to it. (Towards the end of the century there was indeed a dramatic fall in the international demand for weapons systems.)[4] Above all, the market is seen as a neutral form of rationality on which to base social organisation, replacing and reworking those based on forms of 'received authority'.[5] 'The market is expected to produce greater prosperity for all, even at the world level.' 'Nations and cultures have the potential for co-operation without the domination of war.' 'Markets make it possible for the separation of the economy from the political and cultural spheres of existence.'[6]

But, though the markets which are being globalized are indeed economic phenomena, the globalization of market exchange is neither a natural evolutionary process, nor an economic project but a political one, with roots going back to the early 1970s. It is a project of states, which have taken, or been forced to take, deliberate action to support global capital. The very idea that the economy can or must be separated from the political sphere is part of the ideological underpinning of globalization. It exacerbates the insecurities traced in this book.

Though the reach of markets may be global, the process of globalization is extremely – even increasingly – regionally uneven. Though wealth is being accumulated as never before, it is unprecedentedly concentrated and unequal. The global technological base itself is based on centuries of intellectual achievement in the transformation of uncertainty into risk and in the assessment and prediction of risk.[7] But this technological base itself creates not only new risks (whose probabilities can be computed) but also new uncertainties (which cannot). Globalization both reinforces old forms of insecurity and creates new ones of a magnitude, complexity and urgency never encountered before in the history of humanity. While no societies can escape, some create and some bear more insecurities than others. They do so at different scales and in asymmetrical ways.[8]

In 1999, Wolfson College, Oxford, invited a group of scholars to address two aspects of globalization in its annual public lecture series. The first was the manner in which specific components of the global system produce insecurities, what kind and to whom. The second was the actual and ideal responses to them. This was an ambitious project for three reasons. First, a range of disciplines and of paradigms within disciplines inform the analyses.[9] Second, the impact of globalization is specific and local as well as general and global – it depends on a rich diversity of micro-economic and decentralized political foundations. Third, the project is both historical and normative. At the heart of this enquiry is an issue long predating the current era of globalization. It concerns how the state and the market – or politics and economics – can be the repositories of regulative and social order. But listeners rapidly realized that this was also a whistle-blowing exercise, as one after the other, the contributors (who had not heard one another's talks) revealed the inadequacies of existing attempts to respond, regulate or protect and explained the unstable consequences, more often than not unintended, of regulative and protective activity. With two exceptions, this is a set of highly critical audits. Most are disturbing and some, of whose sobriety there can be no doubt, are frankly alarming. However, it is also a set which counters the frequent dismissal of critical analysis as being without a (realistic) constructive project.

The word 'insecurity' refers to that which is unsafe and/or unreliable. It is a cruder concept than risk or uncertainty. Four dimensions of it will be elaborated in this book: (i) physical insecurity – threats to persons, property and our environments; (ii) threats to the economic and political autonomy of states; (iii) instability, particularly of markets; (iv) vulnerability – a susceptibility to damage, closely but not completely aligned with poverty and inequality. But the separation of these dimensions, while necessary for analytical purposes, draws attention away from their interrelationships. These will be explored here.

What are the categories through which to discuss the global creation and bearing of insecurity? They are contested. There is no consensus on how to understand the generation and bearing of insecurities. A scaled range of categories used by contributors will structure this introduction: the world, institutions of global governance, regions of the world (the Organization for Economic Co-operation and Development (*OECD*); the triad: North America, Europe and Japan; the first division of industrializing developing countries; regions unable to industrialise[10]), states, capital, markets, firms and multinational corporations (MNCs), labour, classes of vulnerable people (the 'third world', the poor, the old, the young, unskilled labour, single parent families, finally – and in these accounts residually – 'women'[11]). One category is significantly and provocatively *absent* from most of the reports in this book. This is 'international civil society', the growing set of (inter)networks of non-governmental organisations (NGOs), pressure groups and new social movements which claim a growing influence in the politics of economic regulation as well as political and social rights, justice and environmental responsibility, and to which a growing deference is paid in the post-Washington consensus.[12] Most of our contributors have not needed to introduce them in order to explain either the generation of insecurity or responses to it.[13] The notable exceptions concern social responses to environmental threats and responses to threats to its security by organized labour.[14] There is, of course, another category of organizations of civil society: those which collectively regulate markets under varying conditions of state control or passive complicity, a category of business networks and associations, market committees and international regulatory bodies. Markets (competitive or otherwise) do not function without such collective action. They are studiously neglected in the literature celebrating NGOs and the globalizing role of civil society but they are crucial to outcomes of the real politics of global markets.[15]

This introduction has two parts. In the first, the major themes covered in the rest of the book will be introduced, not seriatim, but woven together in a discussion of the contributors' insights into the means by which specific aspects of globalization generate insecurity, the kinds of insecurities created and the actual (and sometimes the possible) responses of the people and institutions threatened by insecurity. The focus will be on processes rather than on data. However, for the most part (Willett is an exception) the processes and phenomena described are formal and legal. In the second part I will go beyond the scope of the contributions to examine another kind of globalization proceeding apace. This involves both informal and unregistered activity, such as small and clustered industrial firms in the third world and cross-border trade on the one hand, and illegal activity and illegal goods on the other – exemplified by the global trade in illegal arms and drugs. This global underside may be unruly but much of it is ordered and regulated by means *other* than by states. This 'globalized informality' also creates insecurities and those in turn provoke social responses. It is also linked to formal globalization in ways which may reinforce 'formal' insecurities. The globalizing informal economy is much more neglected in research.[16]

Globalization as a political process

Although the word is new, globalization is nothing new. The major powers of the world have been globally interconnected for more than a millennium and Samir Amin provides us with a list of eras. More than one writer sees parallels to the contemporary era in the vivid descriptions of globalization supplied by Marx and Engels in the *Communist Manifesto* of 1848. Indeed, Robin Cohen bounces his analysis of labour off their account. The different kinds of capital have been globalizing in separate ways. Transnational capital has been expanding systematically for over a century. The newest and most engulfing wave of globalization is the response of a set of unique historical events. In the 1970s the US and the UK governments made a response to declining domestic competitiveness, to their balance of payments deficits (exacerbated by the flexed muscles of the OPEC cartel) and to the defensive restiveness of organized labour in response to the crisis of Keynesian welfare systems and of Fordist production systems (see Colin Leys, this volume and 2001). In this project, capital would be freed to expand worldwide. In so doing, competition would be intensified, labour challenged from without and the balance of payments deficit compensated for by financial flows.

Valpy FitzGerald describes the response of finance – an explosion in differentiated financial products, many intended to hedge financial risks and deal in future expectations, a massive concentration of ownership with the most comprehensive global spread of any sector. John Kay describes the response of manufacturing: two trends, one relying on economies of scale and global sourcing and the other on flexible specialization, networks, subcontracting and industrial clusters and both resulting as he sees it in the deconcentration of economic power within sectors of the global economy. In terms of global aggregates, however, ownership has undoubtedly become more concentrated. In the 100 top global economic units there are 53 states and 47 companies. Only 20 countries have GDPs larger than the gross output of the biggest MNC.[17]

Over the last thirty years, as this happened, the main forces reproducing globalization have shifted away from industry (and weapons) and towards technology, information and communications, and the financial means of control of everything else (see Amin's and Leys' analyses in this volume). Some states chose globalization and the rest have had it thrust upon them. In the process, while some states were bludgeoned by conditions attached to international debt into deregulating their economies in ways which have had highly differentiating effects on production and welfare,[18] the Newly Industrialising Countries of Asia (NICs) completed in 40 years a transformation in average wealth, income and well-being which European countries had taken two or three centuries to achieve and which has led commentators to argue for a *pluricentred* global order.[19] Certainly there are three regional capitals of finance, the most globalized sector of all: New York, London and Tokyo. But this apparent pluricentrality poorly disguises the global political hegemony of the US government.

What form does US political hegemony take? At the ideological level, it operates through appeals to liberal democracy as being superior to other forms of political organization, appeals backed materially by conditions attached to loans from the IMF and UN economic institutions, which are dominated by US interests. By these means, non-liberal states are levered into the 'liberal' world order. But their reforms of 'governance' do little to alter undemocratic power relations. These reforms are not necessarily applied in the USA itself, or are practised there with direly disruptive social consequences. A quarter of the world's prison population, two million people, is in the USA. There, some 43 million people are excluded from health care.[20] Nor is the USA enabling the world's most economically powerful states to establish a regulative framework for global capital. Quite the reverse. Corporate taxes fall as a percentage of total taxes globally yet the undemocratic influence of corporations on global governance increases.[21]

How does the political project create insecurity? By at least three means.

First through *poverty*. Poverty and vulnerability result from the operation of a dual set of contradictions. First, in the spheres of political ideas, laws and institutions there is a mismatch between the abstract market principles of private property, 'free' enterprise and equality before the law, and the principles of 'low intensity' forms of modern democracy through which markets are held accountable to the societies in which they function. In low-intensity democracies, businesses are not easily prevented from exercising power outside the reach of electoral accountability. The second contradiction parallels the first in the sphere of the economy. On the one hand there is the actual practice of market regulation (by local states and through a thick mesh of social institutions in which markets are embedded, according to balances of various kinds of power and authority). Social, rather than legal, forms of regulation carry obligations and rights which are exclusive and not general. On the other hand, in the open-ended and unruly deepening of democratic kinds of politics, entire sections of society (deprived of rights at work or to social security) are excluded from participation and power. Both Amin and Susan Willett argue forcefully that the working out of these two contradictions has led to increasing inequality and vulnerability. Such outcomes are not a matter of either contingency or lags but a part of the intrinsic dynamics of global capital. They are much exacerbated by the immobility and segmentation of labour markets, by the creation of labour reserves and the common suppression of the right of labour to organize in countries receiving foreign direct investment.[22]

Dwindling redistributive flows of aid testify to the unimportance of routine poverty to the global economic and political order (the official aim of the United Nations to halve poverty by 2015 notwithstanding). As Willett notes, this intransigent poverty has been blamed famously, by the World Bank,[23] on the internal characteristics of states rather than on the failure or inappropriateness of neoliberal policies (including the Bank's own aid) or the self-interest of the global managerial class (also known as the 'technocracy' or the 'policy elites'), or on the impact on developing countries of transnational capital. When developing states with fragile institutional architectures deregulate, their weak capacity to protect poor people weakens yet more. Many kinds of further instability result. These are listed by Willett: intensified poverty and social unrest, forced migration within state boundaries, flows of refugees across frontiers, robbery and armed conflict.

Second, globalization creates insecurity through the *regulation of wealth*. This works through the politics of markets. How? One explanation is that the regulatory order supplied by states is *threatened* by the global institutions (the IMF, World Bank and the World Trade Organization), which have in turn been subverted to support global capital: international financial capital, multinational corporations.[24] These are argued to have imposed an agenda impervious to electoral democracy. They also impose sanctions on deviant national projects. The agenda is often found to be technocratized and '*de*politicized' through the anodyne terms of its discourse and the manner of its imposition, a conclusion strongly disputed by the contributors to this book who see both discourse and agenda as a distinctive trait of market-driven politics. On this latter interpretation, even development assistance (which has declined in both absolute and relative terms) and NGOs (which bypass formal channels of diplomacy and international relations and may begin to disenfranchise the governments of developing countries) have been subordinated to this project.[25]

Yet a hierarchy of national and international regulative institutions is necessary to provide the essential public goods no longer provided by

national states or by multinational corporations (MNCs).[26] Leys shows
how inadequately this is done at present and how this inadequacy
threatens security. Procedures with 'teeth' are confined to the functions
most important to capital (the management of global communication
and common standards), while the settlement of disputes, the representation of the interests of labour, the stabilization of markets and the
regulation and management of adverse environmental externalities are
poorly addressed.

Procedures linking trade with employment are conspicuous by their
absence.[27] As yet there is no process by which a technical agenda on a
subject apparently as straightforward as the incorporation of labour
standards into trade agreements can be established transparently and
accountably within the World Trade Organization, let alone one by
which the issues can be debated and the institutional architecture for
implementing and enforcing decisions set in place.[28] The WTO is itself
an unruly political arena in which the advanced countries tend to
realign themselves issue by issue, in which compliance is practised,
imposed, delayed and violated asymmetrically and one in which the
developing countries (the G77) are split on most issues and tend to make
unilateral concessions without mutual agreement with each other. Or to
bypass it altogether by solving trade disputes politically. If *thinking* can
help the reform of institutions of global governance, there is at the time
of writing a vast, fermenting vat of normative, managerialist and idealist
literature to go on. It is too early to know whether the unruly coalition
of NGO, environmental and development movements represent social
forces able to give political body to some of these policy proposals.

A third way in which globalization creates insecurity is through *the
reworking of national politics*. The global economic project, driven by
ever-increasing surpluses, is argued to pit itself against the political
project of nation-states in a host of ways. It is generally agreed that a
loss of national autonomy results. 'The global integration of commodity
and capital markets severely reduces the policy options of the nation-
state, disrupts the process of building institutions that govern... the
national economy and weakens the state's capacity to intermediate.'
The economic interdependence of telecommunications and the media
leads to a reduction in 'national interests and sovereignty'.[29] 'The state
is an unnatural and even dysfunctional unit for managing economic
interests in a borderless world.'[30] Regulatory competition will result in a
'race to the bottom' in which a competitive dilution of standards will
rob the OECD 'triad' of the gains (in pay, health, safety, working conditions, social protection and rights to association) made by its labour

movements. Yet there are two counter-arguments each of which finds some empirical justification. First, a 'convergence' theory which sees the regulation of both capital and labour becoming increasingly uniform through the major *regional* blocs, leaving inter-regional differences intact. Second, by contrast, it is argued that capital thrives not only by sourcing at least cost but also by the exploitation of *'regulative loopholes'*. On the latter, opinion is again divided between those who see existing loopholes as transitory, as evidence of the unevenness of political convergence, and others who argue that differences in regulative regimes are structural and, further, that they are necessary to capital which globalizes precisely to take advantage of them.

Leys (this volume and 2001) argues that the three circuits of global capital require *specific* political-environmental conditions. First, all aspects of national policy are combined by finance capital in evaluations of risk. For these, policies bearing on productivity, on wages and on political stability are crunched into single indicators of creditworthiness. Second, foreign direct investment (FDI) in manufacturing plays off tax regimes against subsidies, laws on the health and safety of workers, the price of labour, environmental regulation and the standard of infrastructure. States may compete for this kind of capital at the margins. But once established, FDI exerts direct pressure on national politics. Comparatively little is known about this undemocratic politics which churns in the guts of formally democratic states. By contrast the interests of the third circuit, mercantile capital, in its own freedom to trade, are in perpetual tension with the selective non-tariff protection of labour, of domestic regulations protecting public safety and of social values. Each state has an interest in liberalizing its exports unilaterally. Leys concludes that there is no convincing evidence for a general trend in the reworking of politics. Although the 'loss of options' means a weeding out of diversity in technical policy-making (and a closer consensual binding of national policy elites) it certainly does not mean an *abandonment* of national politics.

The core of the triad is relatively secure. There, the laws protecting terms and conditions of work are being dismantled piecemeal, evaded and pre-empted. The periphery bears the brunt of the insecurities thrown up by both the globalization of the politics of markets and by national political responses to the global economy. Outside the comparative security of the triad and the first division of industrializing nations, a growing number of states is beset by inter-ethnic rivalry (see Willett) and inter-state rivalries (see Ian Brownlie's chapter), yet others by 'spiralling economic crises' (detailed by Amin and by FitzGerald). On the periphery the most insecure are landless unskilled labour, those who are dependent (the young and old) and those responsible for them (women). The global project of catch-up announced by Truman in 1947 has comprehensively failed. The numbers of poor people living on less than a dollar a day increase (even if their proportion declines) and the polarization of incomes and wealth accelerates. The average income differentials between richest and poorest countries which stood at 36 to 1 in the 1950s and 70 to 1 in the 1970s are now 250 to 1[31]

Reacting to this inequality, what Willett terms a 'sprinkling' of groups representing disadvantaged and vulnerable people now reaches out over global communications networks and with local acts of protest to denounce and reject the very idea of 'development'.[32] Some of these movements call for a celebration of the essential value of cultural diversity and 'subsistence' (paradoxically upon occasion the subsistence of peoples with hundreds of years of history of cultural mixing and who themselves may make use of the latest information technology). Others offer more targeted political resistance to environmentally destructive forms of development (particularly dams and timber extraction) while advocating another kind of development in the shape of food security, health, education and infrastructure – all of which require state intervention, a tax base and a process of surplus generation.

Leys sets out to analyse the response to the subordination of national politics to the market, the new forms of global market politics and new forms of national politics. He shows how deliberate political choices have been made to maximize economic growth, abandon controls over finance capital, consolidate and stabilize a regime regulating workers, social security and capital (and loading non-tariff policies with the burden of protecting the national economy) in order to secure national creditworthiness.

Neither Amin nor Leys flinches from outlining an alternative project of political resistance which would empower the casualties of this kind of accommodative political response. Chief among these are full employment, the regulation of markets to increase productive investment, the deepening of democracy around an agenda of secure rights to employment, food security, education, health and social security and the creation of new political institutions at national, regional and global scales. Yet at present non-tariff politics and general procrastination thwart national efforts in this direction. Global governance would require the co-operation of the largest states and MNCs. At present the G7 group is resisting enlargement to G20, to which it has in theory acquiesced. The largest state of all acts as a frankly interested hegemon rather than an altruistic facilitator and thus provokes a politics of reaction.

The politics of capital and the environment

Wolfgang Sachs' argument is straightforward and devastating. The main distinction between nineteenth-century globalization and the current era is that the earth can no longer be free-ridden. It is a finite resource. The technologies driving globalization are creating a global tragedy of the commons under the aegis of private property rights. Furthermore the entire system is driven by a manipulated appetite for consumption on which there is no foreseeable brake. Gains in the environmental efficiency of global capital have so far been made disproportionately at the expense of the natural resource endowment of the *developing* world.

There are two kinds of response to global environmental insecurity: reform the system or do away with it. None of the writers here – including Sachs – has proposed the latter. Reforming the system may make it serve capital better, or pave the way for a less self-defeating way of organizing the world. Under scrutiny, these clear alternatives are found to be composed of hornets' nests of conflicting principles, policies, politics, institutions and unknowable factors. But, for Sachs, mere complexity must not be a deterrent. He sees two elements of a feasible social and political response: drops in consumption by affluent people and a redistribution of tax burdens away from employment and onto the use of energy where the fastest growing sector is air transport.

Global physical security and public order

Susan Willett argues that the globalization of information, technology, finance and manufacturing is undermining the legitimacy of states, especially in the eyes of those excluded from the process, with two consequences. The first is that poor and marginalized people are increasingly emboldened to protest about their conditions – against the states concerned. The second is that, since the regulative power of such states is declining, warlords, mafias and mercenary groups, many of which have an interest in the perpetuation of conflicts, are filling the gap. At another scale altogether, globalized weapons systems and the selective proliferation of nuclear weapons, in defiance of the exclusive set of signatories to non-proliferation treaties (now exposed as toothless), increase the risk of detonation as small states with unstable governments and active zones of conflict acquire the technological capacity to wage nuclear war.[33] Willett describes a global arms market which is increasingly permissive and unregulated – particularly the market in small arms. Although multilateral regulation is the more urgently needed, the establishment of common standards among states with divergent interests could only be achieved at a level which is ineffective. She is driven to conclude that conflicts will not be resolved until the underlying inequitable preconditions are addressed.

Ian Brownlie explains the legal system which regulates global security. This has five elements, all of long standing and owing nothing to the new era of globalization: non-proliferation (dealt with above), the Charter of the UN, the humanitarian law of armed conflict, information and surveillance, and weapons. What is new is open recognition that there is in fact no system. (The enforcement of the UN's Charter depends on solidarity in the Security Council. The latter is contingent on politics, not law. The enforcement of human rights and humanitarian laws of armed conflict is not based in the UN but in regional organizations, and the record on rights such as that of minorities to secede has been inconsistent. UN surveillance has functioned as a threat to peace as well as monitoring threats to peace and information has confused causes and effects of strife. Weapons are globalized in a way which makes them not directly accessible to the Security Council which has formal control over global security threats.) Nor is there a pattern detectable over time in the types of dispute between states, nor a pattern in those disputes that are peacefully rather than forcefully settled, nor is it possible to predict which one of five means of non-violent settlement might be used in the peaceful resolution of international conflicts. The formal UN system can only be activated by consenting states. Negotiation, mediation and conciliation are practised *ad hoc* with means ranging from 'multiple acts of individual recognition' to recourse to the International Court of Justice. The latter has successfully resolved 73 disputes since 1945, though ex-communist states still do not use third party settlement and the US has ceased to be part of its compulsory jurisdiction. However, at the time of writing, there are estimated to be thirty wars being waged, almost all intra-state and therefore outside the scope of the institutions of global order. We consider these so-called 'postmodern' conflicts briefly below.

Global finance

The supremacy of global finance and the priority given to the protection of finance capital are not inevitable. It is a deliberate strategy requiring

floating exchange rates to prevent the depreciation of financial surpluses, the global management of the debt of developing countries, of
the ex-communist bloc and of the deficit of the USA and otherwise the
free movement of finance. It is estimated variously that between 2 and
10 per cent of global financial transactions are directly related to production and trade in the 'real economy'. The rest, the overwhelming
majority, is speculative. But the fact that the balance of political forces
favours capital does not mean that finance capital is secure. These
delinked financial markets are inherently unstable in a way which
nevertheless has direct repercussions on the real economy. FitzGerald
outlines five aspects to this instability. First, financial markets are in
permanent disequilibrium because demand always exceeds supply at the
clearing rate of interest, because risk can never be fully reflected in this
rate. Second, there is a built-in disjuncture between the cost and time of
interpreting information, especially information on the solvency of
states (especially from 'emerging markets' in developing countries) on
the one hand and the intense speed of the necessary reactions on the
other.[34] Technologies of trading are such that shock transmission has
been scaled up. Third, financial markets increasingly deal in future
expectations which are by their nature uncertain. Fourth, existing regulative institutions can intensify the very flaws they were intended to
remedy. The failures of ratings agencies can lead to information-induced
triggers of 'herd behaviour' (exacerbated by the polarized structure of
financial markets) in which there are cascades of private assets deflation
when private commercial debt is suddenly redeemed. Private debt is
then bailed out by states. IMF 'solutions' have exacerbated the most
recent crises by giving a green light to liberalization and short-term
private portfolio investment, precipitating crises, and by imposing uniform austerity packages in their wake, making recovery more difficult.[35]
Fifth, financial investment gets to be biased in favour of the kind of
assets which can be sold fast. Exit and diversification rather than information and direct control are used to contain risk. There is thus an
inherent tendency towards periodic crisis. Banks lend more than they
own and while they are closely regulated domestically, their international dealings are not regulated.[36]

Small developing countries are most vulnerable to the instability of
financial markets. There, a given change has a larger impact on demand,
on prices and production, and through production on labour markets.
Labour in the informal economy, by definition that large segment deprived of any form of social protection, is most vulnerable. The burden
of a global financial crisis falls not so much on investors but on the

households of workers made unemployed as a result of it – and within them disproportionately on women.[37]

It took the threat of destabilization in the triad heartland of OECD countries from the crises of the 1990s to concentrate the minds of policy elites. There is a reasonable degree of consensus about desirable ways to regulate world finance. Four elements are needed: first, a global central bank to supply liquidity to banks as well as states (the IMF currently supplies funds to states alone); second, institutions to assess and guarantee creditworthiness – the regulation of intermediaries and the establishment of market-making banks which would have the mandate to create stability (the Bank for International Settlements having a highly incomplete jurisdiction); third, a legal system for the settlement of financial disputes (none now exists); fourth, a means of co-ordinating the three major regional currencies (the dollar, euro and yen) (existing central banks have a variety of mandates and none includes this role). But this kind of proposal is utopian.[38] What have been tabled are two means of improving the circulation of information. One involves the formalization of the leading industrial and 'emerging market' players so as to improve financial supervision. The second is to increase the power of existing international regulation to monitor international capital markets. They rely on the power of information to reduce risk. Instability is not addressed by them at all. Both these proposals are being resisted by the US government and by international banks. FitzGerald concludes that it is not only poor third world labour that is harmed; what Keynes called 'steady business' is also harmed by this instability. Unlike finance, productive assets are much slower to be divested.

Global manufacturing

One form of global capital creates insecurity for another form in other places. German reunification led to an inflation which then had to be controlled by raised interest rates. The increased exchange value of the mark caused a loss of exports and industrial stagnation, in the fallout from which 7000 jobs were lost in the Netherlands and Northern Ireland.[39] The matrix of social and political institutions shaping global finance capital also shapes productive capital. But there are other sources of insecurity for manufacturing industry: for instance, there is no system of international commercial law beyond the treaty obligations of governments.[40] Key among these sources is political instability. The risk of protectionism threatens production sited in single locations.

So does the need for access to global markets in order to satisfy economies of scale in the core components of composite commodities (however customized they may finish by being). These factors both encourage the dispersal of sites and invite mergers of control. We saw earlier that MNCs exploit small differences in national regulative frameworks for industry. They also exploit the private discretion of officials enforcing such regulations and make it pay the political decision-makers.[41] Liberalization, which should have led to a streamlining of the state, reducing opportunities for corruption, has in practice been closely associated with an explosion of corruption.

Although the number of MNCs has increased from 7000 in 1970 to 38 000 in the mid-1990s, some 500 are responsible for three-quarters of world trade. In a wide range of industries or product groups the world market is controlled by 10–12 firms, often fewer, a structure of competitive or collusive oligopoly whose concentration of control is often underestimated by the absence of statistics on franchising and licensing.[42] Leys reckons that one-third of world output is now under the direct influence of MNCs. But John Kay starts from the fact that the largest and most successful global manufacturing companies rarely hold their ranking in terms of capitalization more than a few decades at the most. And instability at the top has intensified.[43] The current wave of globalization has consolidated a transformation of the commodity composition of the world's largest companies away from those with a competitive advantage in size and scale towards those with competitive advantages in one or a combination of brand, reputation, knowledge and innovation. As a result there is much greater diversity in global manufacturing than ever before. First there are global conglomerates which operate out of the triad. This kind of corporate economy manages the tensions between (i) diversification in products and locations in order to spread risk, (ii) sourcing components according to specific endowments of technology, skill and prices, and (iii) the exploitation of economies of scale in homogenized products, or products with homogenized cores. Kay, however, identifies the fastest growing global companies as being smaller firms, forced to be global because of the small size of their national markets and dealing in highly differentiated heterogeneous products, demand for which tends to be price inelastic (Kay uses the example of a company making industrial fasteners in Luxembourg). Such companies protect themselves by developing highly specific competitive advantages and by finding idiosyncratic 'niches'. Another kind of global firm, one common in developing countries,[44] springs – sometimes at one generation removed – from local agricultural surpluses. Such firms appropriate the open-ended working days, participative supervision and family labour of an agrarian culture.[45] This kind of firm is typically part of a specialized cluster, sometimes extending to thousands of companies, linked through pervasive relations of subcontracting with a flexible and skilled workforce and considerable active co-operation in research and development and marketing. In Italy, clusters specialize in clothes, shoes and food products. In South Asia there are (globalized) clusters for tee-shirts, silk sarees, handbags, surgical instruments, clocks and many other products. Export contracts are qualitatively more comprehensive and information-intensive than local ones. In specifying in advance the price, quality, quantity, terms and conditions of supply, and in sometimes supplying advance credit, inputs and services multinational purchasers achieve an indirect control over small producers which may transfer risk downwards to them.[46] The last kind of global firm is also small but networked, forfeiting price competition to retain trust and reduce opportunism and linked by cross-ownership to exploit regulative differences.[47] With the possible exception of China, however, international manufacturing capital is cautious about sites in developing countries.

Kay makes two points about this variety. First, the development of competitive advantage is a form of protection from insecurity. Second, entire nations may be associated with particular products and/or particular kinds of competitive strategy.[48] Thus a further element in the politics of markets is the diffuse politics of a matrix of cultural and economic institutions conferring a nationally differentiated and path-dependent competitive advantage. Those of the US, for example, are grounded in innovation, brands and knowledge-based products. US regulation *assumes* the opportunistic entrepreneurial behaviour which has contributed materially to its global success. Entire industries are associated with kinds of national advantage. Kay lists advanced electronics, associated with Japan, finance, associated with the US and UK, education-based and audio-visual products with the UK, perfumes with France, clothing with Italy, kitchen goods with Germany. However, it needs noting that the association of industrial sectors or types of commodity with national competitiveness is not set in tablets of stone. 'There is no best system for business', Kay concludes.

The globalization of manufacturing therefore creates a set of important deep structural forces in tension with the homogenizing rules of supranational regulative bodies such as the WTO.

The case of arms and weapons

In 1997 worldwide military spending amounted to $740 bn, making arms officially the biggest manufacturing industrial sector worldwide. Armaments are commodities with the unusual distinction of being in their essence both a cause of insecurity, destruction and abuses of human rights and a means of protection against insecurity. Furthermore, the commodities, while legal, fuel an illegal trade. The sector is also highly differentiated. Willett shows that at one end, the most 'sophisticated' technology is used to extend the aggressive or defensive reach of weapons systems. A technological lead is never long maintained and innovation is closely linked with exports backed by aggressive arms export policies. Exports also contain economic insecurity caused by closures, downsizing and the under-utilization of capacity.

We should note that the USA dominates world exports, accounting for half the world's sales. US sales to governments *increased* throughout the 'peace divided' period of the 1990s from $13.5 bn at the start to $16.5 bn at the end[49] plus a further $1.5 bn of sales to commercial purchasers. The US's exports are four times greater than those of the next ranking supplier (Russia) and nearly twice as large as the combined total of the five next ranked exporters (France, the UK, Germany, China and the Netherlands).[50] Forty per cent of all sales to developing countries come from the US, and about 20 per cent from the UK. The export-driven proliferation of conventional advanced weapons systems is accompanied by the transfer of technological capability, the development of domestic defence industries and the integration of private companies into the global market.

Globalization has restructured this end of the armaments industry in ways which can be said to increase national insecurity. For the first time, civil innovation (in information technology and surveillance) leads military technology. It is out of military control. Second, production is now controlled by international companies rather than by national states. Third, an arms race driven by technology and markets is replacing one driven by Cold War politics. The race is particularly acute in the Middle East (reaching west as far as Turkey) and East Asia, especially Taiwan and South Korea (where marine territory off China is rich in oil and Taiwan is claimed by China). US military expenditure for non-export purposes has also started to increase once more. Fourth, there is increasing uncertainty regarding the final destination of weapons supplies, which are frequently out of the control of suppliers. Fifth, new principles of arm's-length warfare mean that international intervention is increasingly constrained *not* by the nature of the conflict but by the possibility of intervention without human loss – a principle vividly demonstrated by a comparison of the international response to Kosovo in 1999 and Chechnya in 2000.

At the other end of the arms spectrum Willett tracks a massive global diffusion of small arms. The downsizing of military arsenals at the end of the Cold War has released a large supply of – and created markets for – second-hand weapons and spares, often at very considerable discounts. Some exchange of weapons has been free and part of assistance programmes, some of which have been incompatible with the capabilities of recipient states.[51] In 1994 the trade in surplus weapons exceeded that in new ones, an entirely novel development in the global arms trade. These have been crucial in the proliferation of unregulatable intra-state conflicts. Finally, there is a deep reluctance to reduce reliance on nuclear weapons.

In response to the destabilizing accumulations of weapons, the Wassenaar Agreement signed by 33 countries (OECD, Russia and Korea) in 1995–6 promotes transparency and responsibility in trade in conventional and dual-use goods and technologies. A European Code of Conduct on Arms Transfers was also formally adopted in 1999 by member states. The Code established principles and criteria governing the approval of arms exports to countries where they might be used for internal repression or to provoke or prolong conflicts in which human rights violations have been documented by the UN, the Council of Europe or the EU. A further 13 countries on the eastern margins of the EU have aligned themselves with this code. But such codes of conduct are often flouted by their signatories. Even UN embargoes are unenforceable by member states, sometimes for political but mostly for commercial reasons.[52] In the USA, the Code of Conduct for Arms Transfers Act was dropped in March 1999 from the authorization bill to which it had been attached.[53] Willett concludes that the net result is both to widen international differences in endowments of military technology, leading to a global bifurcation between high and low tech armies, and to fuel low-intensity conflict with immensely damaging consequences for psyche, life and property, and leading to gross violations of international human rights and humanitarian law.

Global labour

Labour is for the most part immobilized, but this does not mean it is not globalized. It is incorporated into the 'global political community'[54] constituted by markets. The widening international income inequality is the product of a long historical process of development of infrastructure, institutions and culture. The distribution of endowments and entitlements between individuals in this global political community is quite arbitrary. Some are incorporated in global production systems and some are required for the final consumption of global goods and services. As few as possible in the former. As many as possible in the latter. The legitimacy of the national responses to the global political project depends on a tension between labour as an electoral resource (and therefore needing protection and social support) and labour as a key element in national competition, not only as a class of direct producers for global capital but also as the agricultural and rural workforce supplying basic wage goods for that other working class (and therefore needing control).

Most contributors to this volume identify labour as the ultimate victim of insecurities generated by global capital; increasingly vulnerable to job insecurity and permanent unemployment (see especially Amin and Willett). Labour has not been able to prevent the destruction of the conditions that are conducive to its political organization. Systematic casualization, the intensification of work, the differentiation and feminization of tasks, home working and longer distances between home and work make mobilization much more difficult than formerly, regardless of discouraging legal frameworks (Leys). But Robin Cohen, in developing this theme, also shows how labour threatens capital – through its price, its political instability and its never extinguished potential for political organization. (We might also add, through its extreme reluctance to be dispossessed of land or be freed to have no options but to sell itself.) Opinions divide over whether the perpetuation of economic spaces for petty production – all over the world but especially in developing countries – serves capital (by subsidizing the wage) or challenges it (first by providing labour with the security of an alternative (subsistence) livelihood and second by reproducing poverty and constraining demand for commodities).[55]

The threats of labour to capital and vice versa are not evenly balanced. Capital has the advantage of mobility. Cohen finds that the uneven capitalist transition has had a destructive impact upon labour. As the cost of industrial relocation drops, productive capital has migrated from the triad heartlands; first textiles, then the assembly stages of secondary industry, followed by capital intensive industries, electronics and now information technology and software.[56] As Kay also shows, post-Fordist restructuring has accompanied geographical resiting. This is no simple 'race to the bottom'. The impact of restructuring is felt in increasingly precarious and casualized contracts in parts of the world and sectors of the market from which capital finds it hard to migrate. It is felt in new forms of job-working and subcontracting in its new destinations and in open unemployment where capital can emigrate – exacerbating unemployment caused by technical change.[57] It is felt in shifts in the gender composition of the flexible labour force. Women have taken over jobs previously held by men. Activities in which the labour has been female have expanded. Unorganized, irregular employment, the hallmark of women's wage work, has proliferated. The costs of labour market flexibility have been shifted onto women.[58] Unions have also been suppressed, by forms of organization of production which make the organization of labour impossible and by open coercion, by changes in the legal frameworks regulating organized labour, particularly the ubiquitous erosion of the right to strike, by violations of ILO conventions on wages, health and safety at work and by the weakening of local institutions of enforcement.

Cohen, however, sees labour aligning itself in new ways in response to these threats. Trades unions are finding common cause with consumption interests to prevent price fixing and defend public services. Unions have also supported the reorganization of social security to respond to the more intermittent engagement with employment resulting from flexible specialization and casualization. Their agendas have included training, increased social security entitlements for women, the enforcement of safety regulations and new social obligations such as paternity leave. Unions have also been crucial supporters of pro-democracy movements in Eastern Europe and remain an important element in their domestic politics. The International Trade Secretariats, which are umbrella organizations for economic sectors, have improved the international co-ordination of unions, with some notable successes in campaigns against labour abuses by MNCs. The Non-Communist Apex Body for Trades Unions has recruited unions in the former USSR and its satellites. Now representing 175 millions workers globally, it, along with the International Labour Organization (ILO), seeks the internationalization of labour standards and monitors the repression of labour by governments as well as by MNCs. Finally, unions are linking up with new social movements in their distinctive single-issue mode of politics covering other aspects of identity than work or consumption: on environmental and gender justice, for instance.

New means of politics have been grafted onto older forms of labour militancy which are still active in states in transition from communism, newly industrializing countries and developing countries. Labour struggles are supplemented by the use of global information technology, media exposure, shareholder opposition and consumer boycotts. The extent to which such responses represent an embryonic new mass politics or are efflorescences of sectional interests is not yet clear.

In the heartlands the most vulnerable forms of labour are low skilled, young and female. They are further threatened when social security is individualized and/or funded from redistributivist taxation (which the wealthy, being the universal donors, grow to resist) rather than on principles of social solidarity rooted in universal contributions and entitlements.

Social security and welfare states

Globalization has impacts on the freedom of states to provide social security – pensions, unemployment benefits and measures in support of families. Global finance affects welfare directly through the consequences of debt and of financial crises, through national pressures to woo capital by cutting corporate taxes, through the structural unemployment caused by industrial decline, technical change and spatial restructuring (in Europe) and structural adjustment and liberalization (in developing countries) and the contingent unemployment associated with flexible labour (everywhere). Esping-Andersen regards these chains of causation as no more than counter-orthodox scaremongering. Provided public finances are sound, he maintains, and the sentries of global capital watch for this, welfare states are part of the complex armoury of competitive advantage ensuring the domestic stability needed by FDI. Esping-Andersen's argument is different. In his opinion, newly vulnerable sectors of society owe more to demographic and social changes than directly to globalization. A triple whammy of early retirement, delayed entry into labour markets and structural unemployment reduces the activity rate and affects contributions to pensions. Meanwhile striking drops in fertility exacerbate the ratio between contributors to and receivers of state welfare. Other factors only loosely connected to globalization reinforce the imbalances: the cost of children and the instability of the family. As a result, in Western welfare states there are new constituencies of vulnerable people. The poorly educated and unskilled, the young – especially women and especially women with sole responsibility for children – are inadequately catered for in welfare states geared to providing for the elderly, reforms to which are vigorously resisted by voters, whose median age is rising inexorably and who have a vested interest in the status quo.

Yet the character of a given welfare state results from a social consensus on the weighting of the various threats to welfare and on the capacity of the family (read women) to bear the results of the inadequacies of labour markets. In the Anglo-Saxon welfare system, the response – to fine-tune and target welfare, and to consider the use of a negative income tax, placing a minimum income floor under low paid workers – tends to have the perverse effect of multiplying insecurity. While privatized pensions and other social services tend to be captured by the top quintile of the income distribution (and even there risk pooling is replaced by the individualization of risk), lower down the practice of casualization (intensified under the globalization of manufacturing) enables employers' occupational contributions to be eroded. This has resulted in a huge increase in poverty *after* welfare transfers have been received. The Scandinavian system, which collectivizes the burden of care elsewhere laid on families and under which services are provided which liberate women for work, is extremely costly. The central and southern European system which relies on male social insurance, delegating the burden of other kinds of support to the family (read women) leads to strong resistance to deregulation and imposes such a burden on the growing numbers of women in the workforce that fertility has sharply declined, further exacerbating imbalances between contributors and beneficiaries. Other more radical alternatives – privatization, the citizens' income or 'third way' amalgams of non-profit, co-operative or voluntary provision – are each evaluated by Esping-Andersen in terms of their effects on each of the three models of welfare state and are all found to contain politically unacceptable combinations of inequity, disincentives to economic growth, cost and feasibility. States with nerve are needed. The 'spirited resistance' to attempts to dismantle the welfare state in many parts of Europe – celebrated by Robin Cohen – is also a spirited resistance to a restructuring of welfare in ways appropriate to new domestic vulnerabilities in the era of globalization. Esping-Andersen concludes that growth alone will release resources which might strengthen new political settlements against the opposition of older voters. In its absence he expects 'muddling through' to exacerbate the problems sought to be addressed.[59]

Globalized informality, its consequences for insecurity and its links to formal globalization

In the underdeveloped peripheries of the global system, globalization is said to have four distinctive components. First, globalization has accompanied the enforcement of an agenda of deregulation and privatization associated with structural adjustment loans for otherwise unsustainable burdens of national debt. Second, with technical advances in transport, telecommunications and information technology, physical remoteness from the sites of final demand no longer puts up transactions costs which previously prevented trade. Third, liberalization is argued to have improved the efficiency and increased the scale of operation of proto-capitalists operating previously in the parallel economy, making them free to shake off the borders regarded by neoliberals as anachronistic and producing an integration of regions (which local states have so signally failed to achieve) and an expansion of markets for local agricultural and industrial goods. These trends and tendencies cry out for a critical discussion which is summarized below.[60] Fourth, and by way of contrast, the globalization of trade, transport and information technology, the movement of people, the decline of state authority, the intractable persistence of inequality and poverty are the fertile nutrients for globalized crime, raw material for which is sourced in the underdeveloped world. Indeed, it is said that 'the developing world's most successful transnational corporation' is the organized criminal cartel operating out of Cali, Colombia.[61]

The informal economy is a concept which is highly contested. It is not only activity that is unregistered and untaxed because it falls under tax thresholds,[62] it is what goes on in the interstices of the two parts of the formal sector – the state and corporate business – much of which is also untaxed because tax is deliberately evaded.[63] The informal economy in India can be taken as an example of its size. In 1999 it was carefully estimated by the National Council of Applied Economic Research as accounting for 60 per cent of GDP and of savings, 68 per cent of income and 83 per cent of employment. It is therefore not marginal, not outside the ambit of market exchange or capital accumulation. It is the largest part of the Indian economy.

Worldwide, the informal economy (defined inconsistently by sector, scale, type of exchange, relation to the formal sector and legal status), has the following components:

- Petty production in agriculture and the rural non-farm economy, the biggest single component – regulated parametrically through prices and subsidies and indirectly through physical infrastructure.
- Other organized structures of production, trade and services not regulated by the state.
- The black economy – factor incomes (profit, rent and interest) which are undeclared within the formal sector. In India's black economy,

now making up about half the economy, for example,[64] tax evasion has been estimated as a source of formal-sector leakages which is twenty times more important quantitatively than is corruption. And within this economy:

- Illegal business and trade in legal goods: notably, real estate, gold, inventory, the third world film industry, much of the third world retail sector.
- Production and trade of illegal goods: notably counterfeiting, drugs, arms and prostitution and trafficking.
- Other forms of redistribution such as theft, extortion and corruption.[65]

National informal economies have been unleashed by deregulation. Private sector activities formally registered have been decentralized. Small-scale units have proliferated in sectors previously dominated by MNCs. Public sector or para-statal firms have been privatized, frequently to comparatively small units of capital, and *informalized*. The process is found all over the world from electronics in Latin America to rice milling in West Bengal. It is therefore related to global as well as national restructuring.[66] The informal sectors often appear to be competitive by virtue of the large numbers of firms involved. In practice, more often than not, the informal economy is found to bear a fractal resemblance to the structures of global MNCs described by Leys and Kay: a combination of oligopoly and petty trade. Large firms may preserve petty ones through acts of economic patronage which also control their profit levels (machine tools in south India). Large firms may also offload risk onto and/or seize title from petty operations in the informal economy (large- and small-scale mining in Bolivia and Tanzania). Large firms may coexist alongside petty firms without there being ties between the scales (cosmetics in Nigeria).

Contractual relations are typically networked. For some commentators, network trade reduces transaction costs by relying on trust; for others, network trade expresses forms of market politics and social pressures which do not allow any alternative. In the informal economy power is exercised collusively through overlapping organizations of regulation, co-operation, culture and philanthropy. In *not* being regulated by states, informal activity is not *un*regulated. Rather it is *re*regulated and by a multiplicity of means. The politics of regulation is multifaceted – in some places originating in the defence of businesses from regulation by the state, commonly developing a vital self-regulatory role, enforcing the local terms of participation in markets and the basis of exclusion from them, wringing concessions from the local state either formally or by subterfuge and capture in a politics of opportunism. Other sources of regulative order in informal economies are the family (regulating the family firm) or the kin group; the search for and consolidation of reputation or trust[67] in which oppressive relations may be preferred to the consequences of their loss; collective action; social norms and rules; and last but not least privately organized physical coercion. The explosion of security firms and commercial protection agencies servicing the global economy may equally be a response to the declining adequacy of state security. This is one obvious respect in which informal and formal globalization are linked, for the same firms may service both sectors.

Informalization is consolidating new regulative regimes restoring profits in the face of globalization. This is a dynamic process with its own internal contradictions – most notably between opportunities for entrepreneurship on the one hand and the ruthless cheapening of production costs, the shifting of risks onto client firms and more or less casualised labour on the other.

So *informal* economies are being globalized. They are being adapted to the needs and structures of the emerging single world economy. Some sectors are integral to the process of formal globalization, others are linked less directly with the global economy. Most informal activity – measured in terms of livelihoods – is not criminal. The globalization of the informal economy is usually regarded as a mutation of the conventional economy or as a transitory phenomenon.[68] We will conclude this introduction by examining the ways certain sectors create insecurities, the responses made to them and the linkages made between these sectors and formal aspects of globalization.

Informal globalization necessary to the formal system: offshore financial havens

Over half the world's money is estimated to pass through offshore financial centres (OFCs): an estimated one trillion dollars in 1991.[69] There are at least 41 of them: 18 in the Caribbean and South Atlantic, 14 in Europe, the Middle East and Africa and 9 in Asia and the Pacific. These three sets of regional satellites each operate globally but they each also service a regional financial centre: New York, London and Tokyo. Most are small, landlocked or island territories, interacting with one another in a hierarchy of selectivity and criminality. Each employs a significant part of the total labour force of the territory in which they are sited and generates a significant contribution to legitimate GDP. Off-shore finance is the economic base of these states. While tax havens simply have different (laxer) tax laws and lower taxes or none at all, OFCs provide private and wholesale banking, anchorage for offshore trusts and funds, holding companies and easy insurance and shipping registers. The purposes of all these activities are to evade taxation, avoid closer regulation and escape detection. Finance is the most fungible, instantaneously transmittable commodity, traceable only with great cost and effort, if at all.[70]

Globalized finance cannot operate without OFCs. For reasons of se-crecy (a secrecy the reasons for which range from confidentiality to criminality), while the kinds of links between OFCs and official finance can be painted with a broad brush, the magnitudes of flows cannot. First, OFCs are the destinations of large quantities of capital which have been generated in, but are flying speculatively from, or fleeing, states to whose productive and fiscal project its possessors do not wish it to contribute. This reluctance may be attributed to local mismanagement (as in Russia, although the Washington Consensus sees this as general-ized) or it may be related to international corporate or official financial transfers. Leakages from the official, legal financial system result from overpayments or bribes. These are recycled, sometimes within a single bank, through OFCs for onward lending, perhaps even to revisit the original loan destination.[71] In the early 1990s there were 8 million people with investible surpluses exceeding $1million: an expanding sector for which OFC services of private banking have been created. Second, OFCs are the physical convergence areas for finance capital from a variety of sources: private (retail) and official, global and local, advanced countries and developing ones, legal, corrupt and criminal. Third, OFCs are the sites of stocks of funds from advanced countries for covert security operations elsewhere.

OFCs create insecurities over and above those of the financial system discussed here by FitzGerald. By defrauding states of resources, OFCs abet the process of state delegitimization. Rentier activities flourish at the expense of productive ones because the latter escape accountability far less easily than the former. There are contagious effects on the host economies. Their covert role also adds to physical insecurity.

How does the policy elite respond to OFCs? Hardly at all. Only very lately have there been calls for their abolition, but no suggestions as to how to effect this.[72] FitzGerald identifies the OFCs as major impedi-ments to the reform and regulation of global finance. The toleration of OFCs, their absence from policy discourse on financial reform, paradoxically indicates the essential nature of their role. Disorder is at the heart of the OECD/global financial system. 'Market liberalization' is not only 'capable of impoverishing whole countries, it has paradoxically also made it easier for alternative and destabilising forms of political economy to become established.'[73]

Informal activity linked to the global system in other ways: parallel trade

Where states lack the capacity to enforce their frontiers, goods flow hither and thither outside the enforceable law. Such trade is termed parallel trade.[74] If such goods are dutiable this activity amounts to smuggling, but parallel trade is broader than that. West Africa is a useful case through which to examine other kinds of links with the global system and other insecurities. Despite centuries of cross-border trade, this is nevertheless a region at the very margins of the current global system. Foreign direct investment in the entire sub-Saharan African region declined from 6 per cent to 3 per cent of the total during the 1990s (and two-thirds of this went into mineral exports). Meanwhile, West African cross-border trade has flourished, with a large increase in goods imported from Europe and Asia. Most parallel trade is in legal goods (such as cocoa and cattle), which fuel the inventories of official exports if they finally leave the region. In its commodity composition, it tends to parallel official trade flows and fuels global trade. A small proportion of the currency used for this trade is recycled for speculation through the banking system in Francophone Africa and France.[75] In the eastern states of West Africa this trade has loosened the ethnic composition of trade networks, facilitated private enterprise and accumulation, led to the bypassing of local intermediaries and expanded novel direct links with East Asia and Australia. Trade networks have been restructured. Clientelist relationships of long standing are being replaced by new kinds of contract for educated young intermediaries with feet in both worlds. New forms of brokerage appear.[76] In some parts of the west of this region parallel trade is being criminalized as an illegal global trade in legal goods (diamonds, gemstones and gold) is consolidated to support the internal struggles of collapsed states.[77] The rise of OFCs rooted in Gambia and Liberia is thought to be not unconnected to such trade.

While parallel trade is linked to formal global trade and while this informal restructuring offers opportunities for livelihoods and for accumulation, it also generates insecurities of its own. States lose control over the location and movement of people. Informal business interests grow to be dependent on states which fail to enforce their frontiers in order to sustain this form of capital. To the extent that local states are fully complicit through the patronage and protection of smuggling and the sharing of its rents, they undermine their own formal capacity and resources. Meanwhile rural producers watch the destruction of agriculture and local textiles industries as imports on the parallel global markets undercut their prices, while a sharp fall in the purchasing power of consumers in the franc zone has ruined incentives on the parallel international market for foodstuffs. Capital is diverted from production into trade. Parallel trade expands as networks of networks coalesce. Whereas the networks of post-Fordist flexible accumulation are linked through electronic interconnections and decentralized production, the West African parallel trading networks are shaped by ethnicity, kinship and religion. Rather than being productive, they are distributive. Rather than being a grassroots constituency supportive of liberalization, they form a system resting on inter-state differences in *informal* regulative regimes controlled by those profiting from them.[78]

The informal protection of property rights

For the most part, formal security systems guarantee property rights in the informal economy involving legal goods. But where private property is developing in the absence of legal institutions to protect property rights or to faciliate their transfer, as in the states of the former Soviet Union and the cities of Latin America and South Asia, the physical conditions necessary for market exchange, security of property, are commonly provided by private protection forces often drawn from unemployed ex-security personnel. Their roles cover the physical protection of people, all forms of fixed capital, movable goods and capital in flight and the enforcement of contracts. Large 'shadow states' have developed from parallel flows of tribute (extortion) and expenditure. Protection forces are interconnecting globally. Some integrate protection, (credit card) fraud and counterfeiting, the latter said to be a $200bn business.[79] Others, considered below, protect their own transnational 'value chains' involving global production, trade and finance.

This informalized protection has been argued to be a response to insecurity and to create security, to both protect and provide employment. However, their impact on local capital and the state is unlikely to be other than net adverse: mass capital flight, accumulation under coercive conditions, state plunder or 'primitive disaccumulation' (Burawoy, 1999), creeping mafia control over sectors of the economy with special characteristics such as the need for liquid capital and a labour force vulnerable to intimidation (the construction industry and the disposal of waste are noted in this context), an aversion to investment and reduced growth rates. Extensive mafianization is accompanied by increases in violence, physical insecurity and unemployment (due to its impact on growth and productivity) and by declines in life expectation.

States are generally inexperienced in threats which are not military and do not come from outside. They may also be complicit. Responses are riddled with contradictions. 'Amnesties' tend to be vigorously resisted both by protection forces and by those protected, since they are rarely enforced in ways which reduce the latter's informal payments. The enforcement of the rule of law is easier said than done when the law is shoddy, formally counter-productive but informally highly product-ive for corrupt legislators and shot through with unforeseen conse-quences. Attempts at legal downsizing, and at the shedding of law inappropriate to an informalized system of governance means capitula-tion to law breakers. The state is thereby further delegitimized. What is true for the law is also true for institutions implementing the law.

Illegal global trade

Other forms of globalized trade are illegal and difficult to research. While (small) arms and drugs are best documented, other important globally traded illegal products include art and antiquities, stolen cars, counterfeit goods, wildlife products, nuclear material and other toxic wastes and trafficked women and children for domestic and sexual slavery.[80] Although long antedating the current era of globalization, the increasingly characteristic form is thought to be that of the trans-national criminal organization (TCO). Like transnational corporations (TNCs), TCOs exploit national boundaries, but their objectives are to gain access to goods by circumvention, to elude enforcement and to exploit differences in the criminal justice systems. Like TNCs, some TCOs have a global reach, while others span large, continental regions.[81] While TNCs locate headquarters for tax advantages, TCOs have home bases, entrepots and financial servicing in corrupt, weak and/or collusive states. While TNCs are structured through vertical integration and/or process specialization, TCOs are networked or cellu-lar in organization to reduce risk and resist threats to their control. TCOs are notably embedded in family or ethnicity, forming loose confeder-ations based on kin. While TNCs develop diversified productive portfolios, those of TCOs focus on physical protection, high-tech (coun-ter)intelligence equipment, consumption and expansion of their sector. Contracts are often enforced by a culture of loyalty, riding on pre-existing relations of deference, and by the threat and practice of vio-lence. In host states, formal institutions may be co-opted in a nexus of collusion with state apparatuses and banks. The security of governance and economic growth is jeopardized by such arrangements.[82]

Illegal global trade in legal goods: arms

If an estimated 10 per cent of the global arms trade is illegal, the illegal arms trade runs at $50000 a minute or $2.6bn annually. It supplies individuals, informal protection forces and at least 30 current wars. It is structured through international networks of private dealers. These networks have to be complex and international in order to escape detection.[83] The trade is supplied from the circulation of existing stocks rather than the production of new weapons. It is the insecurity of arsenals which links illegal trade to open regulated global trade. Weapons may be looted from government arsenals. They may be re-cycled regionally from lots purchased by governments with 'end user certificates' approved by lax government sellers. China and the states of the former Warsaw pact are especially implicated in this kind of trade, pressured to earn foreign exchange (often at severe discounts) from surplus stocks of weapons which are long-lasting, relatively low-tech in engineering terms and which have low maintenance requirements. Official importers (governments) may sell onwards to any internal or external group with the capacity to pay, sometimes creating a 'boomer-ang effect' whereby armed forces are faced by weapons supplied by their own government.

It is hard to halt the spread of supply of and demand for illegal small arms. However, the lack of any overt inventory of the arms controlled by 'non-state actors' need not prevent action. Scholars at the Bonn Inter-national Centre for Conversion have proposed the following measures: information sharing; the establishment of a clear and unambiguous legal base of the possession of arms; improvements in the storage and security of weapons; their suppression and destruction. As with the consensus on the stabilizing of global finance so with small arms, im-plementation on the ground has been insipid. The European Union Code, mentioned earlier, has no obligation even to prohibit arms trans-fers to forces not recognizing human rights. The code is not politically binding. In 1997, both the EU (in the shape of the EU Council Working

Group) and the Organization of American States ratified treaties against the illicit trafficking of firearms, but there has been little progress or co-operation between states on the ground.[84]

Global trade in illegal goods: drugs

The value of the global trade in illicit drugs is unknown, but they are without doubt commodities of great economic significance: one UN estimate puts the trade at $400bn p.a. which would make it over 150 times larger than the illegal arms trade. *Seizures* in the US increased from $24m to $86m per annum during the 1990s and totalled $546m. Prior to the current era of globalization the trade was controlled by organized crime groups operating outside the US, La Cosa Nostra controlling an estimated 95 per cent of heroin distributed inside the US in a network operating out of New York and Corsica via Marseilles. Drugs were distributed domestically by 'organized crime families' to networks of street dealers reported by the US Drugs Enforcement Agency to be trading to 'minorities' in low income areas. The system was protected by corrupt relations of complicity with the formal institutions of enforcement. After 1972, when this system was destroyed, the global trade reworked itself, in some places emerging from innocent marketing systems for cut flowers. It is now dominated by organized crime syndicates with epicentres in Peru, Bolivia, Colombia, Mexico and Afghanistan from where cocaine, heroin, methamphetamines and marijuana are distributed. The structure of these global marketing systems is thought to be modelled on that of terrorist groups. It is said to consist of specialized cells separately managing production, transport, distribution, money-laundering, communications, physical protection and recruitment. The most advanced telecommunications, weapons, means of transport and counter-intelligence technologies are used to enforce property rights. According to the US Department of Justice's Drugs Enforcement Agency, the system not only works through parochial relations of control and complicity but also through the corruption of 'entire governments'. Parallel systems of property rights have been enforced and, though its economic consquences are direst among the poor, consumption is socially widespread.

The globalized drugs economy appears to be shifting from forms of regulation and organization based upon kinship and ethnicity to forms based on the co-option and exploitation of formal sector financial, legal and political institutions. It is further linked through the commercial protection firms which operate in the formal and informal global economies. It is linked through the siting of (agricultural) production and through the toleration of processing laboratories. This trade does nothing but exacerbate all forms of insecurity defined at the start of this introduction. Drugs were declared a security threat to the US in 1986.[85] Violence and intimidation are used throughout the value chain. Consumers are criminalized and crime proliferates. Health status declines. The economies of entire states are destabilized. Their political responses are necessarily covert as well as overt and risk complicity and corruption at every stage.[86]

Godson and Williams, reviewing global organized crime, conclude that it 'could prove one of the major security threats of the 21st century' (1997: 112–13), faced with which states are anachronistic and inexperienced. Current responses are a 'hodge podge of separate but poorly co-ordinated programs and policies . . . (creating) confusion about roles and uncertainty' (ibid.: 119): Interpol (co-ordinating 176 national crime bureaux), regional organizations of police co-operation,[87] a UN convention on the prevention of trafficking and a UN Global Action Plan of 1994 against trans-sovereign crime. It is often commented of such symbolic action that it is an achievement in global consensus building and in international *recognition*, but with under-resourcing on the scale reported, one is entitled to doubt even this. Interpol has a budget of $30m and a staff of 270; the UN Plan has a budget of $4m and a staff of 35, while a single TCO may employ upwards of 10 000. There are no international conventions with anticipatory norms of a sort that might even protect future systems of cyber-payments. There is no move towards the international harmonization of law, law enforcement or judicial institutions. There is no systematic co-ordination between specialized units of information within and between states. There is no international social or political movement to isolate safe havens, disrupt supply and demand, insist on the sharing of intelligence or agitate for the removal of incentives.[88] The reasons for this dearth of international regulative zeal may be found in part in the large investments that would be necessary, themselves antithetical to the neoliberal foundations of globalization, in part in the global regulative hegemony of the US.

The unruly politics of globalized informality

There are links between the process of economic restructuring which underpins formal globalization and the informal consequences, some of which, while they serve the interests behind formal globalization, are undermining national economic development – and in developed as well as developing countries. This process is widely thought to encourage celebrations of socially and ideologically manipulated pasts and a resurgence of religious or ethnic fundamentalism, other forms of social unrest, intra-state conflict and new illiberal forms of democracy, termed 'electoral travesties' by Samir Amin. Such events are unpredicted by the paradigms in social science. Willett uses the case of Mexico to show how political instability and intensified and severe poverty following Mexico's reforms were neither predicted nor wanted by the instigator – the USA.

Analyses centred on categories such as states and MNCs are no longer adequate to explain the multiple threats to physical and economic security caused by civil disorder, criminal violence, internal state repression and intra-state wars. In two-thirds of the 30 poorest countries there is either active conflict or an insecure peace. Under these conditions, regulative activity may not 'simply' be informalized, it may collapse.[89] Regional conflicts are no longer being directly sustained by Cold War superpowers; new ones are adaptive, expansive and outside the ambit of global public law. Globalized information and communications technologies lubricate the transfer of cultural products and tend to intensify conflict fomented through social identity. The economist Pranab Bardhan has argued that religion and/or ethnicity are common bases for political mobilization 'because norms restricting entry and exit are more powerful and boundaries less fluid' than other principles of organization. Bonding lowers the costs of collective action and raises its rents.[90] Though strife may be organized around ethnicity or religion, economic interests are often at stake in conflicts *within* the working classes over low-skilled jobs, conflicts between middlemen from minority groups and those (feeling) exploited by them, conflicts over privileged niches for rent-seeking (be they land, commodity markets or state bureaucracies) and those between regional groups over the distribution of taxes, infrastructure and subsidies. New means of sustenance are necessary for such struggles: sometimes commodities for the global market, e.g. diamonds (Sierra Leone), copper (Zambia) and oil. Opposing sides are plugged into global networks for arms, fuel, transport, food, drugs or the international trade in household goods, vehicles, farm equipment, livestock and economic migrants. Where warring groups proceed to transact with MNCs, the legitimacy of the international conventions such as UN trade sanctions is corroded.[91]

'There are obviously no easy solutions in this minefield of contemporary horrors', concludes Bardhan. The most powerful global states and the UN system do not manage such conflicts. Their interventions can exacerbate them. The failure to settle disputes by peaceful means compounds developmental failures and violations of political, economic and social rights.[92] It is not that there has been no response to the economic and political insecurities of informal globalization. Checklists have been provided.[93] The World Bank and other UN economic agencies are working collectively to widen the scope of conditionalities for official credit and aid in order to fuse economic criteria (liberalization), political criteria (electoral democracy, reforms to structures of governance, support to civil society and NGOs) and social criteria (globalized convergence on a rights-based social policy).[94] On the ground, conflict resolution is being privatized, through international NGOs. Globalized surveillance technologies feed into early warning systems of monitoring and evaluation. Novel forms of civil society – mercenary groups, private security companies, private armies – provide protection to property and person (from landlords in South-East Asia to MNCs in Latin America). Given a democratic deficit on the ground which is unrecognized either in diplomacy or in much of the discourse of the 'aid community', it is hard to see who has an interest in *not* perpetuating this unruliness.

However, the unruly underbelly of globalization is not always 'Hobbesian chaos'.[95] More often than not it is ordered in ways which serve the interests of those enforcing their private property rights. Even intra-state conflict powered by ethnic rivalry may have an element of competition for economic resources. Informal globalization is not irrational, it is even sometimes an extreme manifestation of market rationality. It is also not transitional but structural: nourished by the liberalization of economies and the compression of states (which are central to formal globalization) and by unemployment, physical insecurity and declines in state capacity (which result from it). Network forms of commercialization litter the parallel and criminal economies. Primitive and informal accumulation is not simply an era of history pre-dating capital but a process coexisting with advanced forms of capital and business and one in which new units of capital are continually being created. We are only seeing for ourselves what Marx concluded in the mid-nineteenth century: 'Force itself is an economic power.'[96] Both force and economic power have to be much better understood if the real and discursive worlds are to be shaped so as to secure decent living conditions for the mass of the world's people.

Notes

The introduction has been improved by the reactions of Jairus Banaji, Colin Leys, Kate Meagher and David Smith, by literature provided by Richard Higgott, Kate

Meagher and Janine Rodgers and by a website search by Elinor Harriss, to all of whom I am very grateful.

1. Kay, this volume.
2. See Saxenien, 1994; Dunning, 1998; and Lasch and Urry, 1999 for analyses of these new configurations of economy and space.
3. Since democracies do not generally attack other democracies.
4. Willett, this volume.
5. Amin, this volume.
6. The quotations are from, respectively, Sachs, this volume; Gray, 1998: 33; and Bardhan, 1997: 1386.
7. See Bernstein, 1996, for a history of the ideas and technologies involved.
8. An elaborate set of contradictions is involved, 'nested' within each other: between global capital and the environment, between different fractions of capital (finance, manufacturing and trade), between these forms of capital and national states, between supra-state regulative organizations and states, between both and capital, between states, capital and labour, between labour in different locations, between socially protected and unprotected labour, and so on.
9. Law, political economy, development economics, politics, sociology, business and peace studies. The Wolfson Lecture of David Held has been published in *International Sociology*, 2000, and is not included in this book. Papers by Gosta Esping-Andersen and Colin Leys, integral to the project, were incorporated after the lecture series.
10. Amin's classification in Chapter 2 of the regions of capital outside the triad is as follows: (i) the industrializing countries (the former USSR and eastern European satellites, China, South Korea and Taiwan, India, Brazil and Mexico, though these are unable to reduce the proportion of the world population in the labour reserve); (ii) countries with a certain amount of industry but no national productive system: South-East Asia, the Arab states, South Africa, Turkey, Iran and some Latin American countries; (iii) a set with little industrialization: sub-Saharan Africa, the Caribbean; and (iv) the oil countries of the Middle East, not poor but marginalized due to their passive adjustment to the forces of global capital (at least so far).
11. To remedy this, see Hale, 1999.
12. Whereas the Washington Consensus of the 1980s and 1990s allowed for a minimal role for the state, the post-Washington consensus facing global reactions to its legitimacy from developing countries sees an expanded role for 'governance' (which is an architectural cum managerial rather than a political term for government) in: (i) the provision of 'public goods' (few of which are pure public goods as defined by textbooks, the majority of which have been placed in this category by local political consensuses); (ii) public–private partnerships (in which the principle of profit penetrates regions of society previously ringfenced); (iii) 'non-traditional actors': NGOs and new social movements (none of which is democratically accountable) so as better to manage 'social capital'; Higgott, 2000.
13. See Silver and Arrighi, 2000 for an account of the deep structure of interests in favour of protectionism between organized American labour and the US government and the prior resolve of third world states, catalysed beforehand

by UNCTAD, not to allow the 1999 Seattle talks on reform to the World Trade Organization to proceed before the OECD countries implemented at least some of the resolutions of the Uruguay Round which might benefit developing countries, a structure of interests which was reinforced by the politics of mass protest of international NGOs, all of which led to the derailment of the meeting. This outcome has been widely interpreted as indicating the power of international civil social organizations alone.

14. Respectively, Sachs and Cohen, this volume.
15. White, 1993; White et al., 1996.
16. Exceptions include Bach (ed.), 1999; Bayart et al., 1999; Castells, 2000; and Meagher, 1999.
17. Leys, this volume; see also the caution in his footnote no. 3.
18. Though structural adjustment and debt-bonded liberalization are not the only reasons for such differentiation – see FitzGerald and Stewart, 1997, on conflict and Armstrong, 1995, on AIDS.
19. See White, 1988, on developmental states in East Asia.
20. See Esping-Andersen, this volume.
21. See Monbiot, 2000, Latham, 2001 and George, forthcoming, all of whom have long histories of critical activism; but see also Legrain (adviser to the Director-General of the World Trade Organization), 2000: 31.
22. See Bacon, 2000, on the differences of interest between national and sectoral fractions of the global labour force, the suppression of unions and the lack of global enforcement institutions.
23. See the classic report of the World Bank, 1981, advocating structural adjustment.
24. Which increased their foreign investment by a factor of eight during the 1990s.
25. Duffield, 1999; Higgott, 2000; Kamat, 1999.
26. See Held et al., 1999.
27. The ILO, currently charged according to its Director-General with developing 'the social ground rules of the global economy' (quoted in Bacon, 2000) has no capacity to enforce such rules and its jurisdiction does not cover international trade. One alternative is for enforcement to be managed through other global institutions, the most obvious of which is the WTO. 'It's like asking the fox to guard the henhouse' (Brian McWilliams, President of the International Longshore and Warehouse Union). Other union leaders stress the absence of alternatives to a politics of enforcement outside the structure of regulation of capital (ibid.).
28. It is not of course straightforward. Core labour standards include freedom of association and collective bargaining, the elimination of all forms of forced or compulsory labour, of child labour and of discrimination in employment (ILO, 1999). Labour standards are opposed within third world states even by trades unions and NGOs on the grounds *inter alia* that they erode competitive advantage, they are protectionist, they (and the WTO) are part of an exploitative international order, they are an erosion of sovereignty. They are opposed as market distortions by parties representing capital in advanced countries, by multinational corporations, especially financial organizations, since they limit the mobility of capital. They are favoured by trades unions in advanced countries (Hensman, 1999).

29. Bardhan, 1997: 1387.
30. A neoliberal position examined critically by Hashim and Meagher, 1998.
31. Bacon, 2000.
32. Rahnema and Bawtree, 1997 and Sachs, 1995.
33. Bidwai and Vanaik, 1999.
34. Over half of US funds are outside the USA.
35. Stiglitz, 2000.
36. The generation of financial surpluses encourages crisis as a result of speculative investment. In the current era of globalization there have been crises in 1974, 1982, 1987, 1994 and 1997–8 (FitzGerald). Amin argues that the response to the latest financial crisis (by institutions of global governance) is actually using financial resources to destroy the competitive advantage of productive capital in some of the first division of industrializers. Furthermore, agriculture has been squeezed again to provide resources for the reeling non-agricultural sectors of affected economies.
37. Hale, 1999; Jackson and Pearson, 1999; UN, 1999.
38. The apparently sensible 'Tobin Tax' of a very small percentage on all transactions passing international boundaries is also utopian: technically impossible because of the speed, complexity and substitutability of cross-border transactions (FitzGerald, this volume); vulnerable to the trade-offs between the level of taxation, its impact on market volatility and incentives to evade. FitzGerald argues the case for international tax harmonization, which, since taxes paid in host countries would be deductible against tax due in the home country might generate much larger flows of resources than does 'aid'.
39. Leys, this volume.
40. Brownlie, this volume.
41. Harriss-White and White, 1996.
42. Leys, this volume.
43. Legrain, 2000.
44. Schmitz and Nadvi, 1999.
45. Beccatini, 1979; Cecchi, 2001.
46. A (temporary/seasonal) shift of title may be involved; Goodman and Watts, 1994; Watts, 1992.
47. Dunning, 1998.
48. See the critique of national competition policy by Leys, this volume.
49. US Department of Defence, 1998.
50. Stockholm International Peace Research Institute; SIPRI Arms Transfers Project http://www.sipri.se/projects/armstrade/atfproj.html
51. Wulf, 1998.
52. Wassenaar website.
53. Human Rights Watch website: http://www.hrw.org/hrw/worldreport99/arms /arms.s.html
54. The phrase is FitzGerald's, this volume.
55. Bernstein, 1994.
56. Leys, this volume.
57. See Cadene and Holmstrom, 1998.
58. UN, 1999.
59. In the third world and where public finances are not sound, liberalization accompanies the deepening of debt (Prabhu, 1997). Social sector spending is

widely at risk, the more so in the poorest countries (see Meher, 1999, for a regional analysis of states within India). Protective social security is widely considered to be a luxury (Ahmed et al., 1999) and policies to alleviate poverty have been reinterpreted as 'promotive' forms of social security. Seen in this light, policies on education and health are 'preventive' social security. Guhan, 1994, showed that in the developing world protective social security actually protects those least in need of it – typically some 10 per cent of the workforce which constitutes the public sector. The World Bank's safety nets are put in place only for this part of the population if threatened by unemployment due to downsizing and/or privatization. However, skeletal forms of welfare state for the poor or destitute have been shown to be feasible and affordable in countries such as India. Low cost social protection such as practised in East Asian states places heavy burdens on households, and within them on women and/or has differentiating outcomes in private provision (Goodman, White and Kwon, 1998).

60. And see also Meagher, 1999.
61. Williams, 1994: 103.
62. In parts of the economy where the administrative costs of raising tax exceed the revenue stream from it.
63. Breman, 1996.
64. Roy, 1996; Kumar, 1999.
65. Woods, 1998.
66. Meagher, 1995.
67. In which ascribed character (family, ethnicity, locality) are being replaced by acquired characteristics (efficiency, competence, reliability).
68. In Kaplan, 1994.
69. Hampton, 1996; see also Godson and Williams, 1997: 122.
70. Williams, 1994.
71. Boyce, 1992.
72. Gordon Brown, UK Chancellor of the Exchequer, in *The Guardian*, 17.4.00. His argument for the reform of tax evasion is based on the sharing of information within the EU, rather than on levies on the relevant bonds markets, the option preferred in mainland Europe.
73. Duffield, 1999.
74. Parallel trade is *any* circuit of trade operating outside of – and therefore parallel to – existing legal circuits and thus in contravention of legal regulations, whether across or within national boundaries (Kate Meagher, personal communication, 2000).
75. An estimated 10 per cent leakage, not great by international standards; Meagher, 1999.
76. See van Ufford, 1999, for a fascinating account of the changes in the social organisation of the parallel trade in cattle based on Benin.
77. Bayart et al., 1999.
78. Meagher, 1999.
79. Godson and Williams, 1997.
80. Williams, 1999.
81. Examples of the first are the Italian, Chinese, Nigerian and Colombian TCOs. Examples of the latter are said to be TCOs operating out of Japan, Russia, Mexico and Turkey (Godson and Williams, 1997).

82. Williams, 1994; Godson and Williams, op. cit.
83. Two instances reported by CNN in 1995 not only show this characteristic at work but also show the large number of countries involved. The first involved the supply 'pipeline' evading the embargo on Rwanda and exiled Rwandan armed forces. This went through a British company, Miltech, registered offshore on the Isle of Man, and alleged to be linked to an ethnic Indian from Kenya. Miltech apparently supplied Albanian and Israeli manufactured arms to Hutu forces exiled in Zaire. In a second example, an ex-British soldier (sentenced in India in 2000) used Danish funds supplied by a Hong Kong-based Indian with a New Zealand passport to purchase a plane in Latvia to pick up arms in Bulgaria, which travelled via Pakistan to be airdropped to rebels in India (http://cnn.com/WORLD/9611/26/zaire/).
84. Bonn International Centre for Conversion website: http://bicc.uni-bonn.de/ weapons/papers/hwgerf.html
85. Williams, 1994.
86. US Dept of Justice, 1999.
87. Within the EU; America and the Caribbean; within the Baltic states; Southern Africa; the G7 plus Russia (Godson and Williams, 1997: 119–34).
88. Ibid.
89. For instance Somalia, Liberia, Albania, Tajikistan, Colombia, Kosovo, Chechnya.
90. Bardhan, 1997: 1388. Informalization also weakens other bases of political and economic organization, notably unions (Kate Meagher, personal communication, 2000).
91. Willett, this volume and Duffield, 1999.
92. See Ferguson, 1999, for an analysis of the extreme selectivity of rights and of their signatories; see Dhagamwar, 1992, O'Neill, 1994 and Alston, 1994, for the lack of progress in operationalizing claims on states and obligations on the part of states, by means of which rights are enforced.
93. Bardhan's is carefully thought out (1997): guarantees against fears of subjugation, separation of powers, not only between the executive, the legislature and the judiciary but also within the legislature to allow power to all significant parties, the de-ethnicization of state institutions, the establishment of means of redress, decentralization and regional political autonomy, fiscal compromises, positive discrimination, adequate safety nets for social casualties and displaced people, public information and a strengthening of UN peacemaking and arbitration. Last but not least the control and regulation of arms.
94. Wolfensohn, 1999.
95. For this view see Gray, 1998.
96. Marx, 1976: 47.

References

Ahmed, E., C. Hill, A. K. Sen and J. Dreze (eds) (1999) *Social Security in Developing Countries* (2nd edn), New Delhi/ London: Oxford University Press.

Alston, P. (1994) 'International Law and the Right to Food' in B. Harriss-White and R Hoffenberg (eds), *Food: Multi-disciplinary Perspectives*, Oxford: Blackwell, pp. 205–16.

Armstrong, J. (1995) 'Uganda's AIDS Crisis and its Implications for Development', *World Bank Discussion Paper 059–210X*, Washington: World Bank.

Bach, D. (ed.) (1999) *Regionalisation in Africa: Integration and Disintegration*, Oxford: James Currey.

Bacon, D. (2000) 'Can Global Workers beat Globalisation?', Socialist Register Discussion Pages (socialist-register@yorku.ca).

Bardhan, P. (1997) 'Method in the Madness? A Political Economy Analysis of the Ethnic Conflict in Less Developed Countries', *World Development*, 25, 9, 1381–98.

Bayart, J.-F., S. Ellis and B. Hilson (1999) *The Criminalisation of the State in Africa*, London: Institute of AfricanAffairs/James Currey.

Beccatini, G. (1979) 'Dal "settore" industriale al "distretto industriale": alcune considerazioni sull' unita de indagine dell' economia industriale', *Rivista di Economia e Politica Industriale*, 1, pp. 35–48.

Bernstein, H. (1994) 'Agrarian Classes in Capitalist Development', in L. Sklair (ed.), *Capitalism and Development*, London: Routledge, pp. 40–71.

Bernstein, P. (1996) *Against the Gods: the Remarkable Story of Risk*, New York: Wiley.

Bidwai, P. and A. Vanaik (1999) *South Asia on a Short Fuse: Nuclear Politics in the Subcontinent*, New Delhi: Oxford University Press.

Boyce, J. (1992) 'The Revolving Door? External Debt and Capital Flight: a Philippino Case Study', *World Development*, 20, 3, pp. 335–49.

Breman, J. (1996) *Footloose Labour: Working in India's Informal Economy*, Cambridge: Cambridge University Press.

Burawoy, M. (1999) 'The Great Involution: Russia's Response to the Market', Dept of Sociology, Berkeley, University of California.

Cadene, P. and M. Holmstrom (eds) (1998) *Decentralised Production in India: Industrial Districts, Flexible Specialisation and Employment*, New Delhi/London: Sage.

Castells, M. (2000) *The Rise of the Network Society*, Blackwell: Oxford.

Cecchi, C. (2001) 'Rural Development and Local Systems: the Case of Maremma Rural District', PhD Thesis, University of Wales, Cardiff.

Dhagamwar, V. (1992) 'The Disadvantaged and the Law', in B. Harriss, S. Guhan and R Cassen (eds), *Poverty in India: Research and Policy*, New Delhi: Oxford University Press.

Duffield, M. (1999) 'Globalisation and War Economies: Promoting Order or the Return of History?' *Fletcher Forum of World Affairs*, 23, 2, pp. 21–36.

Dunning, J. (1998) 'Globalisation and the New Geography of Foreign Direct Investment', in N. Woods (ed.), *Globalisation*, Special Issue, *Oxford Development Studies*, 26, 1 pp. 47–70.

Ferguson, C. (1999) *Global Social Policy Principles: Human Rights and Social Justice*, Social Development Department, Department for International Development, London.

FitzGerald, E. V. K. and F. Stewart (eds) (1997) *War, Economy and Society*, Special Issue, *Oxford Development Studies*, 25, 1.

George, S. (forthcoming) 'Globalising Rights', in M. J. Gibney (ed.), *Globalising Rights: the Oxford Annesty Lectures*, Oxford: Oxford University Press.

Godson, R. and P. Williams (1997) 'Strengthening Co-operation against Trans-sovereign Crime', ch. 5 in R. Godson, R Schultz and G Quester (eds), *Security Studies for the Twenty-first Century*, Washington/London: Brassey's.

Goodman, D. and M. Watts (1994) 'Reconfiguring the Rural or Fording the Divide: Capitalist Restructuring and the Global Agro-Food System', *Journal of Peasant Studies*, 22, 1, pp. 1–49.

Goodman, R., G. White and H. Kwon (1998) *The East Asian Welfare Model: Welfare Orientalism and the State*, London: Routledge.

Gray, J. (1998) *False Dawn: the Delusions of Global Capitalism*, London: Granta.

Guhan, S. (1994) 'Social Security Options for Developing Countries', *International Labour Review*, 133, 1, pp. 35–53.

Hale, A. (ed.) (1999) *Trade Myths and Gender Reality: Trade Liberalisation and Women's Lives*, Uppsala: Global Publications Foundation.

Hampton, M. (1996) 'Where Currents Meet: the Offshore Interface between Corruption, Offshore Financial Centres and Economic Development', in B. Harriss-White and G. White (eds).

Harriss-White, B. and R. Hoffenberg (eds) (1994) *Food: Multidisciplinary Perspectives*, Oxford/London: Blackwell.

Harriss-White, B. and G. White (eds) (1996) *Liberalisation and the New Corruption*, Special Issue, *Bulletin of the Institute of Development Studies*, 27, 2.

Hashim, Y. and K. Meagher (1999) 'Cross Border Trade and the Parallel Currency Market – Trade and Finance in the Context of Structural Adjustment', *Research Report 113*, Uppsala: Nordiska Afrikainstitutet.

Held, D., A. McGrew, D. Goldblatt and J. Perraton (1999) *Global Transformations: Politics, Economics and Culture*, Stanford: Stanford University Press.

Hensman, R. (1999) 'How to Support the Rights of Women Workers in the Context of Trade Liberalisation in India', in A. Hale (ed.), *Trade Myths and Gender Reality*, Uppsala: Global Publications Foundation, pp. 71–88.

Higgott, R. (2000) 'Global Governance and the Anti-Politics of the Post-Washington Consensus', ESRC Centre for Globalisation and Regulation, Warwick University.

International Labour Office (1999) *Decent Work*, International Labour Conference, 87th Session: Report of the Director-General, Geneva: ILO.

Jackson, C. and R. Pearson (eds) (1999) *Feminist Visions of Development: Gender Analysis and Policy*, London: Routledge.

Kamat, S. (1999) 'NGOs as a New State Formation in the Global Economy', *Exchanges*, 27, December, pp. 3–12.

Kaplan, R. (1994) 'The Coming Anarchy', *The Atlantic Monthly*, February.

Kumar, A. (1999) *The Black Economy in India*, New Delhi: Penguin.

Lasch, S. and J. Urry (1999) *Economies of Signs and Space*, 2nd edn, London: Sage.

Latham, P. (2001) *The Captive Local State*, Nottingham: Spokesman Books.

Legrain, P. (2000) 'Against Globophobia', *Prospect*, 52, pp. 30–5.

Leys, C. (2001) *Market Driven Politics: Global Economic Forces, National Politics and Public Services in Britain*, London: Verso.

Marx, K. (1976) *Genesis of Capital*, Moscow: Progress Publishing House.

Meagher, K. (1995) 'Crisis, Informalisation and the Urban Informal Sector in Sub-Saharan Africa', *Development and Change*, 26, 2.

Meagher, K. (1999) 'Globalisation through the Back Door: Adjustment, Globalisation and Cross-Border Trade in West Africa', Paper at the Conference on Structural Adjustment and Social and Economic Change in Sub-Saharan Africa, Centre for Development Studies, Copenhagen.

Meher, R. (1999) 'Interstate Disparities in Levels of Development', *Review of Development and Change*, 4, 2, pp. 198–224.

Monbiot, G. (2000). *Captive State: the Corporate Takeover of Britain*, Basingstoke: Palgrave Press.

O'Neill, O. (1994) 'Hunger, Needs and Rights', pp. 217–33 in Harriss-White and Hoffenberg (eds).

Prabhu, S. (1997) 'Promotional and Protective Social Security During Economic Reforms', *Review of Development and Change*, 11, 1, pp. 24–51.

Rahnema, M. and Bawtree, V. (1997) *The Post-Development Reader*, London: Zed.

Roy, R. (1996) 'State Failure in India: Political-Fiscal Implications of the Black Economy', pp. 22–31 in Harriss-White and White (eds).

Sachs, W. (ed.) (1995) *Development Dictionary: a Guide to Knowledge and Power*, London: Zed.

Saxenien, A.-L. (1994) *Regional Advantage: Culture and Competition in Silicon Valley and Route 128*, Cambridge, MA: Harvard University Press.

Schmitz, H. and K. Nadvi (eds) (1999) *Industrial Clusters in Developing Countries*, Special Issue, *World Development*, 27, 9.

Silver, B. and G. Arrighi, (2000) 'Workers North and South', in L. Panitch and C. Leys (eds), *Working Classes: Global Realities*, Socialist Register 2001, London: Merlin Press.

Stiglitz, J. (2000) 'What I Learned at the East Asian Crisis', *The New Republic*, 17 April.

Ufford, P. Q. van (1999) *Trade and Traders: the Making of the Cattle Market in Benin*, Amsterdam: Thela.

United Nations (1999) *World Survey on the Role of Women in Development: Globalisation, Gender and Work*, UN Department of Economic and Social Affairs, New York.

US Department of Defence (1998) *Foreign Military Sales, Foreign Military Construction Sales and Military Assistance*, DSCA, Washington.

US Department of Justice (1999) *Overview of International Criminal Organisations*, Drugs Enforcement Agency, Washington.

Watts, M. (1992) 'Peasants and Flexible Accumulation in the Third World', *Economic and Political Weekly*, 25 July, pp. PE90–7.

White, G. (ed.) (1988) *Developmental States in East Asia*, London: IDS/ Macmillan.

White, G. (1993) 'Towards a Political Analysis of Markets', pp. 4–11 in G. White (ed.).

White, G. (ed.) (1993) *The Political Analysis of Markets*, Special Issue, *Bulletin of the Institute of Development Studies*, 24, 3.

White, G. J. Howell and S. Xiaoyuan (1996) *In Search of Civil Society: Market Reform and Social Change in Contemporary China*, Oxford / London: Oxford University Press.

Williams, P. (1994) 'Transnational Criminal Organisations and International Security', *Survival*, 36, 1, pp. 96–123.

Williams, P. (ed) (1999) *Illegal Immigration and Commercial Sex: the New Slave Trade*, London: Frank Cass.

Wolfensohn, J. (1999) 'A Proposal for a Comprehensive Development Framework', World Bank, Washington.

Woods, N. (1998) 'Globalisation: Definitions, Debates and Implications', in N. Woods (ed.), *Globalisation*, Special Issue, *Oxford Development Studies*, 26, 1, pp. 5–16.

World Bank (1981) *Accelerated Development in Subsaharan Africa: an Agenda for Action*, World Bank, Washington.

Wulf, G. (1998) *Conventional Arms Transfers, Surplus Weapons and Small Arms*, Bonn: International Centre for Conversion.

2
Economic Globalism and Political Universalism: Conflicting Issues?

Samir Amin

In the prevailing discourse, market and democracy are considered as indissolubly linked. But neither the concepts nor the realities of what is or could be the market and democracy are subject to question in this discourse. In the same manner, globalization and universalism are conceived as being practically synonymous. The 'global village' constitutes one of the fashionable catchwords which, though bereft of meaning, bear witness to this confusion. In this chapter, I will argue that market/democracy and globalization/universalism are more contradictory than complementary pairs: economic globalization based on the market, and democratic political universalism an explosive nonsense, and that we must rethink the ideas of market, democracy and universalism within the perspective of a historical process which has certainly not reached its term.

The market

The market is invoked in mainstream discourse just as supernatural forces are invoked elsewhere. We are urged to 'believe in the market', which alone 'reveals' (encapsulates) the 'true values' of the hamburger and the automobile, of the square metre of living space in the metropolis, the hectare of rice field, the barrel of petrol, the exchange rate of the dollar, the work hour of the factory labourer in Asia or that of the Wall Street broker, the 'true' price that must be paid to gain access to medical care, university education, to the web.

This discourse is therefore not about the emancipation of human beings and their societies, but of submission to a binding law. The market becomes an absolute, not a concrete network of trade relations classified under the modest category – no matter how important –

known as economic life. It becomes a principle governing all human relations. One can then speak of the market of ideas and that of political 'options' (what a curious and despicable use of words), and probably also of a market in the honour of politicians, like the market in sex (both of which are alive and well – the Mafia knows how to use them). Ethics, which I believe is also a motor of social life, disappears.

For everything there is a supply (whose curve rises on the basis of price) and a demand (whose curve is descending). There is therefore a 'true price' at their intersection. Supply and demand are independent of each other. Nobody asks questions about how they are formed in the real world and their subsequent interdependence, indeed confusion. The sect of 'pure' economists (that is to say those unpolluted by 'politics') was constituted to construct models of this curve, to demonstrate that the market is self-regulating and to give further legitimacy to its work by affirming that the equilibrium which it produces defines the best of all possible worlds. Have these efforts been successful? Certainly not, neither in theory, nor in the practices which they inspire. Since the time of Walras, economics has been employed without result since it has been demonstrated that it is impossible to derive the pattern of supply and demand curves from optimal behaviours (the Sonneschein theorem). Who cares? The style of the sect is like the one used in narrating fairy tales. The Arrow Debreu model, the pride of 'pure' economics, certainly demonstrates that there is, at least, a general equilibrium in the hypothesis of perfect competition. The latter, however, supposes that Walras's famous auctioneer equates supplies and demands. Curiously therefore, the model demonstrates that a central planner perfectly aware of the behaviour of the billions of primary actors who operate in the markets can take decisions that produce the envisaged equilibrium. The model does not demonstrate that the market, *as it really exists*, can achieve this. And if this fundamentalism – the market as religion – is untenable in theory, it is much more so in practice. The pure economist imagines an economy free of all facets of social reality, such as the existence of states, the organized confrontation of social interests (social classes for example), the oligopolistic nature of the main producers' organizations, the interplay of political, ideological and cultural forces etc. It denies what specifically separates social science from the sciences of nature.

But fortunately economic fundamentalism is not the only belief that is possible. One can believe in a God that allows human beings to make their history and a market whose working is regulated. Besides, in reality, the market is always regulated, except in pure imaginary economics. The real option therefore is not regulation or deregulation, but what type of regulation and for what social interests?

I will not discuss here the successive forms that regulation has taken during the history of the last two centuries without which capitalist accumulation would have been impossible. Each of these forms responded to the challenges of the time and place, to the necessary social alliances through which the domination of capital is expressed, forcing the latter to adjust to specific social imperatives. To read politics and history, in which fundamentalists have never shown any interest, makes it possible to understand the meaning and real impact of the market.

The victory of democracy over fascism and those of the peoples of Asia and Africa over ancient colonialism created, after the Second World War, conditions for transparent and efficient social regulations – for a time (as is always the case in real history). The historic compromise between capital and labour in the countries of central capitalism, on the basis of which the welfare state was constructed, also produced the development project that I call national-populist in the Third World and real or at least potential forms of democratic regulation, because they were socially transparent. The state appeared as the instrument for the implementation of these 'social contracts', negotiated compromise and accepted social visions. Its interventions were not those of stupid and awkward bureaucrats, as the neo-anarchist discourse of market fundamentalism maintains; they were instruments for the affirmation of a mature society that knew what it wanted.

The compromises achieved between nations, workers, enterprises, oligopolies, transnationals etc. define the mode of regulation that governs any actually existing society, among others the mode of regulation of its economic life, both at the national level and in international relations. Bretton Woods and fluctuating exchange rates are both modes of regulation. But each expresses the victory of certain interests over others. The universal anarchy/harmony utopia obviates reflection on the modes of regulation that are always present. This is why the economy of contemporary one-sided thinking reduces the instruments of economic policy to two: budgetary policy and monetary policy. This is evidently not true. Other instruments, recognized or hidden, are operated. There are always industrial policies, be they those of the state for example, charged with the task of supporting the establishment of stronger and more independent productive systems *vis-à-vis* the exterior, or be they the expressions of the strategies of private groups of industrialists or financiers themselves (and in this case one speaks, wrongly, of the absence of policies because they are not transparent).

There are always social policies in fact, be they relatively favourable to workers (social security for example) or unfavourable to them. The flexibility of the work market is not the absence of social policies, it is a social policy unilaterally regulated by the strongest – the employers. It is the implementation of the totality of these policies, be it recognized or not, which determines, among others, the state of the external balance, whether balanced or not. And since we live in a world of nations, states, and various currencies managed by various states, the search for a stable external balance is, for all, though in various degrees, unavoidable. The mix of policies – that I call regulation – must take this into consideration.[1]

Social and transparent regulation or opaque and one-sided regulation is always there. Markets don't exist without it, since the forces which operate in the markets are the expressions of social relations. Markets are embedded in these relations. Karl Polanyi reminded us in 1945[2] that, having failed to recognize this, market 'liberalism' produced the two world wars and the Fascist drift. Before him, the classicists – from Smith to Ricardo – then Marx and much later Keynes, had shared, beyond the divergence of their visions, methods and proposals, this recognition that economics is political. In the real world, we do not have to deal with 'markets' simply, but with markets for goods and services that are generally produced by private capitalist enterprises, the majority of them oligopolies, on the basis of defined relations of production (wage labour or self-employed labour which has a semblance of independence but which in fact is a kind of sub-contracted wage labour). In these relations the majority of human beings who only have the strength of their muscles or their brains 'to sell' are, as a result, alienated, in the sense that history of which they are subjects, which they make, appears to them as imposing itself on them from outside. When the human being in question is defined as a 'factor of production' or as a 'human resource', what an acknowledgement of the naïveté of the expression: resources for whom? for what?

Similarly, in the real world, we do not have to deal with 'natural resources' that can simply be treated as 'goods' (commodified), since these resources constitute the basis of the reproduction not only of the material needs of society but also of biological life. However, the rationality of the market is short-term, based on the famous 'devaluation of the future'. In these conditions the dictatorship of the market engenders the progressive and inevitable destruction of the natural basis of reproduction.

In the real world, too, we also have countries, states, nations (call them what you will), and we will have to live with this reality for quite some time. A diversity of national or pluri-national currencies necessarily comes with this plurality of political power. However, mainstream economists assure us that money is a merchandise like any other (it carries a price tag – the equilibrium exchange rate – which assures that of the external balance) and that the market, if it is deregulated, makes it possible to know the 'true price' of the currency: an idea which, by virtue of its expression, appears to be evidence for these propositions. Yet none of the numerous Nobel prize laureates who have not expressed any doubts on this subject is capable of finding an answer to this simple question: which is the true price of the dollar, expressed in yens, that the market is supposed to have revealed to us? 80 or 380 yens? And why, whatever the rate between these two extreme values between which the dollar has in reality fluctuated, has the external balance of the United States remained in deficit? External equilibrium cannot in fact be attained by way of a 'true' exchange rate as revealed by the so-called deregulated market.

Therefore, in practice, what is being proposed to us under the rubric of globalization? Deregulate to the maximum and you will approach the true value of your currency. In practice, for the weak economies in the global system, deregulation does not lead to external equilibrium. Then, we are told: devalue, or let your currency float and devalue spontaneously. The successive waves of devaluation continue indefinitely. And, the height of irony, the more you devalue the more you move away from the purchasing power parity which the defenders of the illusion (the exchange rate equilibrium) pretend constitutes its bottom line.

And who wins and who loses in this game? This is not my domain, the economists concerned would say. And yet, visibly, there are winners and losers. Small winners: the horde of western tourists who can afford to pay for very inexpensive five-star hotels, beyond their reach at home. Big winners: the transnationals. Because simultaneously, in the name of liberalization, globalization and privatization, the sale of the juiciest pieces of the badly managed local productive systems has been ordained to the 'efficient' transnationals. This is how the deal is struck. A national electricity company had constructed a network of production and distribution systems at enormous cost (in the past when the dollar was worth 100 local monetary units). Its juiciest segment (the one that serves the rich districts that can pay) is resold to a transnational while 100 local monetary units are only worth ten American cents. I call this the massive devaluation of the capital laboriously accumulated by the poor, a massive transfer of the value of the capital for the benefit of the rich. This is a more lucid manner of saying how it works out.

Democracy

Democracy is, like the market, a sacred word in the modern vocabulary which has become so current that one rarely asks questions about the history of the emergence of its significance and problems it raises. The idea that, even among the cultivated, the public make of it is based on images, more or less precise: the agora of Athens, and the Greek etymology of the word *habeas corpus*; the human and citizens' rights declaration of 1789; the universal declaration of the human rights of 1948; multipartyism, elections, the separation of powers and the state of law, etc. A long list to which the Asian and African nationalists, sensing that they had been forgotten in the enumeration of the mainstream media, have added the innumerable forms of dialogue in the management of villages in Africa and Asia (Islamic Choura, the Indian panchayat). But no one – beyond the narrow circles of specialists – bothers to reflect on how these institutions participate in the reproduction of a society, or the type of society in question. Democracy is considered simply a good thing in itself which is probably true (in any case, this is my opinion), but certainly not sufficient to understand the successive historic meanings, contradictions and the alternative choices that will determine its future.

First, we have to do with a concept, and a modern reality, that is to say, that has been constituted in conjunction with the formation of capitalism. The forms in which dialogue was organized in the exercise of power in past societies do not have much to do with modern democracy, and the Greek etymology of the word should not distort our understanding; because power, ideology and economic life maintained in capitalist modernity are *sui generis*.[3]

All philosophical systems throughout the ancient world were structured around the idea of a governing cosmic order which imposes itself on human beings and their societies. The task, at best, was to seek out the divine commandments holding sway over them, or else to learn them through the utterances of prophets. The parliaments of the *Ancien Régime* in France, just as the Choura of the Arabo-Islamic world, as well as other institutions of dialogue proper to all ancient societies, were not democratic institutions in the modern sense of the term. In Restoration France, for example, Joseph de Maistre proclaimed that the liberatory aspiration of the Revolution was a chimera to be abandoned, that the law-making madness of modern democracy was to be renounced because 'only God is a legitimate lawgiver', and that the tradition of respect for God's law was to be dutifully obeyed at all times and in all places. Burke was not saying anything different. Just like the Islamic fundamentalists of today, the sentence written by Joseph de Maistre could have been signed yesterday by Ayatollah Khomeini, and today by Sheikh el Azhar. In all these instances the relation between Reason (and the necessary democracy to attain it) and Emancipation is broken.

The modern world is defined by a rupture through which humanity escapes from the commandments of a cosmic order, or rather (in the view of those who see this rupture as progress) humanity frees itself. For me there is no other definition of modernity, and modernity requires nothing more than this philosophical rupture. Thus we see that modernity can never be completed, never be closed. On the contrary, it opens onto the unknown, whose boundaries, though ultimately unattainable, are pushed further backward with each advance in the accumulation of our knowledge with regard to the social realm. Modernity is unending. But it takes on a succession of forms, which vary according to the responses it offers to the challenges confronting society at each moment of its history. The concept and practice of modern democracy find their place within this framework. To say that the human being makes his or her own history, is necessarily to propose an organized social framework in order to make possible a project of emancipation. The latter in turn defines what we call modern democracy.

One then begins to see why modern democracy has nothing to do with the forms of social dialogue of past ages. The modalities of the exercise of power and those of dialogue are of course always linked. But the function of power and the dialogue which underpins it remains, in the old systems, based on the reading and interpretation of tradition, supposedly eternal since founded on divine laws. Modern democracy, on the contrary, fully embraces the right to invention, to produce something new. Herein lies all the meaning of the sign of equality which the philosophy of Enlightenment places between Reason and Emancipation.

The proposition according to which humanity makes its own history represented the birth process of modernity and defined the field of inquiry for social thought, but suggested no answers to the questions posed in that enquiry. Who is the active agent of this history: all individuals, or only some of them? Social classes? Various communities and groups with their own unique qualities and statuses? Nations? Societies organized as political states? And how is this history made? What real factors do these agents put to work? What strategies do they adopt, and why? How, and according to what criteria, do they judge success? What real conditions are transformed by their activities? To what extent do those transformations correspond to the goals of their authors, and to what extent do they diverge? All these questions remain perpetually open. They simply remind us that modernity is a permanently moving process, not a system that is closed and defined once and for all.

The development of modern democracy, which came in response to these issues, therefore has a history. This response crystallizes first of all in the capitalist social project which defines the subject of this history: the bourgeois who is simultaneously the citizen and the entrepreneur. Each led to a strict separation which bourgeois modernity imposes between the political domain, which should be guided by the principles of democracy and economics as managed by private property, free enterprise and market competition.

The democracy in question was and still is therefore exclusively a political democracy. It gradually proclaimed its principles (the rights of the individual, freedom of expression, election, the separation of powers) and invented institutions (legislative houses, governments chosen by electoral majority, independent judiciary etc.). It defined the citizen who had the freedom to exercise these rights. This was first and foremost a man; it was only much later that, in the most advanced modern democracies, similar rights were to be conquered by women. It would also be for a long time the well-to-do man, the property owner who was the sole beneficiary of the right to vote. It was once again necessary to wait for a long time for the struggle of the working class to finally impose universal suffrage. The equation, market = democracy, does not have much to do with historical reality. Modern democracy was imposed by the struggles of the classes that were the victims of the market.

Because the principles of bourgeois modernity were effectively bred in the triumph of the 'market', or to be more exact, the complex of 'private property – enterprise – open competition', these principles have nothing to do with those of democracy. They belong to a totally different sphere.

Modern bourgeois thinking does not at first see the contradiction involved in the strict separation of these aspects of social life. On the contrary, it sees them as two dimensions of emancipation, one of the citizen, the other of the entrepreneur (often the same individual). The idea that other individuals who are neither citizens nor entrepreneurs – women, workers – should enjoy rights is still a stranger to it. Thus, it is no surprise to find that some of the leaders of American independence turned out to be slave owners and that this did not pose any problem for them; they proclaimed themselves to be democrats as well. Equally, it is not surprising that the first modern democratic legislation forbade 'workers' coalitions' and strikes, in such a way as to keep strictly separated the principles of democratic governance of politics and those of economic management through capital, enterprise and market.

To be sure, the history of democratic progress continued, precisely through the affirmation and conquest of new rights – social rights – which challenged the unilateral management of the economy by the market. Here again it was necessary to wait for a long time before these new rights emerged. Up to the Second World War, they continued to remain practically limited to a few rights for workers, organizations (free trade unions, the right to strike) and modest labour legislation. It was only after the war that the working class was able to win, thanks to the defeat of fascism, a political and social legitimacy which it never had before. It was not until then that the welfare state came to be conceived and constructed, inaugurating a new form of social regulation of the market.

It is useful to return briefly to the theoretical issue implicit in our analysis, in order to complete our preceding discussion about the concept of democracy – to whit the meaning of the proposition that the human being, individually and collectively, makes his or her own history. It will be seen at the same time how the separation of the realms of democracy and the market constitutes a fundamental contradiction in the capitalist project.

At every instant, modern social thought is torn between its aspiration to treat human beings as the free authors of their own history and its recognition that they are subject to seemingly objective laws comparable to the laws of nature. Under capitalism, the dominance of economic factors is expressed as the autonomy of economic forces. Like natural forces, these act as realities answering to objective laws. In the dominant discourse there is a perpetual insistence on a supposedly unavoidable submission to these notorious economic laws (which vulgarizing rhetoric encapsulates in the phrase 'the market'). In vaguer and often cruder forms of this rhetoric, reference is made to laws of nature, and even to a 'state of nature', to which people would be as subject as they are to objective forces. Recall, however, that the Enlightenment modernity defined itself with a call to *escape* from supposedly natural laws and to give full authority to the law-making citizen. But a retrogression towards submission to these alleged demands of nature is always lurking in the recesses of bourgeois thought. From nineteenth-century social Darwinism to aggressive contemporary insistence on genetic and 'neurological' explanations of social phenomena, this deviant conceit is perpetually present. Yet it is forcefully expressed only under certain conditions, and therefore it is essential to specify them.

The movement of history does not proceed along a straight line and in a single direction. It is made up of moments of advance in some direction, of hesitations, of retreats, of blind alleys, of choices at forking pathways. During periods of tranquil progress, it is always very tempting to think of the historical process in linear terms. These are periods which the political economy of the system interprets as phases of accumulation ensuring reproduction of the social relations primary to the system. During those moments, history seems to be going, naturally and inevitably, in a known direction. Those are moments during which social thought seems capable of producing powerful and coherent doctrines, those of the 'great narratives' (such as the bourgeois democratic project, the socialist project, or nation-building projects) which current social thought, in deep crisis, treats as objects of ridicule.

On the other hand, when the social equilibria that hitherto had ensured the calm reproduction of society have turned topsy-turvy, when no one can foresee the direction in which society will move once its equilibria have been restored, the crisis also becomes manifest in the collapse of those big, reassuring, intellectual structures. Their weak points become yawning gaps. Such periods are marked by the fragmentation of social thought, and this fragmentation provides fodder for wayward conceits that direct it away from its needed reconstruction. My interpretation of contemporary history treats it as having moved out of a period of the former sort which foundered in the current crisis.

Therefore, is modernity outlived, as is complacently uttered in current fashionable discourse? Not in the least. For if modernity simply means that human beings make their own history, then it is a long way from becoming outlived. Undoubtedly, in times of deep crisis like the present, there is a great temptation to go back to a premodern stance and claim that while human beings believe that they make their own history, in reality history takes place quite apart from their activity. In other words, there is a temptation to claim that what happens goes in no direction that anyone can even discover, let alone hope to influence by constructive and consequential action, and accordingly to suggest falling back on the unambiguous stance of trying to manage this meaningless history as well as possible. To manage as well as possible, then, means the democratic management of pluralism at the grass-roots level, the organization of so-called 'conviviality', the improvement of this or that aspect of social life. The counterpart to this is acceptance of the essential features of the established system, including the rule that the market dominates everything, i.e., capitalist political economy. The motives leading to these conclusions are understandable. They stem from disarray consequent on the exhaustion and even collapse of the great projects marking the preceding stage of history, not only the socialist project but also that of the nation-state and various others. But to understand these motives is not the same thing as to believe that this situation may last, let alone that it will last forever as is proclaimed in the 'end of history' thesis.

The so-called postmodernist critique thus fails to see that modernity, always incomplete, is today confronted with a challenge, not to renounce its fundamental principle, but to go ahead with its implementation by inventing the new.

Preceding the postmodernist propositions is an extensive rhetoric asserting 'the failure of modernity'. The least that can be said on the topic is that this superficial discourse has no analytic foundation whatsoever. The modern epoch is also the epoch of humanity's greatest achievements, accomplished at a pace immeasurably greater than that which marked premodern times. Modernity achieved enormous progress in material production and scientific knowledge. Likewise, democracy advanced, despite its limits and occasional setbacks. Social progress was achieved despite its limits; and even ethical progress too. The idea that each human life is irreplaceable, the idea of happiness, the idea of individuality irreducible to membership in a familial or ethnic collectivity – these are all modern ideas. Certainly these results of progress (and I have no qualms about using that currently unfashionable word) did not come about through continuous movement along a straight line. They had to be won, they are always threatened, and there are setbacks which are always accompanied by enormous crimes. But this is no reason to throw out the baby with the bath water and to mutter 'things used to be better'. Nor is it a reason to simply say that because of 'failures' we must give up on the foolhardy struggle to go forward and instead be content to simply cope with the present reality – that would be to take a leap which I consider neither necessary nor useful.

Modernity is still unfinished, and it will remain so as long as the human race continues to exist. Currently, the fundamental obstacle setting its limits is still defined by the social relationships specific to capitalism. What the postmodernists refuse to see is that modernity can progress further only by going beyond capitalism. Unfortunately this possibility seems inaccessible at the present moment. For the 'failures' of modernity, and the aggravation of conflict that has brought with it that wave of violence (recognition of which is the source of the postmodernist thesis), result from the evolution of that same capitalism and show that it has reached the end of the historical path at whose earlier stages it could still, despite its specific contradictions, appear synonymous with progress. Today the choice 'socialism or barbarism' is truly the choice confronting the human race.

We are in fact living in times characterized by a disequilibrium in the balance of social forces to the benefit of capital, and to the detriment of labour. The temporary product of the erosion of the postwar systems of regulation, is far from being a utopian dream of 'deregulation'; it is, in reality the one-sided regulation by capital. Social rights conquered after a hard struggle by the popular majority are put into question. Democracy returns to its bourgeois origin: that of political management alone, while economics is handed over to the diktats and vagaries of the market. The result is what I call a 'low intensity democracy'. The citizen (and today it is everybody) can vote freely, for the right or left. This is no longer of any importance, let alone effect, because his or her future as worker (or as an unemployed person) will be decided elsewhere, in the 'market'. The vote loses its meaning, and a crisis of democracy is the result. In countries where people believed democracy to be entrenched, it wobbles: most evidently in the abstention of the majority of the electorate in the United States (and not by happenstance the poorest half). Is the devaluation of what is called the political class in Europe not a symptom of the same dangerous erosion? In Third World countries manifestations of this crisis are even more violent. The erosion of societal, national populist projects has no doubt found an opening in the desirable recognition of the virtues of free expression and political pluralism. But this opening coincides with a degradation of social conditions, for which the imposed model of globalization (which will be examined later), is largely to blame. Also, the process of political democratization had hardly gained momentum before it quickly lost legitimacy again in the eyes of the popular majority. What can be expected of this fancy pluralism, electoral travesty and the weak powers they produce? Do the escalations of religious fundamentalism and ethnic strife not already suggest that disaster is not far away?

And yet, this crisis coincides with a new leap in the development of productive forces. The rapid progress of the scientific and technological revolution, of information and robotics, has already quickened what I have called the necessary withering away of the diktat of value, that is to say, the market. Unbelievable paradox: the harbinger of a potentially spectacular emancipation is accompanied by the deepening of the double crisis engendered by the one-sided management of the economy by the market, and by the reduction of democracy to weak political management.

Globalization, which I take up now, aggravates this major contradiction of capitalism, and intensifies the explosive market/democracy conflict to a degree of unprecedented violence.

Globalization

Globalization has equally become a 'catchword', so much abused in popular discourse that one is no longer sure of its real meaning. Taken in its most ordinary sense – the existence of relations between the various regions of the world, intensive enough to have some effect – globalization is as old as the world, even if it is easily agreed that the intensity of these relations today is considerably greater than in the past. But as with 'market' and 'democracy' it is once again crucial to identify the specific characteristics of each of the successive phases of this very long history of globalization, to analyse its mechanisms and, by so doing, to link the successive forms of globalization to the social systems of the world's various regions in their mutual relations with each other.

There existed – at least for the old world (Eurasia and Africa) – a system of globalization that I have elsewhere described and analysed over the long duration of two millennia from 500 BC to 1500 AD.[4] The so-called silk roads, the transfer of technologies (be it the compass, printing or gunpowder, to take examples reproduced in all elementary school books) and the spread of religions, all testify to the reality of this ancient globalization – to the point that when Vasco de Gama lands on the coast of India in Calicut in 1498, he is surprised to find Christians there. It is likewise known that the Uigurs were Nestorians before being converted to Islam; that Islam travelled to China and Indonesia and that Buddhism travelled all the way from the Himalayas to conquer Mongolia, China (for a time), Japan, Sri Lanka and the countries of South-East Asia, so that Alexander the Great, and then Christians and Muslims, found it in Afghanistan.

That globalization – which did not include so-called pre-Columbian America – operated according to a very different logic from that which subsequently became capitalist modernity. The three 'centres' of the old globalization (China, India, the Middle East) accounted for 80 per cent of the population of the globe. In addition, that globalization was not polarizing, in the sense that the development gap between the various regions it linked, was, for almost all of the populations concerned, very modest, not exceeding a ratio of two to one; also in the sense that nothing fundamentally prevented retarded regions from catching up with the most advanced. The discourse of modern globalization affirms that globalization provides an opportunity, and that the peoples concerned may take advantage of or miss it depending on internal factors. Curiously, this affirmation, which is precisely unrealistic as far as modern globalization is concerned, was true in the past. It is instructive that the greater part of Europe, which until about 1000 AD was on the periphery of the global system of the time, more or less lagging behind in development as does Africa today, was able, over the remarkably short time of three centuries, 'to catch up' and even to prepare to 'overtake' the old centres.

Globalization in its modern form was constituted following the Industrial Revolution which, between the eighteenth century and the beginning of the nineteenth century, marked the beginning of the fully fledged form of capitalism. The mercantilist transition between 1500 and 1800 could be interpreted from this point of view as a fight between the old (feudal) mode of production and the new (capitalist) one, and also as a fight between the old global system (which swung between three centres – Chinese, Indian and Middle Eastern) and the new system, integrating the Americas and organized by the new and upcoming Atlantic Europe centre. I will not dwell on this crucial turning point which I have discussed elsewhere.[5]

The new globalization, however – that of capitalism – is polarizing. In two centuries, from 1800 to the end of the twentieth century, it has been able to reduce the population of the centres of the system – whose frontiers have not changed much and which generally embrace the contemporary 'triad' (the United States, Canada, Western Europe, Japan) – to 20 per cent of the population of the planet. The gap in the level of development between these centres and the vast regions of the world which have become their satellites, has continued to widen, over the last two centuries, to the point when the ratio mentioned earlier, which was two-to-one in 1800, is sixty-to-one today. The polarization that is characteristic of modern globalization is phenomenal, without precedent in the entire past history of humanity.

The key question which this raises is whether this polarization is immanent to the global expansion of capitalism, that is to say, produced by its governing internal logic, or only the result of various concrete, multiple and specific conditions that have all, as if by chance, operated in the same direction: that of making it impossible to catch up. The prevailing discourse does not broach this issue, content to repeat ad nauseam that 'globalization offers an opportunity' etc. Nonetheless it seems curious that none of the people concerned in Asia, Africa and Latin America have been able to seize this 'opportunity', except those few newly industrializing countries permitted to do so by their geopolitical locations.

Instead, I maintain that polarization is immanent in the global expansion of capital. This is because the 'world market' in question remains deeply unbalanced by the single fact that it remains truncated; constantly widening its commercial dimension (trade in goods and services) and in the domain of international transfer of capital, this market remains segmented with regard to labour and to the international migration of workers, both of which remain subject to controls. On its own, this truncated nature of the world market is bound to engender polarization, independently of the thousand and one concrete specific conditions that, according to conjunctures and policies, can spur the acceleration of growth here, or slow it down elsewhere.[6] Liberal discourse pretends to be unaware of this reality and, as a result, remains inconsistent. A really coherent liberal should insist on the opening of borders in every dimension. Then, trade, capital flows and the migration of workers would create conditions for the homogenization at the world level, of an authentic globalization of the economy. Marx and Engels thought in 1848 that the bourgeoisie would do this, would have the courage to carry their project to its proper conclusion. They overestimated its revolutionary capacity. The end result was therefore a globalization of capital but not of the economy, which, on the contrary, is distinguished by the centre/periphery dichotomy that continues to worsen.

The polarization of actually existing world capitalism also has its own history in which one can recognize distinctive stages. During one and a half centuries – from 1800 to 1950 – this polarization was practically synonymous with the division between industrialized/non-industrialized countries. This simple duality was challenged after the Second World War. Already, the Russian Revolution from 1917, then that of China, allowed each 'to catch up' (through industrialization) and to construct new social relations inspired by Marxist socialism. The political successes of national liberation movements in Asia and Africa and the Latin American 'desarrollismo', in turn, imposed an overhaul of the previous scheme of polarization. All were expressions of the revolt of peoples of the periphery, victims of polarizing capitalist globalization.

Capital was forced by this new relation between social forces more favourable (or less unfavourable) to the peoples of the periphery 'to adjust'. And it did so with such success that it has been able 'to reintegrate' into the global system societies which, in various degrees, had attempted to make themselves autonomous. Much closer to the concept of a 'capitalism without capitalists' (with regard to the former USSR) or 'state capitalism' (with regard to countries of the Third World) than to that of original socialism, the models in question attained their historic limits after having fulfilled their real function of initiating a transition to 'normal' capitalism – that is to say, capitalism with capitalists. But the societies in question were reintegrated into the process of capitalist globalization without having been able to construct themselves into really new centres. The explanation of this reality is certainly complex, varying from one country at a given time to the other. The internal social, political and ideological dynamics proper to these societies certainly share a major responsibility in this history (or more precisely these particular histories). But I will assert that, beyond these concrete and diverse conditions, two major realities dominated the scene of this history.

The first concerns the shift of the centre of gravity of the forces that produce and reproduce polarization. Formerly this was located in industry. That is no longer the case. In its place, I have advanced the thesis that the advantages that allow the historic centres (the triad for short) to maintain their dominant positions in spite of the industrialization of the peripheries are located in what I have called the 'five monopolies'[7]: technological initiative; the control of financial flows at the international level (the most internationalized facet of capital); access to the natural resources of the entire planet; control of the means of information and communication; and, last but not least, a monopoly of weapons of mass destruction. Through the use of these five monopolies the triad puts industries of the periphery in the position of sub-contractors, similar to what was, at the dawn of capitalism, the system that put handicraft workers at the mercy of mercantilist capital.

In this analysis, what I have elsewhere called the law of globalized value has passed through successive forms, each specific to each of the phases of polarizing globalization. The first form, unequal trade, which belongs to the phase defined by the dichotomy industrialized/non-industrialized countries, gives way to new forms of extraction of the surplus produced in the 'globalized' peripheries. The case of Korea, to which I will return, perhaps illustrates better than any other the nature of the dynamics of the new polarization. This analysis, of course, is in contrast with the rosy 'success stories' in which the World Bank specializes.

The second form of 'globalized value' has to do with the persistence of a 'reserve' labour force, which the globalization of the peripheries (including socialist peripheries) during the last half-century was not able to absorb. The concept that I propose to consider here is founded on a distinction between two categories of workers: those who are integrated in efficient modern forms of production and as a result are actually or potentially competitive (to various degrees), and those who are excluded (not only the unemployed, of course, but also workers in sectors with low productivity, in agriculture, services, and what is sometimes called 'the informal sector'). The distinction is certainly relative and is not always easy to portray statistically. But it is, in my opinion, significant.[8]

Historically, in countries of the triad, capitalism was able gradually to absorb the 'reserve' in what I will call 'the active army'. It had no fixed time within which to accomplish this. The thesis of the globalization of developing countries through a similar absorption of labourers became canonical thanks to the work of Arthur Lewis.[9] Conventional thinking (that of the World Bank, for example) never went beyond this. And yet the facts demonstrate that such an absorption is impossible within the context of the prevailing logic of the accumulation of capital. And the reasons are almost obvious. As long as the productive forces develop, modernization requires a relative mass of increasingly expensive capital and relatively less and less qualified manpower. This inability of capitalism to absorb a 'reserve' that has become a growing proportion of the population of the globe defines the historical limit of this social system, the irrationality of its rationality.

By examining the degree of advancement of the societies of the periphery in the Industrial Revolution and the proportion of their 're-serve' labour force one gets a striking picture of the magnitude of the challenge facing humanity as a result of capitalist globalization, and the diversity of the forms in which it is expressed.

A challenge which, nonetheless, it appears, also concerns the centres themselves. A reserve army is indeed on the road of reconstitution here for twenty years or so (the unemployed, the poor, the excluded and the marginalized). I will not intervene here in the debate on this set of problems:[10] are they the products of 'transitory' changes,[11] or do they represent a trend that is bound to worsen by reason of the nature of contemporary scientific and technological revolution?

The kind of revolutions that shook the peripheries of the system during the twentieth century, and particularly during the second half of the period, the challenge of their radical nature, led up to the constitution of three layers of societies more or less engaged in modernization and industrialization.

The first layer embraces all the socialist or former socialist countries (the USSR, Eastern Europe, China), South Korea and Taiwan, as well as, to a lesser degree, India and the major countries of Latin America (Brazil and Mexico). These countries entered the Industrial Revolution, in the sense that they constructed systems of national industrial production, as a result of which they are either effectively competitive (Korea is the best example) or at least are potentially so, though this does not exclude the possibility that they may yet undergo involutions in actual practice.

But none of them has been able to reduce its reserve army to the same proportion to the centres in the analogous stages of their development. It seems reasonable to estimate this reserve at 40 per cent for Russia, more for Brazil and Mexico and at a much higher proportion – in the neighbourhood of 70–80 per cent – for India or China. Korea and Taiwan are perhaps the two exceptions to the rule, which some exceptional local and international conditions can explain.

The second layer consists of countries where industries have been established, by transnational capital or the local state, but in which it would be difficult to identify the existence of a national productive system. Some of the industrial units dispersed within them may be competitive, others not; but the local system as a whole is not. It is difficult to say that these countries have 'achieved' their industrial revolution. I group in this category those countries of South-East Asia whose capitalism is subject to qualification, not without reason, of 'proxy capitalism' or 'ersatz capitalism',[12] the Arab countries (Morocco, Algeria, Tunisia, Egypt, Syria, Iraq), South Africa, Turkey and Iran, and some countries of Latin America. Considering a lot of individual data for each of these countries, their aggregate labour reserves vary between 50 and 70 per cent of the population.

The third layer is constituted by countries which have not yet entered industrialization (sub-Saharan Africa, the Caribbean, and some west Asian countries). In these countries the aggregate reserve nearly constitutes the totality of the population.

It will be noticed that my classification is silent on some of the oil-producing or mining states whose rental economy does give the appearance of wealth (in terms of income per capita) simply because they are sparsely populated. Like the American protectorates of the Gulf, these countries are, in spite of their financial clout, passive participants in the world system, in reality almost as 'marginal', from this point of view, as countries of the third group. Marginalization, which I have defined in terms of the passive position occupied in the world system (that is to say the submission to the exigencies of a one-sided adjustment), is not synonymous with poverty. Marginalization and poverty clearly tend to go together, but there are exceptions – the marginalized 'rich'. In practice, only the most prominent peripheral countries try to impose themselves as active participants of the world system, to force centres of the triad to adjust to the exigencies of their development. As will be seen, this ambition is bound to occupy a central position in future conflicts.

The analysis that I have outlined here, of modern globalization seen in its economic dimension, which is dominant, will perhaps now help us see more clearly its complex and ambiguous relationship with political, ideological and cultural universalism.

Universalism

The concept of universalism, that is to say, one of a discourse destined to apply to all human kind, equally has an ancient history.

What I called the metaphysical revolution, which extends from the fifth century BC to the seventh century AD, was based simultaneously on the tributary mode of production and the domination of the metaphysical ideology of the age.[13] The fact that Confucius, Buddha and Zoroastre belong to the same century, about 500 years BC, and that two centuries later Hellenism produced the synthesis of cultures of the Middle East, thus preparing the terrain for Christianity and Islam, are facts constituting, for me, manifestations of this universal aspiration. The setting of tributary society nonetheless determines its upper reaches and limits. My thesis on this essential point is that in the societies that pre-dated capitalism the ideology of metaphysical alienation fulfilled a dominant function in the reproduction of the legitimacy of power, and that economic life was subjected to the logic of this dominant function. Power was the source of wealth; and it was necessary to wait for capitalist modernity to see the relationship between these two terms inverted.

The grand universalisms of the tributary age conquered enormous spaces that constituted themselves into distinct cultural areas, but none of them was able to impose itself on the entire planet. One could therefore be tempted to read the history of the two millennia that preceded the formation of capitalistic modernity as those of, on the one hand, class struggle within the tributary social systems, in the manner of Marx, and on the other, a 'conflict of cultures' (religions and civilizations) perhaps in the manner of Huntington (making all necessary reservations about the simple and superficial theses of this sociologist of foreign affairs). But in reality the conflicts of the time were far from assuming this dominant cultural dimension. Within the large cultural spaces in question, numerous and diverse political authorities shared and competed for the control of the tributary extraction of surplus and their conflicts were those that, in fact, occupied centre stage. Even the Crusades, which are often presented as an epic battle between Christianity and Islam, were in fact 'Frank wars' (as they were called by the Arabs at the time) conducted by feudal lords of the European periphery (mainly France, England and Germany), and as much against Byzantium as against the Khalifate. It was an offensive of an ascendant periphery against the centre dominant at the time (Hellenistic Byzantium and the Khalifate).

This chapter of universalism has in any case been closed. 'The human being makes his or her history' constituted the new central core of modern universalism, associated with capitalist expansion. However, capitalism conquered the entire planet, imposing a dominant economic logic on all its component societies. Inversion of the relationship between politics and the economy, and conquest of the planet, went hand in hand. However, since this economic conquest is far from being homogenizing, and has on the contrary exacerbated the polarization of wealth, modern universalism found itself – and still finds itself – confronted with a challenge to which it has not provided an answer.

The human beings that are said to make their own history are, as a result, Europeans and Europeans alone. Eurocentrism – this particular distortion of the ideologies and perspectives of the dominant world – is not just one among many manifestations of the 'conflict of cultures'. It is the expression of the contradiction peculiar to the polarizing expansion of globalized capitalism, a modern product, a fabrication that goes back again to the eighteenth century, concomitant with the age of Enlightenment.[14] It has nothing to do, for example, with the view that western Christians of previous ages took of 'infidels', whether Muslim or others.

The globalization of actually existing capitalism, that is to say of a polarizing system, does not have much to do with the cultural dimensions that are so central to the discourse of 'the westernization of the world'. Technocrats of the system will always have some trouble in understanding that the 'global village' is a hollow expression. If I put quotation marks around 'westernization', it is because the term is misleading. In fact, the dominant culture of the modern world is not 'western' but capitalist.

Nevertheless, the dominant culture of capitalism has not been able to take root in the system of peripheries, because the latter are victims of the world's polarization. The main aspect of this culture – commodity alienation – is accepted. I will even go further to say that protests against it are more pronounced in the richer societies of the centre than in the poor of the periphery, whose peoples aspire to a little bit of this consumption of which only the privileged can see the limits. But other aspects of this culture – the universal values of capitalism (the spirit of enterprise, respect for the law, the plurality of opinion), like those of its alternative socialist critique (overcoming commodity alienation, democracy with a social content) – are not generally accepted with ease, because the polarization that exists deprives them of all their positive content.

Depending on local conditions, the traumatized societies of the periphery will sometimes lean towards the adoption of the values of the capitalist culture in question (democracy and the spirit of enterprise, which the liberal fractions of the national middle class have sometimes championed) or of their socialist critique. Alternatively, the disappointment and chaos that unfailingly follow the failure of the liberal bourgeois (or para-socialist) attempts to implement capitalist democratic ideas, can lead to a relapse into a neurotic celebration of the past; religious fundamentalism and the resort to ethnicism are both manifestations of this. The dominant system then tries to accommodate, even tries 'to recuperate', these returns to the past (which do not threaten the real domination of capital in any way), through light and sweet talk in praise of 'diversity'. The facile discourse of postmodernism pretends to ignore the fact that there are two very different kinds of diversity: first, those which focus on the future and call for a plurality of the creative faculties in building a future that lies beyond capitalism; and those sterile kinds, that focus on the heritage of the past. The latter can be summarized in a caricature: one hand brandishes the symbol of your diversity (the Koran, or the flag of an ethnic group for example) as long as the other holds a bottle of Coke.

Globalization and insecurities

The internal contradiction specific to capitalist modernity thus sets the economic dimension of polarizing globalization against the political project of the autonomy of nations of the periphery aspiring 'to catch up'. According to successive conjunctures in historic phases, this contradiction was either exacerbated or attenuated.

Three systems occupied centre stage from 1945 to 1980–90: the welfare state in the capitalist countries of the centre, Sovietism in the East, populist national projects in the Third World.[15] Each of these systems was based on a distinctive logic of strong market regulation, to the point where the second system (the Soviet) nurtured the illusion of having reduced the sphere of intervention of the market to almost nothing.[16] The mechanisms conceived at Bretton Woods for the management of the international monetary system and within the context of the UN negotiations concerning trade and investments (notably within UNCTAD) were also systems for the regulation of globalization. The countries of the East, without receding into autarky (except when it was imposed from the outside, as was the case with China from 1950 to 1972), also tried to master their external relations to a greater degree than before.

These forms of regulation brought about a general upsurge in economic growth and the period witnessed unprecedentedly high growth rates, in all three regions of the global system: the West, the East and the South. The negative assessment of the period by the extremists of neo-liberalism – the society of Mont Pelerin – that speaks 'of the failure' of the models of the time, even of their 'irrationality', is a perfectly ideological judgement (in the worst sense of the term), negated by the facts.

The regulations in question did not, however, attenuate the fundamental contradiction of the system, between the expansion of the accumulation of capital and the entrenchment of democracy. In the welfare states of the West, the practice of political democracy was scrupulously respected as never before (one thinks of the fascisms of the period between the two wars). But this political democracy was not social democracy except in the sense that it was accompanied by the extension of social rights (forms of social security) without bringing about the socialization of the control of production. It therefore ended up with a manipulative and depoliticizing 'massification' that gradually eroded the sense of democracy. In contrast, in the countries of the East and the South the regulations put in place were socially oriented in the sense that the economic growth they engendered benefited, in various degrees, wide segments of the masses; but they were accompanied by almost wholly non-democratic political and cultural policies. This clamp-down on pluralism was legitimized by discourses that held that it was necessary 'to develop first', and that democracy would come later. Official ideologues of Sovietism, theoreticians of Latin American 'desarrollismo' and politicians at the service of the western powers (symbolised for example by Huntington) were in perfect agreement on this point.

The overall result was, therefore, the reinforcement of commodity alienation and the destruction of the natural environment. The hope that the systems of the East and the South would be able to erase the heritage of polarization was itself also gradually erased. Even though at one time and in certain areas they did make it possible to reduce the impact of this polarization, the contradiction between accumulation and democracy resurfaced. The three systems of regulation, plus the one which operated at the global level, attained their historic limits and their erosion led to the triumph of neoliberalism of the society of Mont Pelerin. But, contrary to the theoretical affirmations of this sect, this change would not catapult the entire global system towards unprecedented heights, but on the contrary, would trap it in an accelerating spiral of crises. Within a few years the policies put in place in the name of the neoliberal utopia had produced generalized chaos. And once again, contrary to the simplistic thesis that places the sign of equality between market and democracy, the latter found itself exposed to extreme vulnerability by the much vaunted unilateral dictatorship of the market.

And the challenge cannot now be met by a return to the past, a 'remake' of previous forms of regulation. Not only does that idea not take into account the critical reading of the post-Second World War period that I have just proposed; it also fails to consider the major changes, at all levels, produced precisely by the successes of the postwar half century period (industrialization of the peripheries, democratic aspirations, the questioning of commodity alienation, awareness of environmental degradation, new forms of the law of value, moves beyond manufacturing and Taylorite industrialization, etc.). These are the new challenges. They can only be met by looking ahead, towards the future, without nursing a nostalgia for the past, recent or distant.

The collapse of the systems of regulation of the postwar period opened a period of capitalist crisis. The shift in power relations in favour of capital, represented by the dominance of the transnationals, while it did indeed produce a meaningful rise in the profit margin, was only possible on the basis of a relatively stagnant – sometimes even in contracting – global demand, as a result of the unequal distribution of income, as much at the various national levels as in the global system.

The crisis manifests itself, in fact, in a growth of the surplus (produced by that of profit) which cannot find an outlet in the expansion of productive investment (for lack of dynamism in demand), and for which the system undertakes to create an alternative financial outlet, in order to prevent the capital depreciation which this imbalance could cause. What is known as 'financialization' of the system (that is to say, the priority given to the protection of financial investment at the expense of productive investment) therefore constitutes a strategy for the management of the crisis.[17] From this point of view, financial globalization becomes a strategy, and is not the product of an objective constraint, as the discourse which pretends to legitimize it maintains. This strategy of financial globalization is constituted, for its part, by equally well known elements: the floating of the exchange rates (which gives ample room for speculation), the management of the external debt of countries of the Third World and the former socialist bloc and the external deficit of the United States. The intervention of the IMF, ordaining the opening of capital accounts for the liberalization of transfers, aims at widening the field of this globalized 'financialization'.

The results of this financial globalization are already visible. From 1980 onward the international financial transfers curve takes off and detaches itself from the growth of world trade and productive investments. The bulk of international financial movements concerns transfers between countries of the triad. This explains why no matter what the comparative real interest rates are in the United States, Japan and Germany (with which the European Union is aligned) and regardless of the wide fluctuations of the exchange rate in the case of the dollar, the American deficit has persisted. Incidentally this refutes the theory according to which the meeting of the supply and demand for money reveals the 'true' exchange rates which are supposed to adjust the balance of payments.

But a part of these movements of funds heads towards countries in the periphery. Floating capital finds in them opportunities for short-term investment, making it possible to pillage laboriously accumulated local surpluses, as was the case during the 'financial crises' of Latin America (Mexico in 1982, tomorrow Brazil?), South Africa (following the movement of capital towards this country avoiding South-East Asia since its crisis of 1997), and no doubt Russia and others tomorrow. Large capital flows also moved to East and South-East Asia.[18]

The influx of capital into South-East Asia led to inflation in real estate and stock markets. As the best economists of the region had predicted as far back as 1994, it was bound to lead to a financial crisis. But these nonconformist economists were not believed; the World Bank and the IMF rejected their forecasts until the collapse was at hand.

The so-called South-East Asia crisis[19] marks a turning point in the future trend of the management of globalization. It announces the coming collapse of globalized management of the financial surplus of capitalism in crisis. It is, indeed, interesting to observe that national governments in the region in question reacted in a manner that has really, for the first time, disproved the certainties of the G7 and the institutions at its service. China and India, in effect, are no longer considering opening their capital accounts. Korea and the countries of South-East Asia are looking towards the same direction, that of the restoration of national control over the movements of capital. Countries of Latin America and some others, possibly including Russia, could imitate them and the Non-Aligned Movement (NAM) could become 'Non-Aligned on Globalization'. The G7 was not insensitive to this real danger that threatens to put an end to financial globalization, transferring the risks of the depreciation of capital back to the triad. Did the G7 not acknowledge that it was necessary to 'regulate' international capital flows barely two weeks after the crisis exploded? A few days earlier the same word, 'regulation', was still forbidden. The chief economist of the World Bank, Stiglitz, followed suit and suggested a new formula for crisis management which has been called a 'post-Washington consensus'. Even Mr Camdessus discovered that total deregulation did not offer only advantages. Of course the key people responsible for globalized management only initiate a counter-offensive to enable them to remain masters of the game. It is necessary to save capitalism from neoliberalism, declares George Soros.

Indeed the global economic war has begun. The crisis of South-East Asia, and especially that of Korea, is its financial dimension, a minor crisis similar to the many witnessed by Great Britain and France after the war. It has been observed that the 'fundamentals' proper to the countries of Asia have remained healthy, and, measured in terms of deficit in proportion of the GDP or durability, the Korean crisis is less severe than that of the United States. And yet the dominant capital – backed by the diplomacy of the United State and Japan – is not content with proposals of reforms to the local banking and financial systems. They try to seize the opportunity to dismantle the Korean productive system – nothing less – under the pretext that the latter is dominated by monopolies! The same logic made the IMF oblige the United States (whose crisis is more severe) to sell Boeing for example (which is a monopoly, it would appear) to its European competitor Airbus (also a monopoly!). If he were to have proposed such a solution, Mr Camdessus, irrespective of his French nationality, would have been fired immediately by Clinton!

The collapse of the financial globalization strategy opens a new phase of serious international conflicts. Was it wrong to predict from analysing financial globalization, that the latter would in the end be the harbinger of geostrategic conflicts and perhaps, through them, of a return of nationalistic affirmations of sovereignty, far from the 'end of history'? Of course, such conflicts are not 'conflicts of cultures' *à la* Huntington, but conflicts of societies. The major conflict that would probably break out quickly is that which has already ranged the dominant powers of the triad against those who govern societies of the first order of the periphery. But we can also foresee an amplification of contradictions within the triad, on whose development will depend, to a large extent, the dynamics of the construction of the European Union.

Will these conflicts retain a purely mercantile dimension and remain confined to shocks of strategies of the dominant classes? Or will the upsurge of the social struggles engendered by the collapse of the management policies of the crisis raise them to significant social and meaningful alternative policies? In Europe, these struggles will necessarily centre around the project of the European Union possibly to give it some progressive social content.[20] China will lean towards one direction or the other of the national project.[21]

In any case we are, in my opinion, entering a new period of conflict and social struggles. The neoliberal policy of 'competitive deflation' (globalization unilaterally regulated by transnationals – and financialization) is already in crisis. In record time it has seriously aggravated all the social problems that peripheral capitalism had never seriously tackled hitherto – particularly the agrarian question – and has aggravated poverty, social dislocation and social exclusion to an unprecedented degree, marginalizing whole countries and even an entire continent. In the developed capitalist centres, it has brought back to this front job insecurity and permanent unemployment. Major social movements, like those of the landless in Brazil and unemployed in France, have already assumed the dimensions of a political challenge. These social struggles are bound to strengthen and become more widespread, because the inevitable devaluation of capital will give rise to violent conflicts over who pays the bill. The G7 and its instruments (including the military strength of the United States and the media at its service) are already trying to shift the weight of the crisis to the popular classes in the countries of East and South Asia. They have already been able, through the reduction of the prices of raw materials (oil and tropical agricultural products) to further marginalize the most vulnerable countries of the periphery and to shift onto their peoples the burden of impoverishment of their economies. Tomorrow, they will probably try to shift part of the bill onto the pensioners in the private pensions systems (in the United States, in Great Britain especially), since it is less difficult to reduce retirement benefits than wages!

Will it be possible, in such conditions, to develop strategies for common struggles, globalized in their own way? Will the reconstitution of a reserve army in the capitalist centres themselves make it possible to create a new popular internationalism? Will the conjunction between the struggles for the democratization of political and social systems in the peripheries, and the rejection of the G7's crisis management plans, give rise to such a new internationalism? The answers to these questions will depend on the development of the struggles of the people who, in the final analysis, are the subjects of history.

This does not mean that it is useless to propose possible alternatives to enable us to 'move out of the crisis'. The debate around these questions will certainly help the social movements to see things more clearly, to formulate effective strategies. But I must say without mincing words that it is not difficult to conceive these alternatives on the basis of principles that, it seems to me, are obvious: the regulation of markets at all levels making it possible to return to full employment and the reduction of reserve armies in the peripheries; the reorganization of capital markets so as to channel capital into productive investment; rebuilding financial and monetary systems with a view to organized regionalization plans; creating conditions for a new negotiated globalization; the democratization of societies and the reinforcement of the ties between the rights of persons, the rights of citizens, and social rights (the right to security, to work, to education and health care). These changes would certainly require the establishment of appropriate new institutions, both at the national level (by inventing new forms of state intervention) and at the regional and international levels. It is not difficult to conceive the modalities on which to base the institutions to replace the World Bank, the IMF and the WTO, nor reforms that could relaunch the UN (in the management of trade and transfer of capital and technology, through a regenerated UNCTAD, for the security of peoples and nations). These alternatives are inscribed in the perspective of the construction of a polycentric world, assuring peoples and nations levels of autonomy that would enhance democratic and social progress, in other words enhance 'another difficult globalization'.

Difficulties are not situated, in the main, at the levels of 'technicality' of the mechanisms and institutions to be conceived. They are situated at a totally different level: in the social and political forces able to impose it.

Conclusion

We now come to the conclusion of this presentation of challenges, with a fundamental question: how is history made?

My view of history is summed up in the thesis that I have described as 'under-determination' (as opposed to 'over-determination' of the

Marxo-Althusserian vulgate).[22] In this spirit, I analyse the logics proper to each of the constituent processes of social reality and study its specific concrete contents, be it the logic of capitalist accumulation (for the modern times), that of a particular type of system of power, or those of ideological or/and religious systems. These logics are not, *a priori*, either fatally complementary (in conformity with the concept of over-determination of the market discourse for which everything simply adjusts to that particular economic logic) or necessarily contradictory. Yet a particular consistency is always finally produced in one way or another, determined by the actions of subjects of history and unknowable in advance. Human liberty is situated in the choice that societies make and that determines the particular coherence in a given concrete society, at a given moment of history. It is not therefore a liberty conceived without constraints.

The choice between different possible alternatives is permanent. I believe we are at a moment of history, where the better and the worse are both equally possible. Capitalism, in its development, has passed through two successive phases and the second has exhausted its course.

There are now many signs indicating that capitalism has entered a third phase of its development: the ongoing scientific and technological revolution, computerization and robotics, decentralization of productive systems,[23] involving the expansion of the tertiary sector and the decline of the share of industrial manufacturing.

The dominant interpretation of these transformations is that they must necessarily bring progress. The naïveté of this thesis is apparent the moment one realizes that it is not technique that commands history, as McLuhan asserts, but the struggle for its control, and that the economics which sets the system in motion is itself embedded in social relations. The conjunction of these transformations only indicates that we are indeed at a crossroads and that the alternatives have to do precisely with the social relations that are ignored in the dominant discourse.

The development of historic capitalism is that of the continuous exacerbation of its three contradictions: i.e. commodity alienation, global polarization, destruction of the natural base.[24] None of these changes mechanically implies the reversal of these trends. But each of them could make this possible, on condition that prevailing social relations are re-ordered in an appropriate direction.

Informatics and computerization on the one hand, the growing centralization of capital on the other, are challenging the concept of value and announce its possible withering away. The near disappearance of direct labour as a result of robotized work processes abolishes the autonomy of every singular chain of production to make it an indissociable element of social production taken as a whole. Besides, the new forms of re-skilled labour amplify the interdependence of production and abolish the concept of competitiveness at the level of the productive unit.[25]

The decline of industrial production in the centres of the system, and the explosion of the so-called tertiary activities there, are ambiguous phenomena. Some of these activities, dictated by scientific, or even social, progress, potentially hold the promise of being used for the better organization of society. One could easily include in this category the more effective equipment and other advances in medicine, and the general expansion of knowledge and education. But many other such activities are merely means of organizing the waste of the surplus generated by the rising productivity of social labour.

This waste is necessary in order to facilitate the reproduction of the unequal distribution of income. It also exacerbates mercantile forms of economic management. The 'costs of selling' – advertising and so on – are the expressions of such bloated capitalism in decline. Here again, one sees that the relative decline of manufacturing industry does not bring back the world of 'before the Industrial Revolution' (as in the fashionable discourse of the 'end of the working class', the 'end of smutty factories' etc.). Economic activities remain more than ever controlled by oligopoly capital whose centralization continues endlessly. Here again one finds that capitalism is unthinkable without politics at its service, a politics of a renewed alienation, legitimizing inequality both in the distribution of the social product and in the organization of power at all levels, from the enterprise to the state. Production would remain regulated, in appearance by the 'market', in fact by coalitions of dominant capitalist interests. More than ever this capitalism of the third era appears as the antithesis and not the synonym of the market. For more than ever its reproduction would require the continuous and active intervention of the state, of policies manipulated to serve its interest, and the reduction of democracy to the status of decorative rhetoric.

At the level of the global system, ongoing changes are bound to further exacerbate polarization. The 'five monopolies', discussed earlier, are at the root of this aggravation of the trend towards global inequality, in spite of the successes of industrialization in the peripheries of the system. However, these monopolies have 'extra economic' dimensions ignored by 'pure economics'. Their obvious political dimensions, which the arrogance of military superpower exemplifies everyday,[26] illustrate once again that the economy is embedded in social relations of which politics constitutes only the visible topmost layer.

In this perspective, capitalist expansion could continue for a long time, while drawing on the gigantic reserves of labour which I mentioned earlier, by organizing a kind of global putting-out system. This system would resemble a kind of apartheid at the world level, maintained by military violence. The global system of capitalism of the third era will thus run the risk of being nastier than those of its previous phases.

But it also stands to reason that this is not the only possibility. This evolution makes it possible to consider new social relations emancipated from the commodity alienation of productive industry, of which the institution of the 'citizens' income' could constitute the first step,[27] starting the long transition to socialism, defined as the social mastery of production. The peoples of the periphery no longer accept the destruction that polarization represents for them. Bridges can be constructed by establishing an active solidarity between this refusal, on the one hand, and the democratic aspirations of the peoples of the centres, on the other. Systems of regulation at the global level could then enhance the potential to bring about positive changes, the progressive reduction of polarization and the construction of a pluricentric world, another condition for the long transition to global socialism.

The contradiction which I started from is the one that opposes, on the one hand, the economic logic of capitalism (popularized by the discourse of the market) and the logic of globalization which it commands, and on the other the democratic aspirations and those aiming at the emancipation of the popular classes and nations that are victims of the system. This contradiction is not near to being resolved. As long as this contradiction is dominated by economic logic, capitalist society will increasingly become barbarous. But if forces of emancipating democracy manage to impose themselves, even if gradually, then the third era of capitalism will become that of its own decline, opening up the long transition to socialism.[28]

Notes

1. What is known as deregulation is in fact nothing more than another form of regulation whose nature is hard to discern because it is unilateral. As a clear example, the WTO is a curious institution: if markets can really be deregulated, why the need for an institution assigned to regulate them? And the WTO does regulate markets, while condoning, in the corridors, the dominant segments of capital (the transnationals) to negotiate between them compromises that concern them. This so-called 'deregulation' is simply a shameful

regulation and at the same time essentially non-democratic. The proposed MAI (Multilateral Agreement on Investments) is even more cynical: it replaces legislation by states, potentially democratic, with laws made by transnationals and, moreover, erases the principle of the separation of powers, since in the courts of arbitration that it proposes, the transnationals will be both complainants and judges.

2. See my critique of the theory of the self-regulating market in S. Amin, *Spectres of Capitalism: a Critique of Current Intellectual Fashions*, New York: Monthly Review Press, 1998, ch. 8. See also Bernard Guerrien, *L'économie néoclassique*, La Découverte: Repères, 1996. Giorgio Israël, *La mathématisation du réel*, Le Seuil, 1996. Hakim Ben Hammouda, *Les pensées uniques en économie*, L'Harmattan, 1997.

3. Samir Amin, *Spectres of Capitalism*, op. cit., ch. 2.

4. Karl Polanyi, *The Great Transformation*, Boston: Beacon Hill, 1994, 1st edition 1944.

5. See my views on modernity and critique of postmodernism in S. Amin, *Spectres of Capitalism*, op. cit., ch. 6, and the bibliography at the end of the book.

6. Samir Amin, 'The Ancient World System versus the Modern Capitalist World System', *Monthly Review*, 14, 3, 1991, pp. 349–85 (and the bibliography appended to the article).

7. Cf. S. Amin, 'A propos of Re-orient', unpublished paper.

8. On the globalized law of value, see: S. Amin, *Les défis de la mondialisation*, Paris: L'Harmattan, 1996, ch. 3.

9. Samir Amin, *Capitalism in the Age of Globalisation*, London: Zed, 1997, esp. ch. 1 ('The Future of Global Polarisation').

10. See ref. note 8.

11. Even though, persistent over several decades and perhaps affecting a quarter or a third of the population, as in the case of Great Britain, the 'problem' already embraced dramatic dimensions.

12. Yoshikara Kunio, *The Rise of Ersatz Capitalism in South East Asia*, Manila University Press, 1988.

13. Samir Amin, *Eurocentrism*, London: Zed Press, 1989, part 1.

14. Ibid., part 2.

15. Samir Amin (ed.), *Mondialisation et Accumulation*, Paris: L'Harmattan, 1993, Introduction.

16. The formal opposition between 'market economies' and 'centrally planned economies' should be qualified. S. Amin, *Spectres of Capitalism*, op. cit., ch. 5.

17. Cf. S. Amin, *La gestion capitalist de la crise*, Paris: L'Harmattan, 1995. S. Amin (ed.), *Mondialisation et Accumulation*, op. cit; also S. Amin, *Capitalism in the Age of Globalisation*, op. cit., chs 1, 2, 5.

18. The motivations here were more diverse. Strong growth (in China, Korea, South-East Asia) attracted them there (to link them to productive investment, of good or poor quality, in any case nourished by the illusion of prosperity without danger). This strong growth, exceptional at the world level, was nonetheless due to a large extent *not* to deregulated opening-up (as the World Bank Reports put it) but on the contrary, to the regulation maintained in this region through the management of national strategies. That these strategies were effective and intelligent in the long run or,

debatably, whether they attracted our sympathy or appeared negative in their social and political dimensions, are different problems. The attraction of these funds for Asia was reinforced when, as from the 1990s, some of these countries (especially in South-East Asia) equally took their turn in opening capital accounts. They found themselves further strengthened by the opportunities that would emerge in China and in India with the envisaged opening of their accounts.

19. Samir Amin, 'The Challenge of Globalization', *Review of International Political Economy*, 3, 2, Summer 1996, pp. 219–30.
20. See Jomo Sundaram (ed.), *Tigers in Trouble*, London: Zed, 1998, especially chapters by K. S. Jomo, Walden Bello, Ha-Joon Chang and others. See also in S. Amin (ed.), *Mondialisation et Accumulation*, op. cit. the contributions of Suthy Prasartset and Georges Aseniero.
21. Samir Amin, *Capitalism in the Age of Globalisation*, op. cit., ch. 6 ('The European Case').
22. Samir Amin, *The Future of Maoism*, Delhi: Rainbow, 1998, especially pp. 133–44: 'Is There Really any Chinese Model?'
23. Delocalized production, managed from a distance, sub-contracting, etc.
24. Samir Amin, *Les Défis de la Mondialisation*, op. cit., conclusion, section 1.
25. Samir Amin, *Spectres of Capitalism*, op. cit., ch. 5.
26. See Willet, this volume.
27. See Esping-Andersen, this volume.
28. Samir Amin, *Les Défis de la Mondialisation*, op. cit., Conclusion.

3
Global Capitalism and National Politics

Colin Leys

Introduction

How are the national politics of medium-sized industrial countries affected by the formation of a global economy? Many have predicted a drastic diminution of their significance. Mathew Horsman and Andrew Marshall, for example, predicted in 1994 that 'at home, states will be able to control access to their territories (although illegal immigration may be difficult to control), run welfare programmes, establish and maintain national education and training standards, create or retain health-care programmes. They may even invest in infrastructure, subsidise businesses, dictate work-rules. But their ability to do these things will be severely limited on several fronts...'[1]

But in how many cases is the subordination of states to market forces really likely to go as far as Horsman and Marshall imagine? Or will it go further? How severe are the limits states will experience? Will all states be able to retain public health-care programmes and subsidize businesses, or just some, and if so which? What specific mechanisms are involved, and what are the conditions within which they operate? Are there no countervailing tendencies and mechanisms at work?

For although it has become a cliché that lifting controls over trans-border capital movements subordinates politics to the market, this is not self-evident. At first sight, the end of the Bretton Woods era of national economies subject to control by elected national governments might seem to entail a shift from the subordination of economics to politics to a sort of rough equality between the two, rather than a subordination of politics to economics. States need capital for investment, employment and tradable output. The owners of capital need states to provide political security, material and legal infrastructure,

75

educated, disciplined workers and consumers dependent on wages and private pensions. In the abstract, states – that is, politics – look just as well placed as capital to come out on top.

So if politics have become subordinate to market forces, this is initially the result of a political choice, whose essential logic is as follows. First there must be a cultural preference that assigns an extremely high priority to consumption. Then there is an acceptance – explicit or implicit – of the argument that consumption will grow fastest if the owners of capital are left free to move it wherever they think it will fetch the highest return. Next, the relative scarcity of capital means that every state must try to ensure that its national 'regulatory regime' is at least as attractive to capital as those of near-competitor countries.[2] The wide differences between national incomes per capita means that some states will always be willing, or feel obliged (by economic desperation), to offer better terms than others, because they have less to lose and more to gain. This gives rise to the temptation to 'dive to the bottom', i.e. to reduce the requirements laid on capital towards those of the 'cheapest' country: the lowest effective tax levels, the fewest trade union rights, the most minimal health and safety regulations, and weakest environmental controls.

This is only a tendency, which is offset by many other factors. A large domestic or regional market, a highly educated workforce, a modern infrastructure, sophisticated communications systems, or congenial and safe living conditions for corporate executives, all enter the equation when corporations and banks are deciding where to invest or hold their cash balances. These considerations, processed by the teams of analysts employed by corporations, are summed up in the movements of the capital and currency markets. In any given country, a shift in any variable or parameter that the markets judge sufficiently negatively reduces the inflow of capital (or may result in an outflow) which is reflected in a weakening of the currency or a rise in interest rates, or both. As either of these raises the cost of living, and tends to reduce the prospective rate of growth, politicians will generally do their best to avoid them. So the tendency remains for 'regulatory regimes' to be continually weakened as states compete for capital, unless they agree to present a common front (as in the short-lived project for harmonization' in the EU during Delors' presidency of the European Commission).

To the extent, then, that in larger economies significant areas of economic policy have been removed from the reach of politics and given over to be decided by market forces, this reflects a primary, political decision to do so as a means of attaining faster economic growth.

But the mechanisms which then take over the direction of affairs from politics, like the capital and currency markets, and bargaining between states and TNCs, quite quickly become self-enforcing. In relation to any one medium-sized country, the 'discipline of the markets' can be very powerful, most clearly in relation to macroeconomic policy, as the French learned in 1983, the British in 1992, the Mexicans in 1994 and the East Asians in 1997–98.

A worldwide crisis like that of the 1930s would undoubtedly change matters: the 'market' would be discredited again and new national revolts against 'global capital' could be expected. But short of this, so long as voters still value consumption above other goals, and believe that existing global arrangements represent their best chance of maximizing it, the enforcing power of 'the market' remains; the decision to liberalize is a Faustian bargain with market forces. The economic costs to any individual country of opposing 'the market' rise as its economy becomes more and more integrated into a worldwide one, and political choices are correspondingly narrowed. With the end of the Bretton Woods era of capital controls, therefore, all countries have increasingly tended to find themselves in the situation that has long been familiar in the former colonies, in which powerful external economic forces shape domestic development and the state is too dependent on foreign capital to be able to subject it to effective control.

The formation of a global economy

The 'golden age' of global capitalism under the Bretton Woods regime saw an unprecedented expansion of output and trade, but it also gave rise to new developments which undermined the system.

First, sustained worldwide growth led to a steady increase in the number of countries in which capital could be profitably invested. As material and legal infrastructures and urbanized low-wage workforces became available in more and more places, one industry after another found it profitable to invest in them: first, labour-intensive industries such as textiles and the simple assembly stages of secondary manufacturing started to move, then capital-intensive industries such as automobiles and chemicals, then higher technology-based industries like consumer electronics, and finally – by the 1990s – information-based industries like financial services. By the 1970s capital had many more options than had been the case in 1950, let alone 1914.

Second, scientific and technological advances in both production and transport greatly reduced the cost of moving production from one place to another. Between 1930 and 1990 sea freight costs fell by 50 per cent, and air transport costs by 80 per cent.[3] Production could also now be divided up in new ways, with different stages distributed among sites in different countries, the most labour-intensive in low-wage countries, and so on. On the other hand, the capital-intensity of new technologies, and the rapidity of technological change, meant that producers of relatively high value-added products (including services) could not hope to recoup their costs quickly enough unless they sold them on an international scale. This, coupled with the fear of reviving protectionism, led to a growing surge of foreign direct investment (FDI) from the mid-1980s onwards, especially in the form of acquisitions and mergers, as companies based in the so-called 'triad' of Europe, the USA and Japan sought to secure access to each other's rich markets (in the first half of 2000 a record $1.88 trillion of acquisitions and mergers were recorded worldwide, and throughout the 1990s about 27 per cent of all such transactions were transnational).[4]

Third, dramatic advances in information technology permitted a growing number of transnational corporations (TNCs) to develop the communications and organizational capacity to begin to treat the whole world not just as a single market, but as a single production site – or at least, a limited number of regional sites, producing broadly similar products.[5] Research, development and production itself could now be co-ordinated almost as effectively across the globe as across a country or even a city in the past. The fact that this involved operating in many different national jurisdictions meant that TNCs established large legal and technical departments to negotiate with governments and engage in 'regulatory arbitrage' (getting the greatest advantage out of the differences between national regulatory regimes).

Fourth, with the recovery of the Axis countries after the Second World War, and intensifying international competition, the United States moved from being a major creditor country in the late 1940s to becoming the world's largest debtor, leading to President Nixon's unilateral decision to abandon the convertibility of the US dollar in 1971. This was followed in 1973 by the abandonment of fixed exchange rates between the world's leading currencies, and a corresponding explosion of activity on the currency exchanges, driven partly by companies' attempts to hedge against the risks of future currency fluctuations in their foreign operations, and partly by speculative activity. By 2000 about $2 trillion of currency were being exchanged worldwide every day, dwarfing not only the value of the currencies needed for the exchange of goods and services (world exports were worth $5 trillion), but even more the foreign exchange of any national central bank. This meant that a government could no longer influence the exchange rate for its currency by intervening in the currency market, as the British government learned on 'Black Wednesday', 16 October 1992, when, in spite of the expenditure of £10 billion of the country's foreign exchange reserves, the pound sterling was driven by speculators out of the European Exchange Rate Mechanism and devalued by 15 per cent.

Fifth, effective control over the movement of capital began to be abandoned with the rise of 'offshore' banking. Beginning in the 1950s, owners of US dollars who wanted to keep them outside the jurisdiction of the US government began to deposit them in special dollar accounts in banks in Paris and London. These so-called 'Eurodollars' were later joined by other currencies which also came to be called Eurocurrencies, even though they were increasingly deposited in non-European banking centres as well. So many interests were served by the practice that both the US and other governments acquiesced in it until by 1987 the combined value of all these 'offshore' accounts totalled $4 trillion.[6] Deposits on this scale meant that borrowers had ample opportunities to borrow major currencies outside the regulatory jurisdiction of the governments which had issued them. In 1981 the US government belatedly tried to rein in the Eurodollar market but found that foreign banks would not co-operate.[7] It responded with a wholesale deregulation of US domestic banking. Other governments with major financial sectors were forced eventually to follow suit so that all national controls over capital movements quickly became less and less effective and by the mid-1980s had been mostly abandoned, leading to the formation of a single global capital market and permitting the surge of FDI mentioned above.[8]

Sixth, successive rounds of negotiations had modified the General Agreement on Tariffs and Trade. By 1990 average tariff barriers had fallen to less than 5 per cent;[9] and in the Uruguay Round of negotiations, concluded in 1994, agricultural products and 'intellectual property' (i.e. the increasingly important information and media industries) were brought within the scope of the Agreement.

Seventh, in 1989 the communist regimes of the USSR and Eastern Europe collapsed, while reforms were also opening up China to investment and production by private capital. Even Cuba and Myanmar began to solicit capitalist investment. By the late 1990s North Korea was virtually the only country in the world still fenced off from global capital.

This list of factors leading to 'deregulated' or neoliberal globalization includes most of those usually cited, but it omits the extremely important political dimension. Many accounts of globalization portray it as primarily driven by technological changes and 'impersonal' market forces. But even the most seemingly impersonal of the developments listed above had a political dimension. Governments had it within their power to try to resist the change that was occurring, or to try to channel it in other directions, but rarely tried. There were certainly temptations to deregulate the domestic financial sector ahead of other countries;[10] but the main driver was the initial commitment to deregulation by the USA and the UK, which immediately made it more costly for other countries not to conform.

Even this formulation, however, presents the formation of a global economy in such a way that neoliberal domestic policies that became virtually universal in the 1980s and 1990s look like a purely rational, enforced response to a primarily economic imperative confronting governments. But globalization was also first and last a project to defeat 'socialism'. Both the US and the British economies had experienced slow growth and declining international competitiveness in the 1960s. In both these countries politics became polarized, between defenders of the postwar 'settlement' (the UK term) or 'national bargain' (the US term) – in which the state played the role of both manager of the economy and provider of social services and social security – and those who feared that private capital risked losing its power and authority. One side of the New Right's successful campaign to roll back 'socialism' or 'liberalism' was to attack its domestic base in the labour movement through anti-union measures and higher unemployment, privatization, reducing taxes on capital, and 'deregulation'. The other side was ending controls over capital movements and reducing trade barriers, exposing the domestic workforce to competition from imports from countries with lower-paid workers and weaker regulatory regimes and at the same time making it harder, if not impossible, for any future government to reverse these changes. (The Canadian Minster for International Trade declared that the Free Trade Agreement with the USA was needed 'to ensure that no future Canadian government could ever return to those bad old nationalist policies of the past'.)[11] The result of capital mobility, combined with the other factors mentioned above, was the rapid formation of a global economy which quickly generated market forces that impinged on national states and governments with altogether new force. The deregulation that was undertaken in response to this pressure, however, enjoyed strong support from business and the right-wing parties throughout the OECD for domestic political reasons as much as economic.

By 1990 a new global economy clearly existed. A company could sell its goods or services virtually anywhere, production could take place almost anywhere, capital could be invested more or less anywhere, profits could be remitted from anywhere. This did not mean there was a single, homogeneous worldwide market, or that foreign capital could be invested, or foreign goods sold, as easily in Japan as in Canada. Non-tariff barriers of all kinds remained, and distinctive national tastes did not change overnight, although international sales of US-made films and television programmes, and the penetration of foreign markets by firms like Toyota, MacDonalds and Blockbuster Video were slowly homogenizing tastes. But to a degree unknown in 1914, firms could consider all the countries of the world as parts of a single market, and more and more were beginning to do so. Moreover, advances in production technology had made it much easier to vary the product to suit particular regional or even national 'niches' in the world market. As Eric Hobsbawm put it, 'for many purposes, notably in economic affairs, the globe is now the primary operational unit and older units such as "national economies"... are reduced to complications of transnational activities'.[12]

The modern global economy

'Globalization sceptics' have argued that reports of the 'death of the nation state' have been greatly exaggerated, that the proportion of world output traded internationally only returned to its 1914 level of roughly 13 per cent in the early 1990s, that most large companies have heavy investments and roots where they are headquartered, and are still owned largely by nationals, whether institutions or individuals, and that nation-states remain crucial to the operation of the global economy. This is all true, yet it misses the point. There are fundamental differences between the global economy of 1914, and that of the early 1990s, and they do not lie in the ratio of transnational to global trade, although that has now well surpassed the 1914 level. They lie in a series of developments in the new global economy which have led to what Leo Panitch has called the 'internationalization of the state' – nation-states becoming increasingly agents of the agenda of transnational capital.[13] The two most signigicant differences lie in the creation of global financial markets, and the global production and marketing of manufactured goods and services by TNCs.

Global financial markets

By the end of the 1980s 'deregulation' and computerization had resulted in the elimination of most significant geographic barriers in all kinds of financial activity. Besides the phenomenal growth of the currency and derivatives markets, securities and bond markets had also been global-ized. Stocks of companies in Japan could be traded as easily in Frankfurt as in Tokyo, and bonds issued by Volkswagen or the city of New York could be bought as easily in London, or vice versa. When the London stock exchange closed, the New York exchange was already open, and when it closed, Tokyo took over until London opened again.[14] Although there were some important hold-outs against free capital movements, including India and China, generally the owners of capital were now free to move it more or less anywhere. Through satellite-based infor-mation technology they were also acquiring the capacity to evaluate with greater accuracy and speed more and more alternative ways of investing or banking it worldwide. Net international bank loans rose from 0.7 per cent of world output in 1964 to 16.3 per cent in 1991. Bond issues grew at about three times the rate of world output between 1973 and 1995. Derivatives expanded 'astronomically', to a total value in 1996 of $321 trillion, more than world GDP.[15] According to Gowan, in 1999 a small number of highly secretive US-based 'hedge funds' – firms speculating in foreign exchange derivatives – had between them access to something like $30 trillion of bank loans to bet against national currencies. Gowan reasons that their successive attacks on foreign cur-rencies must have had the approval of the US government. In effect they were financial privateers, a modern version of the private pirates li-censed by the British government in the eighteenth century to raid enemy merchant shipping. The scale of the funds they could borrow explains why the notorious collapse in 1998 of the Long Term Capital Management Fund, with its Nobel economics prize-winning directors, necessitated the mobilization of $3.5 billion of tax revenues to bail out banks that would otherwise have collapsed.[16]

TNCs and global production

By the end of the 1980s TNCs were responsible for more than half of all the world's trade in manufactures, and perhaps three-quarters of all trade in services. According to one estimate, in 1994 the 500 largest TNCs controlled three-quarters of all world trade. TNCs also controlled 80 per cent of all land under export crops, and the marketing channels for a large number of primary commodities.[17] Foreign direct investment also made TNCs omnipresent. By the mid-1980s the value of production by TNCs' foreign affiliates had overtaken the value of world exports.[18] At the same moment, FDI in service industries overtook FDI in manu-facturing, and for the first time FDI as a whole expanded faster than financial flows.[19]

A high proportion of the assets of both the manufacturing and the service sectors in most OECD countries thus came to be owned by big transnational companies, and by the late 1990s about one-third of all international trade consisted of intra-firm transactions (and much more in the case of major industrial exporters – for instance over 50 per cent of the trade of both the USA and Japan).[20] Large TNCs are, moreover, by definition oligopolists, with considerable market power. François Chesnais suggests that the most significant indicators of concentration are now world market shares rather than national ones, and notes that 'in a wide range of industries and product groups the world market is shared by 10–12 firms, and often fewer'.[21]

Yet even these data tend to understate the scale of TNC dominance of the global economy, thanks to the growth of corporate networks. A firm may derive substantial profits from a country without owning any plant or employing a single worker in it, through franchising, licensing and similar contractual relationships.[22] 'Network' firms, consisting of webs of legally independent units linked by cross-ownership or contracts, have become more and more common, as have alliances of a looser kind between companies with no cross-ownership or standing contractual links, on the lines of the Japanese keiretsu.[23] A statement, therefore, to the effect that 'the world's top 300 industrial corporations now control . . . 25 per cent of the world's $20 trillion stock of productive assets' has become hard to interpret.[24] Their power to determine the use of the world's productive assets may well be larger. The UN estimated in 1994 that 'overall, as much as one-third of world output may now be under the direct governance of TNCs, with the indirect influence certainly much greater'.[25]

The need to operate globally in order to survive has in any case enormously expanded the number of TNCs, from 7000 in 1970 to 60 000 by the late 1990s, with 508 000 affiliates.[26] This means, from the perspective of national politics, that even a quite small company by world standards may be fulfilling specific tasks in a tightly integrated global production and marketing strategy directed from overseas. The most important directing centres are the headquarters of a limited number of very large TNCs. In 1990 fewer than 300 American firms accounted for three-quarters of all transnational activity by US companies, and about 150 British firms accounted for four-fifths of all British FDI.[27] Of the world's 100 largest TNCs in 1992, 29 were American, 16 were Japanese, and 44 European.[28] The significance of TNCs in domestic politics can be summed up in two broad generalizations. First, since they are often very large organizations (in 1997 the largest 100 TNCs had total sales of $39 billion and assets of $42 billion) they often literally outgun national states in terms of negotiating resources, as well as having considerable economic leverage.[29] Most industrialized countries have bigger GDPs than the gross revenues of most TNCs, but TNCs are free to deploy their resources single-mindedly in pursuit of their limited goals in a way few states are, and sometimes the scales are reversed to a significant extent. For instance TNCs regularly borrow and spend more than the states of quite large countries. In January 2000, America Online raised $160 billion to take over Time Warner, four times the GDP of Nigeria. Or to take another example, US banks – now heavily represented in London – spent $15 billion on information technology in 1990 alone, while as late as 1996 the annual expenditure of the entire British government on information technology in 1996 was estimated at about $3 billion.[30] In general, states have long since lost whatever communications advantage they may once have had over companies. Corporations are also sophisticated lobbyists at the supranational as well as national levels of power.[31] In short, 'transnational corporations should now be put centre stage' in any realistic analysis of domestic politics, not just in the analysis of international relations.[32] Second, TNCs are profitable in large part precisely because of their political capacity, especially their leverage in negotiations with host or prospective host governments, often backed by diplomatic interventions by their 'home' states. TNCs can get regulations altered (or maintained) to their advantage or they can exploit the existing pattern of regulatory differences, getting labour-intensive work done where unions are weak and wages low, declaring taxable profits where taxes are lowest through 'transfer pricing', and so on.[33] The phenomenon of 'network' firms – firms consisting of many legally separate companies, but with complex interlocking shareholdings allowing for unified overall control – is usually explained in terms of the 'positive externalities' this can yield from specialization, greater flexibility and so on; but the ability of a TNC to escape regulatory costs by 'dissolving' itself into a network is hardly less important.

> Because the firm determines its own size [in deciding what bit of a network, legally speaking, it will 'be'], it also chooses the limits of its legal responsibilities, which in turn provides an open invitation for the evasion of mandatory legal duties. The practice of corporate groups of creating autonomous profit centres, in order to secure, alongside (legitimate) efficiency advantages, at the same time (illegitimate) risk displacement and liability limitation, supplies ample material here.[34]

Liability to taxes is especially significant, since the power to tax is the foundation of national sovereignty. Yet the complexity of contemporary TNC financing, combined with the network form of organization, enables TNCs to limit the bite of all but the biggest and most determined national tax authorities. Picciotto notes that:

> TNCs ... have opposed attempts at strengthened regulatory cooperation [between states]. Instead, they have developed legal structures for transnational corporate capital which take advantage of the ambiguities, disjunctures, and loopholes in the international tax system. Indeed, the growth of the TNC, in the characteristic form of an international network of related companies carrying on businesses in different countries in a more or less integrated way, is to a significant extent attributable to the opportunities it has to take advantage of regulatory differences, or 'regulatory arbitrage'.[35]

So we should not be surprised to learn that both corporate tax rates and the marginal personal tax rates for high income investors fell in almost every OECD country from the mid-1980s to the mid-1990s,[36] or that 'perhaps half of the industrialized world's stock of money resides in or passes through tax havens'.[37] It is sobering to reflect how far the political salience of personal taxation in the OECD countries in the 1980s and 1990s, and the devastating impact on public spending of voters' 'tax aversion', were due in part to the fact that so much corporate income was escaping tax altogether.

While even modest-sized states backed by electoral majorities clearly remain able to face down even the largest TNC, the balance of power has undoubtedly shifted. Perhaps the best comparison is between most states today and municipalities in the past. In the era of national economies, corporate investment decisions were made on the basis of variations between different locations in the country in terms of labour supplies, infrastructures, proximity to markets, local taxes and the like. Today, in the neoliberal global economy, national 'regulatory regimes' themselves have become part of the pattern of local conditions (or 'complications', as Hobsbawm says) which transnational companies take into account and work hard to change.

The effects of global market forces on national politics

In the long run the most important effect of globalization is the way the new global accumulation system reshapes the social structure of all countries – their class structure, ideology and political organization – and hence the balance of political forces in them. With the loss of national state control over the accumulation process, this reshaping is more dramatic and unconstrained than before, although not otherwise unfamiliar. The restructuring of production, under the pressure of global competition, is increasingly expressed in a global process of concentration through mergers and acquisitions on an unprecedented scale, as corporations jockey for position to become worldwide oligopolists.

In countries of the 'north', productivity gains are achieved with magnified social costs as companies shed all sentimentality in face of intensified cross-border competition. Abrupt announcements of thousands of 'job losses' become commonplace as manufacturers shift production to lower-cost sites and retail chains and banks and other 'service industries' seek profits from merging overheads, closing branches and transferring labour costs to their customers. Factor-price equalization (aka the 'law of value'), now operating on a global scale, drives wages towards world norms and restructures the workforce of even the richest countries in line with the new geographical options open to capital. This leads to a marked shift in the division of national income between capital and labour in the main industrialized countries and to a decline in real wages for less-skilled work, reinforced by higher unemployment and casualization. At the same time world demand for highly skilled labour has raised its price, while the increased returns to capital, and the reduction of taxes on them, have dramatically expanded the global cadre of millionaires (to nearly six million in 1998) and billionaires (358 in 1995).[38] The combination of these processes has thus already produced patterns of inequality (and disparities of power) not seen since the 1920s (if not the 1880s) in some countries of the 'north' – signalled by new terms, such as 'the excluded', 'winners and losers', 'A and B teams', 'two-thirds one-third society', and the like: and new levels of crime and preoccupation with crime and physical security of property and people, new patterns of regional differentiation within countries as well as between them, and new problems of migration, driven by economic desperation as much as by war and state collapse.[39]

On top of these effects of globalization are the consequences of shocks or crises, amplified by the scale of the speculative capital now available and the lack of controls over it. Already in 1990 the IMF was concerned at the 'pyramiding of financial transactions on a relatively small base of real transactions', but financial capital has vigorously opposed any serious reconstruction of the global 'financial architecture'.[40] The scale of some of the shocks, however, and their social and political consequences, have become very great and far-reaching. In 1982, when Mexico defaulted on its national debt, it 'threatened to bring down the entire international banking system at one stroke'.[41] In 1994, when the Mexican neoliberal bubble burst and the peso collapsed, the international rescue effort co-ordinated by the US government consumed $48 billion. Ordinary Mexicans' living standards fell overnight by 20 per cent, and it was estimated that repairing the damage would consume the net growth of the whole of Latin America until the year 2002.

The Mexican case is typical of the way the costs of overcoming the crisis were borne by the most vulnerable people. The costs were felt outside the region too: the peso crisis led to capital flight from other countries quite unconnected to Mexico, as far away as East Asia, and the East Asia crisis of 1997–8 had similar effects, notably in Russia.[42] In a world where an estimated 86 million people are employed by TNCs, virtually every significant local economic crisis has significant transnational effects.[43]

To trace the impact of the forces just outlined on the social formation of even a single country is a major task. For an industrial country the analysis must include, first, the decline of most 'northern' workers' 'social power' – their ability to threaten production by withdrawing their labour; second, the dissolution of the old class boundaries, and with them the basis on which political parties once rested in most countries of the 'north' – a dissolution linked to the rapid decline of manufacturing employment and the rise of service work, the casualization and also the growing 'feminization' of wage and salaried work, the re-emergence of home-working, the expansion of consumption by those in work; third, the dissemination of shareholding, both individually and through pension funds; fourth, the growing dependence on self-provided pensions as the value of state-provided pensions declines; and fifth, the individualization of culture and the commodification and privatization of daily life. Political consciousness has also been profoundly affected by the 'mediatization' of life both at work and at home, as well as of party politics. And almost everyone is affected by profound cultural changes caused by falling transportation costs, new forms of entertainment, and the simultaneous multiplication of choice and homogenization of tastes. National politics are also put increasingly in question by the dissolution of national borders, sometimes on the initiative of national states (as in the EU), sometimes not (as with the various east and South-East Asian 'natural economic territories').[44] Sometimes, as in parts of sub-Saharan Africa, what is dissolved is not just borders but the state itself. Even a century that had become blasé about change was aware, at its close, of a fresh unleashing of forces famously described a century and a half ago: 'Constant revolutionising of production, uninterrupted disturbance of all social conditions, everlasting uncertainty agitation ... All old-established national industries have been destroyed or are daily being destroyed. They are dislodged by new industries, whose introduction becomes a life and death question for all civilized nations...'[45]

This kind of country-specific analysis, however, is beyond the scope of this chapter. Here we can be concerned with only the most general and direct impact of global market forces on the governments of nation-states in the short term. The ways in which financial capital and productive (goods and services) capital affect national state policy are somewhat different (even though much of the capital in the financial markets at any given moment belongs to non-financial TNCs).

The impact of financial markets

Taken together, the global capital, derivatives and currency markets are supposed to register the collective judgement of the owners of capital of the profitability of the overall mix of economic and political conditions in each country when all factors, including the risk of adverse government policies, are taken into account: 'capital is now so mobile that markets will ensure that holders of financial assets receive roughly the same, risk-adjusted real return everywhere. Any country that offers significantly lower returns will experience capital outflow and a rapidly depreciating exchange rate.'[46] This means that government spending and fiscal policy are heavily constrained, in the short term, by the markets' judgement of what they should be. 'The power of the bond market has forced discipline on to governments everywhere' and Keynesian macroeconomic policies are no longer an option for the government of one country acting alone.[47]

Further, if the option of devaluing the currency is given up, whether through monetary union with other countries, or by tying the currency to, or even adopting, a stronger one (as in 'dollarization'), no cushioning by devaluation is possible. Then a politically determined reduction in interest rates can only precipitate a capital flight. So virtually no scope remains for traditional macroeconomic policy-making at the national level. Cerny summed up the consensus as follows:

> Governments have all found their capacity to intervene in the domestic economy significantly altered, reducing their power to pursue

comprehensive economic strategies and differentiating and compli-
cating the kind of market interventions which they are led or forced
to adopt. The interaction of changing financial market structures on
the one hand and states on the other has done more than production, trade or international cooperative regimes to undermine the
structures of the Keynesian welfare state and to impose the norms of
the competition state, while at the same time narrowing the param-
eters of competition still further.[48]

But this loss of 'Keynesian capacity', important though it is, has tended
to divert attention from the tendency of financial markets to constrain
all areas of policy, not just macroeconomic policy. In theory at least, the
financial markets register the collective judgement of the owners of
capital on the balance of the advantages and disadvantages of a country's total 'economic regime'. They do this continually and with the help
of increasingly elaborate and easily accessible databases that determine
the grades awarded to governments and public organizations by credit
rating agencies. Plans which the experts employed by these agencies
dislike, whether or not they affect public spending, have an automatic
negative effect on interest rates.[49] Proposals to tighten the regulation of
money markets, for example, or impose new obligations on the managers of pension funds to become long-term investors in domestically
based companies, will undoubtedly be penalized. More generally,
market analysts routinely estimate a 'political risk factor', expressed as
a premium on the current interest rate on government bonds which
discounts the possibility of future political changes unfavourable to
capital. 'Left labour' governments in the 'north' have consistently had
to face a risk premium of 1 or 2 per cent.[50]

Pressures from markets for goods and services

Non-financial TNCs differ essentially in that they represent capital that
is committed in the relatively long term to particular lines of production
of goods or services. Their role can be examined in relation to, first, non-
tariff barriers to trade, and second, non-tariff barriers to investment,
including the quaintly named 'structural impediments'.

As tariff barriers to global trade grew steadily lower under the Bretton
Woods arrangements, non-tariff barriers (NTBs) of various kinds came
more clearly into view, affecting an estimated 18 per cent of world trade
in 1992.[51] Some of these barriers, such as state purchasing rules that
confine bids for government contracts to domestic companies, serve
national interests in defence, food security and so on. Others, like

complex bureaucratic customs procedures, or safety or health tests not applied to domestically produced goods, are essentially general protectionist alternatives to tariffs; a third category are domestic social practices or arrangements, sometimes reinforced by law, that express longstanding and cherished national values. The most commonly cited example of the last kind of NTB are the Japanese keiretsu or 'families' of companies doing business with each other based primarily on long-term relationships of trust, and only secondarily on price (so that cheaper foreign suppliers are excluded). Another example is Japan's Large Retail Store Law which protects small Japanese retailers from elimination by supermarket chains, in order to maintain employment in the retail sector and preserve a pedestrian-based local community shopping culture.[52]

The main pressure to lift non-tariff barriers to trade comes from foreign companies anxious to break into local markets. Governments also get involved, through lobbying and diplomatic efforts, in trying to reduce other states' non-tariff barriers (and defend their own). This is especially likely if they have balance-of-payments difficulties, and if their ability to influence their balance of trade in other ways has been reduced by the weight of intra-firm transactions in their country's foreign trade (when up to half a country's foreign trade consists of intra-firm transactions, such traditional macroeconomic measures as are still available to influence the trade balance, such as credit expansion or contraction, become relatively ineffectual).

Pressure to remove non-tariff trade barriers can cut deep into sensitive areas of national culture and social practice.[53] The member states of the EU initially aimed at eliminating such barriers through 'harmonization' – i.e. adopting common standards and rules. When this eventually proved too difficult and controversial, harmonization was dropped in favour of 'mutual recognition' – i.e. subject to certain grounds of exception, any product or service that could legally be sold in one country could be sold in them all. 'The mutual recognition of standards as the principal means of removing border barriers has in itself a strongly deregulatory effect, as the least demanding national standard will become the European standard.'[54] In effect 'mutual recognition' legitimated the least onerous regulations and set up incentives for all EU states to adopt them.

But TNCs are almost by definition concerned less with access for exports than with productive investment, which makes them interested in a much wider range of policy issues than the regulations specifically applying to their products. John Dunning, a pioneer of TNC studies, concluded that:

if the government of one country imposes too high a corporation tax, firms – be they domestic or foreign – may decide to relocate their value-added activities in another county where taxes are lower; or, in considering where to site their new plants, firms may choose that country with the least burdensome environmental constraints, or whose government pursues the most favourable industrial policy, or which offers the most advanced telecommunications facilities or the most attractive tax breaks for R and D activities. Indeed... *anything and everything a government does which affects the competitiveness of those firms which must have some latitude in their cross-border locational choices must come under scrutiny.*[55]

Thus the scope of the 'regulatory regimes' which states compete to 'lighten' for non-financial TNCs may, like the scope of the concerns of the capital markets, be very wide. What is more, states may often be technically 'outgunned' by the legal expertise that TNCs can command.[56]

Yet the tendency of 'regulatory competition' to lead to a 'dive to the bottom' is offset by political pressures on states to prevent the dilution of standards, whether to protect a special interest or some more widely shared one. The result is not so easy to predict as many pronouncements by advocates of deregulation imply. Even under the EU's Single Market Act – the most favourable case from the perspective of firms, since the law obliges states to recognize each other's standards – effective resistance is mounted and outcomes are determined by complex combinations of reason, interest, the relative strengths of the participants and so on, rather than always ending in an inexorable competitive lowering of standards.[57] Nonetheless, it is equally clear that states no longer have the last word. Indeed there is no last word, since there is always a potentially lower standard than the one that presently exists, which some country may choose to adopt, and TNCs constantly renew their attempts to induce one government (or regional body) after another to do so.

To sum up this discussion: we find that the impact of 'market forces' on national politics has enormously increased, whether affecting macroeconomic policy generally through the financial markets, or microeconomic policy through pressure from TNCs and their home governments, and the autonomy of most states – apart from the USA and, perhaps, oil-rich states like Saudi Arabia – has been greatly reduced in relation to them. National policy-making is now pervasively influenced by this new circumstance.

State responses

There is an obvious conflict between the logic of capital accumulation, which drives the global economy, and the logic of legitimation, which drives politics in all states with free elections. The former gives priority to the needs of capital at the expense of labour, and at the expense of public-sector funding on which most public goods and social services depend. The latter depends on catering to these other needs. In the era of national economies, the conflict between these two logics was contained, however erratically, by capital's relative immobility. Globalization has for the first time separated the fields of operation of the two logics. Can this last? It is too early to say. In the meantime the possible responses of national states are limited.

First, states can still try to pursue macro- and microeconomic strategies to reduce unemployment, which is the single most important determinant of welfare, and of government popularity. The scope for doing this can sometimes be greater than it seems in theory, at least in the short run. Vincent Cable points to protectionist 'anti-dumping' measures that may be taken with strong public support, and which governments may get away with for quite a while by bending the rules (or simply ignoring them), or by relying on deeply 'embedded' non-tariff barriers which hamper investment by foreigners and protect domestic firms from foreign takeover.[58] Most states do what they can in this line, however contradictory it may be to their general support for global liberalization: 'there is ... an underlying tension and contradiction in the policies of most governments: embracing certain aspects of globalization and loss of sovereignty while resisting others in the name of the sovereignty of the nation-state'.[59] This does involve costs, however, in terms of taxes, prices and profitability, and in the long run there will be resistance from those who have to pay them.

Second, states can co-operate to try to establish a global state, or something approximating one. Conflicts of interest between the world's 180 countries – not to mention the USA's resistance to giving up its *de facto* control over the global economy – would make this difficult, even if the owners of capital did not mobilize strongly to prevent it. For example, while all countries will ultimately suffer disastrous consequences if the ozone layer is destroyed, a global agreement on banning production of the CFCs responsible for its rapid erosion could only be obtained by allowing the late industrializing countries to go on producing them after production will have ceased in the advanced industrial countries.[60] In any case, capital strongly resists the establishment of anything resembling effective global regulation, even the long-canvassed 'Tobin tax' on speculative capital movements, arguing that is not only undesirable but also technically impossible.[61] For the foreseeable future a global state capable of regulating the global economy is a utopian dream.

This conclusion is not significantly qualified by the institutions of 'global governance' that have come into existence, or into greater prominence, as a result of globalization. In addition to organizations like the EU, NAFTA, ASEAN, MERCOSUR, etc., which have been created mainly to promote regional trade liberalization, other supranational regulatory institutions have come into being in response to a demand for international public goods that neither markets nor nation-states will provide and (positive or negative) externalities that they cannot capture.[62] But the public goods that are provided for in this way are those that chiefly concern private capital – e.g. the rule of law and dispute settlement needed for an open system of trade and investment; common standards for weights, measures and interconnection; management of global communications networks like aviation, telecommunications, and sea-lanes to prevent congestion and disasters; management of environmental concerns like Antarctica and like the atmosphere and oceans (to stop cross-border pollution as with acid rain and sewage dumping in shared areas like the North Sea).[63] Of course financial stability, the rule of law and telecommunications are also important to ordinary people, but public goods like a healthy environment, stable employment conditions and freedom from crime – which are today just as 'global' as financial stability but which, while very important to ordinary people, are either less important to capital, or are positively opposed by it – are much less well provided for. Of the effective international regulatory structures that do exist, many are provided for by global capital itself.[64] There is a striking contrast between the relative effectiveness of, for example, the IMF or the Bank for International Settlements, and the relative ineffectiveness of most of the agencies set up and treaties made to reduce pollution.

Third, if it is not practicable to create a global state capable of regulating capital, a group of reasonably compatible partner states can try to create a regional one. This was one of the impulses behind the EEC and remains a reason for the continuing push for closer political union by left-leaning European federalists, reflected in (among other things) the Social Chapter of the Maastricht Treaty, which was supposed to lay down minimum standards of employment. The weakness of the Social Chapter's final provisions, however, and the declining interest of most EU states in upholding them, are also significant. The EU has always reflected the interests of capital more strongly than those of labour.

A fourth option is to pass the buck downwards – devolution or 'subsidiarity'. In effect, local political authorities are left to do what they feel they can within the constraints set by the market in their areas. Provided it is done in such a way that local people feel they have an appropriate share of whatever national resources there are, this option has the merit of relieving the central government of some of the responsibility for decisions which are in any case more and more severely constrained. It is also a useful response to the popular misconception (assiduously fostered by neoliberal politicians) that power has been 'taken away' from people and transferred to regional authorities ('Eurocrats' in Brussels), when in reality it has been ceded to capital, with the EU acting primarily as a facilitator of the transfer.

A fifth option is to seek alternative strategies for enhancing 'national competitiveness'. These always have a strongly ideological as well as substantive character, as the following definition by Vincent Cable shows: a ' "national competitiveness" strategy recognizes that capital is mobile, that companies are increasingly global, that governments have little talent for "picking winners", and that competition occurs, eventually, between companies rather than countries. Nonetheless, *a sense of national economic purpose can be created around the idea of* "competitiveness"; creating a pool of highly educated and flexible workers, an efficient infrastructure, *sound money and a good quality of life*. Such a competing nation is then well placed to operate as an open economy, attracting mobile financial and human capital.'[65]

Instead of talking about policies for 'national development', then, politicians propose alternative ways of 'positioning' their countries in the global marketplace. Their ability to do much about this is very questionable, but for most countries there still appear to be some alternative options, with different implications for different elements of the population; and in the less competitive industrial countries advocating some other country's allegedly successful 'model', such as 'Rhineland capitalism' or the 'Hong Kong model', became for a time a standard form of ideological competition. This was an interesting demonstration of the levelling effects of globalization. Politicians in ex-colonial countries have always had to think in this way, looking for policies that would change the structure of their countries' economies so that their 'insertion' in the global economy would be more advantageous. Now politicians in all countries had to think in these terms.

A recent American-led school of thought has proposed an analysis of the way 'northern' counties differ in their responses to globalization, according to the character of their pre-existing political and industrial institutional structures and cultures, using a deliberately simplified and economistic model with which reality can be compared. In this model globalization is understood simply in terms of expanded markets for traded goods and services. Its prime impact on national life is to alter people's 'preferences', according to whether they gain or lose from this change. Both among capitalists and among workers there are winners and losers, especially according to whether they are in the internationally 'tradeables' sector or not, and in the case of workers, according to how far they have scarce skills, these shifts destabilize pre-existing alliances and settlements, such as those underpinning the Keynesian welfare state. How far they do this, or how quickly, depends on various aspects of domestic politics, seen as an 'institutional structure', including in particular the trade union movement, the electoral system, and the constitutional system itself. This structure shapes the way people's altered preferences are expressed and how they affect politics. Those who are losing out, press for state resistance to, and protection from, the newly powerful global market forces, and politicians are under electoral pressure to comply. Some 'institutional structures', such as the strong 'corporatist' or 'co-ordinated' systems of so-called 'Rhineland' capitalism (or its East Asian variants), may allow politicians to keep the pre-existing political system more or less intact for some time. But over time the economic costs of doing this are apt to become too great. Policy options are limited by the new mobility of capital. Eventually something has to give. Typically, one of the shocks to which the global system is prone creates an opportunity for a new political coalition to come to power and make changes to the institutional structure which will give future governments greater immunity from popular pressures. In what is felt as a general crisis resulting from such a shock a new government may be able to reduce trade union powers, alter the electoral system, limit the 'veto' powers of interest groups through constitutional change, or devolve powers and responsibilities to non-elected bodies or local elected bodies. What changes are made, and how far they go, are also deeply influenced by the pre-existing institutional structure.[66] In particular, David Soskice points out that co-ordinated production regimes of the 'Rhineland' or the 'East Asian' type are all outcomes of long histories of institution-building and deeply 'embedded' in social structures and cultures. Where they do not already exist they are not in fact available as alternative 'strategies' to be 'adopted' as solutions to the problem of international competitive-

ness. In such 'uncoordinated' economies the only realistic short-run
option is to adapt as fully as possible to the discipline of market forces:

> In the Anglo-Saxon economies in which business was not organized
> so effectively [as in the co-ordinated economies], this lack of business
> co-ordination meant that the institutional capacity for re-regulation
> [following globalization] was missing, as was political power, in these
> liberal market economies, governments – both left and right – were
> forced or chose to implement wide-ranging deregulation as the only
> available framework in which companies could remain or become
> internationally competitive.[67]

This makes sense, but as Garrett and Lange remark, 'such a political
economy [as the highly schematized one assumed in such a model]
does not exist'; but they add, to understand the complex interactive
processes involved 'it is necessary first to isolate their independent
effects'.[68] But whether their deductive approach succeeds in doing this
is debatable. For one thing, in treating the change in the transnational
environment as purely exogenous their model immediately excludes the
all-important interconnections between domestic political agendas and
the formation of the global economy and the forces that operate in it.
And in treating the changed global context of domestic politics as
purely economic the model makes a further break with reality. To take
a few examples at random, the political influence over European media
policy of the American film industry, or the role of American companies
on European economic policies generally through their dominant role
in the US delegation to the WTO, or the influence on the US State
Department and NATO on EU policy towards its own eastward extension, are all hard to model in terms of the 'new institutionalism'. But
since no account of domestic politics in Europe in the age of the global
economy that excluded such important factors could hope to be very
useful, the methodology adopted by this school does not seem very well
adapted for this purpose.

Convergence?

Because all regimes are exposed to the same global context, many
writers have speculated that over time they will tend to converge towards a standard model, with increasingly 'homogenized' institutions.[69]
Against this, Hollingsworth and Streeck argue persuasively that there are
too many counter-tendencies, and that in any case, uncertainty as to

what 'best practice' really is, in a world of rapidly shifting performance requirements, makes the quest for a 'winning formula' for national competitiveness liable to be self-defeating.[70] Hollingsworth and Streeck, however, assume that states have at least some freedom of choice: but students of capital markets, such as Philip Cerny, assume on the contrary that the 'competition state' is obliged to become 'the main vehicle, the pre-eminent carrier, of "embedded financial orthodoxy"'.[71] This would seem to imply a long-run tendency for regulatory competition to erode the group-based regimes, since higher short-term returns to capital are available in the capital-based systems. This tendency has already made significant inroads into the once-celebrated Swedish model, and threatens the original 'Rhineland' model too.[72]

To prevent this, powerful states, controlling access to investment and sales in important markets, would need to collaborate, in effect to re-establish some constraints on capital movement. This is very unlikely to happen without a major global crisis. Otherwise the 'Anglo-American' or liberal market model, backed by the huge scale of the US economy and the hegemony of the 'Washington consensus', especially in the 'epistemic community' of international finance, seems destined to prevail, with what long-run costs in terms of legitimation, and consensus-based (not to mention democratic) politics, can only be surmised.[73] As Joachim Hirsch has argued, it was the containment of capital accumulation within a plurality of sovereign states that underwrote the system's stability and legitimacy. Governments could mobilize citizens, whose social relations are otherwise constantly being dissolved by the market, to feel united by a common national identity which make the essential class compromises possible.[74] If states gradually lose the capacity periodically to submit the logic of accumulation to collective demands for equity and a wide range of unmet needs, it is not clear that legitimation can be sustained. On the other hand, it is not clear either that capital accumulation can be sustained without such legitimation. Public order is only the most elementary of the non-market conditions for accumulation on which capital depends, but even that is undermined by 'self-regulating' global capitalism.

Contradictions of the global economy

How stable is the global field of forces in which national politics now takes place? How far is it inherently contradictory? Is the narrowing of the scope of national politics, and its increasingly reactive and subordinate character in relation to the forces at work in the global economy, likely to

continue? And if it is, can democracy survive it?[75] That the global economy is unstable no one really doubts. David Held et al. comment that
'regulatory instruments to manage systemic risks often fall far short of
those necessary to deal with them effectively. In this respect the absence
of any substantive attempts, following the East Asian crisis to re-regulate,
at an international level, short-term capital flow, is indicative of this
problem. Given the potentially volatile nature of global financial
markets, and the instantaneous diffusion of financial information between the world's major financial centres, systemic risks continue to
pose a permanent threat to the functioning of the entire global system.'[76]
As Louis Pauly observed in 1995, 'a collective movement away from
capital decontrol may be undesirable, but it remains entirely possible. If
it were not, then the world's central bankers and finance ministers would
not fly into paroxysms of anxiety whenever a major financial institution
gets into trouble, or a major borrower threatens to default. To them,
mismanagement of systemic risks and the consequent disintegration of
international markets remain all too imaginable.'[77]

The so-called 'neo-medieval' global political system, lacking any sovereign body, that existed in 2000, was clearly vulnerable to crisis. Yet the
USA, especially, has much too much to lose from a widespread collapse
not to mobilize its own resources, and those of other wealthy countries,
to try to prevent it happening, as when it organized the Gulf War,
contained the Mexican economic crises of 1982 and 1994, and imposed
settlements of a sort in Bosnia in 1995 and Kosovo in 1999.

In the long run, however, the most serious threat may well come less
from shocks of this nature, dangerous as they are, than from globalized
capitalism's lack of any 'regime of accumulation' to match global spending power to productive potential. Bennett Harrison, for example,
thinks that chronic lack of demand will undermine global growth:

> while networks and strategic alliances may have improved the coord-
> ination of global production, they can do nothing by themselves to
> stabilise and coordinate global demand...Without some sort of
> global demand management, no amount of institutional tinkering
> on the supply side will be sufficient to restore long-run global eco-
> nomic growth.[78]

Barnet and Cavanagh agree:

> An astonishingly large and increasing number of people are not
> needed or wanted to make the goods or to provide the services that

the paying customers of the world can afford. The gathering pressures of global competition to cut costs threaten the vast majority of the 8 billion human beings expected to be living on earth in the first quarter of the twenty-first century with the prospect that they will be neither producers nor consumers.[79]

To the extent that rapid growth rates in the industrializing countries of Asia lead to growing exports to them, as well growing imports from them, the older industrial countries that can shift efficiently to meeting that demand should experience only transitional economic difficulties. Even this, however, would entail political tensions, while for countries that are unable to adapt quickly, the repercussions could be very serious, yet states will face greater and greater difficulties in easing the pain. To quote Susan Strange once more:

> state authority has leaked away, upwards, sideways, downwards. In some matters, it seems to have gone nowhere, just evaporated. The realm of anarchy in society and economy has become more extensive as that of all kinds of authority has diminished... The state was once the guardian of national security; its right to loyalty and obedience and its authority to levy taxes rested fundamentally on that role. If the role goes, and if it is then insuffi-ciently replaced by the welfare role of the state as guardian against economic insecurity... it is little wonder that its authority declines.[80]

But the transition to a globalized economy still has a great deal of its course to run. How serious the loss of state authority is cannot really be known until the politics of nations are really studied in their global context, a task that has still largely to be undertaken.

Notes

1. Mathew Horsman and Andrew Marshall, *After the Nation-State: Citizens, Tribal-ism and the New World Disorder*, London: Harper Collins, 1994, p. 246. Hors-man and Marshall were at the time practising journalists.
2. There may occasionally be a world-wide glut of capital (real interest rates may be temporarily zero or even negative), but even when that is the case the fact that goods and services are increasingly produced for global markets means that there is always competition between potential alternative locations for individual productive investments.

3. David Held, Anthony McGrew, David Goldblatt and Jonathan Perraton, *Global Transformations: Politics, Economics and Culture*, Stanford: Stanford University Press, 1999, p. 170.
4. *World Investment Report 1999*, p. 95. The process was, however, not symmetrical, in that while Japan was a major source of outward FDI, it accepted hardly any inward FDI.
5. Stephen Thomsen, 'Regional Integration and Multinational Production', in Vincent Cable and David Henderson (eds), *Trade Blocs? The Future of Regional Integration*, London: Royal Institute of International Affairs, 1994, pp. 109–26.
6. Richard J. Barnet and John Cavanagh, *Global Dreams: Imperial Corporations and the New World Order*, New York: Simon and Schuster, 1994, pp. 109–26.
7. Eric Helleiner, *States and the Reemergence of Global Finance*, Ithaca and London: Cornell University Press, 1994, pp. 136–8. The opposition was led by the Bank of England and the Swiss National Bank, both of which benefited from the Euromarket.
8. For the process of regulatory competition that led to the rapid globalization of financial markets in the 1980s see 'The Deregulation and Re-regulation of Financial Markets in a More Open World', in Philip G. Cerny (ed.), *Finance and World Politics: Markets, Regimes and States in the Post-hegemonic Era*, Aldershot: Edward Elgar, 1993, pp. 51–85.
9. *World Investment Report: Transnational Corporations, Employment and the Workplace*, New York and Geneva: United Nations, 1994, p. 123.
10. Eric Helleiner pointed out that trade liberalization (the reduction of national tariffs and non-tariff barriers) requires collective action (countries seek reciprocal treatment), but states can gain from reducing their financial regulations unilaterally, so that states would be tempted to derive the benefits of a closed financial order (such as increased policy autonomy and more stable exchange rates), while 'free riding' by unilaterally liberalizing their markets to gain advantages for their national financial systems (*States and the Reemergence of Global Finance*, p. 197). Helleiner also cites the common training, experience and outlook of the world's main central bankers; the fact that the USA and Japan had interests as lenders of last resort that made them give leadership in financial matters that had no equivalent in trade; and the fact that 'trade liberalization is generally controversial because the costs in terms of lost jobs are readily visible and they are borne by concentrated populations, whereas the benefits in terms of lower consumer prices are less tangible and more dispersed. Financial liberalization arouses less controversy because the kinds of costs discussed at Bretton Woods are dispersed at the macroeconomic level, whereas it provides direct benefits to specific individuals or groups operating at the international level' (*States and the Reemergence of Global Finance*, p. 205).
11. Quoted by Manfred Bienefeld in 'Capitalism and the Nation State in the Dog Days of the Twentieth Century', in Ralph Miliband and Leo Panitch (eds), *Between Globalism and Nationalism: Socialist Register 1994*, Merlin Press, 1994, pp. 103–4.
12. Eric Hobsbawm, *Age of Extremes: the Short Twentieth Century 1914–1991*, London: Abacus, 1995, p. 15.
13. Leo Panitch, 'Globalisation and the State', in Miliband and Panitch (eds), *Between Globalism and Nationalism*, pp. 60–93.

14. Strictly speaking there was actually a three-and-a-half hour gap between the close of the stock exchange in New York and the opening of the exchange in Tokyo and another hour's gap between closing in Tokyo and re-opening in London.
15. David Held et al., *Global Transformations*, pp. 204–8. On derivatives and risk see FitzGerald, this volume, and Adam Tickell, 'Unstable Futures: Controlling and Creating Risks in International Money', in Leo Panitch and Colin Leys (eds), *Global Capitalism Versus Democracy: Socialist Register 1999*, pp. 248–77.
16. Peter Gowan, *The Global Gamble: Washington's Faustian Bid for World Dominance*, London: Verso, 1999, pp. 95–100.
17. John M. Stopford and Susan Strange, *Rival States, Rival Firms*, op. cit., p. 15; Peter Dicken, *Global Shift*, London: Paul Chapman, second edition 1992, p. 57. The proportions of the various commodity markets controlled by TNCs were: over 80 per cent, wheat, maize, coffee, cocoa, tea, pineapples, forest products, cotton, tobacco, jute, copper, iron ore, bauxite; 70–80 per cent, rice, bananas, natural rubber, crude petroleum, tin; 50–70 per cent, sugar, phosphates.
18. *World Investment Report 1993*, p. 130.
19. Ibid., p. 134.
20. Held et al., *Global Transformations*, p. 247.
21. François Chesnais, 'Globalisation, World Oligopoly and Some of their Implications', in Marc Humbert (ed.), *The Impact of Globalisation on Europe's Firms and Industries*, London: Pinter, 1993, pp. 15–16.
22. Susan Strange, 'The Defective State', in *What Future for the State?: Daedalus*, 124/2, Spring 1995, p. 59.
23. Chesnais ('Globalisation', p. 17) thinks that 'the entry of the Japanese keiretsu as major competitors in the late 1970s and their large-scale penetration through investment into the US economy. . . gave the onset of global oligopoly its irreversible character and made international cross-investment an imperative strategy for the survival of large firms'. On 'networks' see also Gunther Teubner, 'The Many-Headed Hydra: Networks as Higher-Order Collective Actors', in Joseph McCahery, Sol Piciotto and Colin Scott (eds), *Corporate Control and Accountability*, Oxford: Clarendon Press, 1993, pp. 41–60.
24. Barnet and Cavanagh, *Global Dreams*, p. 423, citing 'back-of-the-envelope' calculations by the editors of the *Economist*.
25. Ibid., p. 135.
26. *World Investment Report 1999*, p. 6.
27. Dicken, *Global Shift*, p. 49.
28. *World Investment Report 1994*, p. 8. These UN figures naturally do not cover transnational criminal organizations, although some of these function in many respects like legal TNCs and have comparable assets. A survey by Louise I. Shelley ('Transnational Organized Crime: an Imminent Threat to the Nation-State?', *Journal of International Affairs*, 48/2, 1995) notes that the Medellin syndicate, the less successful of the two Colombian drug cartels, was said to have at least $10 billion worth of assets in Europe, Asia and North America in the late 1980s, equal to the average assets of the four Swedish TNCs included in the UN's top 100 list in 1992 (pp. 480–1). Barnet and Cavanagh (*Global Dreams*, p. 389) report estimates of between $100 and $300 billion as the annual worldwide profits from the drugs trade, implying

the existence of numerous powerful transnational enterprises. As the role of 'offshore' banks in laundering criminal profits implies, and as the BCCI scandal showed, the boundary between TNCs and transnational organized crime is not always clear. The growing significance of international organized crime in the global economy and the parallels between it and both TNCs and states was noted by Susan Strange in 'The Limits of Politics', in *Government and Opposition*, 30/3, 1995, pp. 305–7.

29. *World Investment Report 1999*, p. 6.

30. Susan Strange, 'The Name of the Game', in N. X. Rizopoulos (ed.), *Sea-Changes: American Foreign Policy in a World Transformed*, New York: Council on Foreign Relations, 1990, p. 247; Barnet and Cavanagh, *Global Dreams*, p. 386; *Guardian*, 30 January 1996.

31. For instance Vivien A. Schmidt, writing about the European Union, notes that 'business privileged access to supranational decision-making ensures that policy interactions have shifted from an almost exclusive reliance on national government bargaining [i.e. bargaining between the member governments] to one that includes, if it is not dominated by, business actors in the transnational sector' ('The New World Order, Incorporated', in *What Future for the State*, op. cit., p. 80).

32. Susan Strange, 'Rethinking Structural Change in the International Political Economy: States, Firms and Diplomacy', in Richard Stubbs and Geoffrey R. D. Underhill (eds), *Political Economy and the Changing Global Order* (London: Macmillan, 1994), p. 111.

33. Held et al., in *Global Transformations* (p. 277), cite an estimate by Rousslang that transfer pricing 'saves' MNCs (multinational corporations) 'around $8 billion' in taxes, but add that 'this is only around 4 percent of worldwide taxable income of manufacturing MNCs' and 'of secondary importance to profits and government tax revenues'. The significance of the word 'only' here is not clear. If MNCs' average tax rate were, say, 10 per cent, the tax 'saved' in this way would presumably be equal to 40 per cent of their tax obligations, hardly a secondary consideration from their point of view.

34. Teubner, 'The Many-Headed Hydra', p. 58, quoting H. Collins, 'Ascription of Legal Responsibility in Complex Patterns of Economic Integration', *Modern Law Review*, 53, 1990, p. 731.

35. Sol Picciotto, 'Transfer Pricing and Corporate Regulation', in McCahery et al., op. cit., p. 387. Picciotto's major study, *International Business Taxation* (Oxford: Clarendon Press, 1992), describes the elaborate ways of corporate tax avoidance, and the hitherto rather ineffectual responses of international co-operation between national tax authorities, in dispassionate detail.

36. Michael Wallerstein and Adam Przeworski, 'Capital Taxation with Open Borders', *Review of International Political Economy*, 2/3, 1995, pp. 425–45. The authors criticize the view that this flowed necessarily from capital mobility, arguing that provided the full cost of investment is tax deductible, as it usually is, only fear of tax *changes*, and not the absolute level of tax on profits, affects investment flows.

37. Anthony Ginsberg, quoted in Barnet and Cavanagh, *Global Dreams*, p. 89. In a survey of the capital income tax situation in the EC in the early 1990s, Peter B. Sorenson concluded: 'Governments in Europe should seriously consider whether they wish to retain personal taxes on income from capital in reality

and not just on paper. If the answer is in the affirmative, they must soon take steps to ensure that such taxes can actually be enforced in an integrated European market. This will be a very difficult task, involving sensitive issues such as bank secrecy laws, and requiring a cooperative attitude from non-EC countries. If EC governments refuse to face this challenge directly, the days of the personal income tax as we know it may be numbered' ('Coordination of Capital and Income Taxes in the Economic and Monetary Union: What Needs to Be Done?' in Francisco Torres and Francesco Giavazzi (eds), *Adjustment and Growth in the European Monetary Union*, Cambridge: Cambridge University Press, 1993, p. 378). At the end of 1999 the problem remained largely unaddressed.

38. On millionaires recruited from corporate executives with stock options see Wally Seccombe, 'Contradictions of Shareholder Capitalism: Downsizing Jobs, Enlisting Savings, Destabilising Families', in Leo Panitch and Colin Leys (eds), *Global Capitalism Versus Democracy: Socialist Register 1999*, pp. 76–107. Merrill Lynch estimated that the nearly six million High Net Worth Individuals (i.e. owning a million dollars or more), who collectively owned $21.6 trillion in 1998, would own $32.7 trillion by 2003 (Merrill/ Lynch/Gemini Consulting, *World Wealth Report*, www.ml.com/woml/ pressrelease/19990517.htm). The 1995 figure of 358 billionaires is taken from the *UN World Development Report 1996*. In 1997 *Forbes Magazine* reported that the 225 richest people in the world owned a total of $1 trillion between them, an average individual fortune of $4.5 billion each (*Human Development Report*, New York: UNDP 1998, p. 30).

39. Cable notes the emergence in the older industrial countries of what used to be the hallmark of 'third-world' societies: 'for the educated and moneyed section of the population, the opportunities presented by globalization – travel, wider experience, promotion – are great. We thus have one, potentially large, disadvantaged, alienated and powerless element in society, and another which is flourishing but has less of a stake in the success of any particular country' ('The Diminished Nation State', in *What Future for the State?*, p. 43).

40. International Monetary Fund, *International Capital Markets: Developments and Prospects*, Washington: IMF, 1990, p. 1.

41. Eric Helleiner, 'Explaining the Globalization of Financial Markets', *Review of International Political Economy*, 2/2,1995, p. 332. On the way crises have been contained, see Helleiner, *States and the Reemergence of Global Finance*, op. cit., Chapter 8.

42. Held et al., *Global Transformations*, p. 213.

43. *World Investment Report 1999*, p. 265.

44. On the 'Greater China' NET, Jordan and Khanna write: 'Taiwan and the PRC are in the position of reacting to domestic pressures to further liberalize trade and investment, while being constrained from doing so by their security concerns. This is particularly true for Taiwan, whose smaller economy is more susceptible to being dominated by the booming PRC economy. These governments' only option is to try to manage and channel growing interdependence to their own possible political advantage because the economic and political costs of halting economic flow are too high' (Amos A. Jordan and Jane Khanna, 'Economic Interdependence and Challenges to the Nation-

State', *Journal of International Affairs*, 48/2, 1995, p. 443). Other NETs studied in the article are North-East Asia (Japan, North and South Korea, north-east and far eastern Russia), and four South-East Asian NETs: the Indonesia–Malaysia–Singapore Growth Triangle; the Indonesia–Malaysia–Thailand Growth Triangle; the Golden Quadrangle embracing northern Thailand, Yunnan Province in China, and northern Myanmar and Laos. A nascent fourth NET in this area is also referred to, linking Brunei to parts of Indonesia and the Philippines.

45. Karl Marx, *The Communist Manifesto*, ed. Frederic L. Bender (New York: Norton, 1988), pp. 58–9.

46. Ben Steil, 'Competition, Integration and Regulation in EC Capital Markets', in Cable and Henderson (eds), p. 27.

47. Hamish Macrae, '1996's Financial Markets', *The World in 1996*, London: Economist Publications, 1996, pp. 124 and 127.

48. Philip G. Cerni (ed.), *Finance and World Markets: Market Regimes and States in the Post-hegemonic Era*, Aldershot: Edward Elgar, 1993, pp. 79–80.

49. Timothy J. Sinclair, 'Passing Judgment: Credit Rating Processes as Regulatory Mechanism of Governance in the Emerging World Order', *Review of International Political Economy*, 1994, pp. 133–50. Whether the credit agencies or their clients make intelligent use of the data they collect may be doubted, in view of the failure to foresee either the Mexico crisis of 1994 or the East Asian crisis of 1997–8.

50. In a study of 15 countries from 1967 to 1990 Garrett found that 'the financial markets always attached interest rate premia to the power of the left and organized labor' and that these premia appeared to increase with greater capital mobility. 'Presumably, these results reflect the market's skepticism about the willingness of governments to pursue "prudent" macroeconomic policies where the left and organized labor are powerful' ('Capital Mobility, Trade, and Domestic Politics', p. 95).

51. Held et al., *Global Transformations*, p. 165, citing S. Page, *How Countries Trade*, London: Routledge, 1994, Chapter 4.

52. Ronald Dore, 'World Markets and Institutional Uniformity', in Geraint Parry (ed.), *Politics in an Interdependent World*, op. cit., pp. 59–60. This is an instance of the difficulty of distinguishing between production and service and trade and investment in the modern global economy. The Law featured strongly in the US–Japanese Structural Impediments Initiative negotiations in 1998–90 partly because of the desire of the US toy chain, Toys-Я-Us, to open branches in Japan.

53. In the US–Japanese 'Structural Impediment Initiative' negotiations in 1988–90, the Japanese for their part were concerned with reform of the American education system, the adoption by the US of metrication, and improving US savings behaviour (Cable, op. cit. p. 34).

54. Alasdair Smith, 'The Principles and Practice of Regional Economic Integration', in Cable and Hederson, *Trade Blocs?*, p. 29.

55. John H. Dunning, *Globalization: the Challenge for National Economic Regimes*, Dublin: Economic and Social Research Institute, 1993, p. 15 (italics added).

56. Yves Dezelay has pointed out that the huge global firms of corporate lawyers that have emerged do not just supply a demand created by regulatory arbitrage by TNCs, and regulatory competition between states, but also play an important role in driving the whole process: 'One of the main factors dis-

rupting the national systems of regulation results from the competitive pressure exerted by the forum shopping for regulatory regimes to which multinationals of expert services incite their clients' ('Professional Competition and the Social Construction of Transnational Regulatory Expertise', in McCahery et al., op. cit., p. 203). They also write a great deal of the academic law on the subject: 'these new experts practise the art of double-dealing by guiding their clients through the regulatory maze which they know all the better for having been, to a great extent, its designers' (p. 204).

57. Jeanne-Mey Sun and Jacques Pelkmans, 'Regulatory Competition in the Single Market', *Journal of Common Market Studies*, 33/1, 1955, pp. 67–89. In one of their two case studies, Britain and Ireland banned the sale of upholstered furniture that was not impregnated with flame retardants. Ten other EC states took them to the European Court of Justice but in the end the matter was left to be sorted out politically. In the second case, France prevented Barclays Bank from offering French customers interest-bearing current accounts, which were legal in Britain, but Barclays accepted the ban rather than pick a fight with the French government; i.e. the decisive consideration was again political, in spite of Barclays' apparent legal rights.

58. Cable, 'The Diminished Nation State', pp. 39–40.

59. Ibid., p. 41. In spite of the inconsistency involved most neoliberals advocate governments retaining the power to curb immigration.

60. For a survey of the environmental threat posed by the globalized capitalist economy see Held et al., *Global Transformations*, Ch. 8.

61. For a comprehensive review of the Tobin tax idea and the practical and political problems it raises, see Mahbub ul Haq, Inge Daul and Isabell Grunberg (eds), *The Tobin Tax: Coping with Financial Volatility*, New York: Oxford University Press, 1996. One of the contributors, Peter B. Kenen, calculated (p. 110) that a tax of 0.05 per cent on spot transactions would have been feasible (i.e. would not have provoked excessive evasion) and would have yielded $100 billion in 1992 and $150 billion in 1996 – figures which both explain some of the opposition, and form a useful contrast with the level of official development aid (ODA) to low income countries of $29.9 bn in 1992 (World Bank, *World Development Report 1995*, Washington, Oxford University Press, 1995. The World Bank did not publish total ODA after 1993, possibly because it was declining.) At this feasible level of taxation, however, Kenen assumed the tax would have no effect on the volume of transactions – i.e. it would do nothing to reduce financial volatility because if it was large enough to reduce volatility it would be evaded.

62. Public goods: goods which no one can be prevented from consuming and whose consumption by one person does not prevent their consumption by others.

63. Vincent Cable, 'The Diminished Nation-State', in *What Future for the State?*, p. 37. Held et al., in *Global Transformations*, pp. 54–5, cite a figure in the mid-1990s of some 2500 inter-governmental organizations, holding some 4000 conferences a year, and over 5000 international non-government organizations. Cable's list of evolving 'global regimes' includes the Internet, the ECME, the International Settlements, the IIF, the MIGA, the TRIPs/TRIMs, CODEX, the World Trade Organization, the International Telecommunications Union, the International Labour Office, the CITES, the World Meteoro-

logical Organisation; but not, for unexplained reasons, the World Bank or the International Monetary Fund or any UN institutions (op. cit., pp. 35–6).

64. Cable, in 'The Diminished Nation State', cites the International Securities Markets Association and the Bank for International Settlements as cases in point, and notes that some global regulation is partly state – and partly privately – provided and some is provided by states pooling their sovereignty (as in the World Meteorological Organization) or by treaties. He summarizes the recent evolution of what he calls 'global regimes' along a continuum from strong national and weak global rules, to the opposite, for thirteen spheres of concern, from computer networking and currency markets to the environment and migration (ibid. p. 38). It would be interesting to compare the degree to which there is global regulation of any kind with the degree to which the benefits go primarily to capital or primarily to non-owners of capital, but to my knowledge this has not yet been done.

65. Cable, 'The Diminished Nation State', p. 48 (italics added).

66. The founding text for this school is Robert O. Keohane and Helen V. Milner (eds), *Internationalization and Domestic Politics*, Cambridge: Cambridge University Press, 1996, especially the chapter by Peter Lange and Geoffrey Garrett, 'Internationalization, Institutions, and Political Change' (pp. 48–75). See also Garrett's chapter in the same volume, 'Capital Mobility, Trade, and the Domestic Politics of Economic Policy', and introductory and concluding chapters by the editors; Geoffrey Garrett, *Partisan Politics in the Global Economy*, Cambridge: Cambridge University Press, 1998; and Herbert Kitschelt, Peter Lange, Gary Marks and John D. Stephens (eds), *Continuity and Change in Contemporary Capitalism*, Cambridge: Cambridge University Press, 1999.

67. David Soskice, 'Divergent Production Regimes', p. 134.

68. Geoffrey Garrett and Peter Lange, 'Internationalization', p. 69.

69. Ronald Dore, in 'World Markets' (op. cit.), explores some of the forces tending towards uniformity.

70. In J. Rogers Hollingsworth, Philippe C. Schmitter and Wolfgang Streeck (eds), *Governing Capitalist Economies* (New York and Oxford: Oxford University Press, 1994), Chapter 11.

71. Cerny, *Finance and World Markets*, p. 80. For identical conclusions see Held et al., *Global Transformations*, pp. 229–30.

72. Cf. Albert, *Capitalism Against Capitalism*, Chapter 9, 'The Rhine Model in Retreat'; and Birgit Mahnkopf, 'Between the Devil and the Deep Blue Sea: the German Model Under the Pressure of Globalisation', in Panitch and Leys (eds), *Globalisation and Democracy*, pp. 142–77.

73. See Marc Humbert, 'Strategic Industrial Policies in a Global Industrial System', *Review of International Political Economy*, 1/3, 1994, p. 458, using language closer to that of the 'regulation school', makes a very similar observation: 'In a nutshell, a nation's territorial structure of production is the outcome of the articulation between the logic of the nation's societal system and the logic of the global industrial system. But both logics are usually different – in some cases they are clearly antagonistic – leading to somewhat orthogonal [sic] evolutions.' I think, however, that they are always different and always contradictory – i.e. mutually necessary as well as mutually antagonistic.

74. Joachin Hirsch, 'Nation-state, International Regulation and the Question of Democracy', *Review of International Political Economy*, 2/2, 1995, pp. 267–84.
75. 'The result is a strengthening of business . . . and a weakening of the nation-state overall, in the particular the voice of the people through legislatures and nonbusiness, societal groups . . . In other words, deliberative democracy may also suffer . . . Overall, democracy is at risk' (Vivien Schmidt, 'The New World Order', pp. 76–7).
76. *Global Transformations*, p. 234.
77. Louis W. Pauly, 'Capital Mobility, State Autonomy and Political Legitimacy', *Journal of International Affairs*, 48/2, 1995, p. 387.
78. Bennett Harrison, *Lean and Mean, the Changing Landscape of Corporate Power in the Age of Flexibility*, New York: Basic Books, 1994, pp. 30–1.
79. Barnet and Cavanagh, *Global Dreams*, pp. 425–6.
80. Strange, 'The Defective State', pp. 56 and 70.

4

Globalization and Sustainability

Wolfgang Sachs

Symbols are more powerful the more meanings they are able to admit. They actually live on ambivalence. The Cross, for instance, counted both as a token of victory for conquerors and as a token of hope for the vanquished. That ambivalence raised it above the fray; a single clear message would have meant that it divided rather than united. The same may be said of the image of the blue planet, now a symbol unchallenged by either Left or Right, conservative or liberal. Whatever their differences, they are all fond of adorning themselves with this symbol of our epoch. To fall in with it is to announce that one is abreast of the times, in tune with the world, focused on the future, truly prepared to set off into the new century. In this picture are condensed the opposing ambitions of our age. It is hoisted like a flag by troops from enemy camps, and its prominence results from this plurality of meaning. The photograph of the globe contains the contradictions of globalization. That is why it could become an all-weather icon.

No sooner had the image become available, in the late 1960s, than the international environmental movement recognized itself in it. For nothing stands out from the picture as clearly as the round margin that sets it off from the dark cosmos. Clouds, oceans and land masses gleam in the wan light; the earth appears to the observer as a cosy island in a universe unfriendly to life, holding all the continents, seas and living species. For the environmental movement the picture's message was plain: it revealed the earth in its finitude. That circular object made it obvious that the ecological costs of industrial progress could not be shifted forever to noplace, that they were slowly building up into a threat to all within a closed system. In the end, the externalization of costs belonged to the realm of the impossible. In a finite world, where everyone was affected by everyone else, there was an urgent need for mutual care and attention, for more thought about the consequences of one's actions. Such is the holistic message and, certainly, it was not without some effect. Since the days when a few ecologists launched an appeal that was so full of foreboding, the image of the planet as a closed system has steadily gained currency and even recognition in international law. The conventions on ozone, world climate and biodiversity prove that the perception of the earth's biophysical limits has attained the supreme political consecration.

For some time, however, ecologists have no longer had a monopoly on the image. At various airports, in the endless passageways between check-in and exit, a well-lit publicity board has been visible in recent years that strikingly expresses a different view of globalization. It shows a background with a laconic text: 'MasterCard. The World in Your Hands'. The hurrying passengers are being told that, wherever they fly in this big wide world, they can count on the services of their cards and slot themselves into a global credit and debit network. The credit card empire stretches out across all frontiers, with purchasing power in any location and accounting in real time, and its electronic money transfers ensure that the traveller is always provided for. In these and numerous other variations, the image of the planet has turned since the 1980s into a emblem of transnational business; hardly any company in telecommunications or tourism – not to speak of the news industry – seems able to manage without it.

This has been possible because the picture also contains quite a different message. In its detachment from the pitch-black cosmos, the terrestrial sphere stands out as a unified area whose continuous physical reality causes the frontiers between nations and polities to disappear – hence the visual message that what counts is perhaps the boundaries of the earth, but certainly not political frontiers. Only oceans, continents and islands can be seen, with no trace of nations, cultures or states.

In the picture of the globe, distances are measured exclusively in geographical units of miles or kilometres, not in social units of closeness and foreignness. The satellite photographs generally look like renaturalized maps, seeming to confirm the old cartographical postulate that places are nothing more than intersections of two lines – those of longitude and latitude. In marked contrast to the globes of the nineteenth century, which sharply delineate political frontiers and often use different colours for different territories, any social reality is here dissipated into morphology. The earth is depicted as a homogeneous area offering no resistance to transit – or only resistance caused by geographical features, not by human communities and their laws, customs or purposes. Every point of the hemisphere turned towards the observer can be seen at the same moment, and this simultaneous access of the human gaze suggests the idea of unobstructed access on the ground too. The image of the planet offers the world up for unrestricted movement, promises access in every direction, and seems to present no obstacle to expansionism other than the limits of the globe itself. Open, continuous and controllable – there is an imperial message too in the photographs of the earth.

The image symbolizes limitation in the physical sense and expansion in the political sense. Little wonder then that it can serve as a banner for both environmental groups and transnational corporations. It has become the symbol of our times across all the rival world views, because it brings to life both sides of the basic conflict that runs through our epoch. On the one hand, the ecological limits of the earth stand out more clearly than ever before; on the other hand, the dynamic of economic globalization pushes for the removal of all boundaries associated with political and cultural space (Altvater and Mahnkopf, 1996). The two narratives of globalization – limitation and expansion – have acquired a clearer form over the past three decades and fight it out both in the arena of theory and the arena of politics. The outcome of this struggle will decide the shape of the new century, if not the fate of the blue planet.

The rise of the transnational economy

Since the mid-1970s, when the Bretton Woods system of fixed exchange rates gave way to floating parities determined by the market, the world economy has witnessed the collapse of boundaries in a process that started slowly but has gradually speeded up. Of course, the quest for raw materials and markets had for centuries been impelling capitalist companies beyond their national frontiers, but only in the last few decades has an international order been created that works programmatically towards a transnational economy with open borders. Whereas all the first eight GATT rounds since the war dismantled more and more tariff obstacles to the exchange of goods, in line with the traditional ideal of free trade, the last of these, the Uruguay Round, and the newly constructed World Trade Organization have laid the legal foundations for politically unregulated movement of goods, services, money capital and investment right across the globe. The Uruguay Round, concluded in 1993, drew more widely the circle of freely tradable commodities and also deregulated 'software products' such as planning contracts, copyrights, patents and insurance. Controls on the movement of capital, allowing easier inward and outward financial flows, have been progressively removed over the past twenty years, first in the USA and Germany, then in the mid-1980s in Japan, and finally in the countries of the south. In order to make foreign investors feel more at home everywhere, the WTO (and the OECD with its provisionally stalled multilateral investment agreement) have imposed on each state an obligation to accord at least the same rights to foreign as to domestic investors.

A utopian energy is at work in all these initiatives. This can be seen in the ever more frequently declared intention to create a 'level playing field', a global arena for economic competition in which only efficiency counts, unfettered and undistorted by any special local traditions or structures. All economic players are supposed to have the right – at any place and any time – to offer, produce and acquire whatever they want. Up to now, this free play of the market has been hindered by the dizzying diversity of the world's social and legal orders, which have grown out of each country's history and social structure. The aim now, therefore, is to wrench economic activities from their embeddedness in local or national conditions and to bring them under the same rules (if any) everywhere in the world. There should be no blocking, weakening or interfering with market forces, because that leads to efficiency losses and sub-optimal welfare.

This utopian model of economic globalization also features the earth as a homogeneous area, to be crossed at will by circulating goods and capital. Only supply and demand, and in no case political priorities, are supposed to speed up or slow down these flows and to point them in the right direction. The world is conceived as a single huge marketplace, where factors of production are bought at their cheapest ('global sourcing') and commodities are sold at their highest obtainable price ('global marketing'). Just as in satellite pictures of the planet, no role is played by states and their particular laws. Places where people live are foreshortened to mere locations of economic activity. And yet, to the continual annoyance of the neoliberal heaven-stormers, societies everywhere prove sluggish and resistant. The globalizers thus have the onerous task of adapting base reality to ideal model. Their mission is tirelessly to overcome obstacles to the free flow of commodities and thus to make the world comprehensively accessible. That is precisely the programme of the WTO's multilateral economic regime.

In the last few decades, of course, a material infrastructure has also been created for transnational integration. Without the global network of telephone lines, glass fibre cables, microwave channels, relay stations and communications satellites, there would be no open-border world – or at least not as a routine part of everyday life. For electronic data flows – which can be converted into commands and information, sounds and images – eat up kilometres at the press of a key or the click of a mouse. Geographical distance ceases to be of any significance, and since the costs of the transfer and processing of data have dramatically fallen, worldwide interaction has become the daily bread of the globally oriented middle classes. Thus, electronic impulses translate what the external view of the planet already suggested: the unity of space and time for any action in the world. In principle, all events can now be brought into relation with one another in real time for all parts of the earth. Whereas the picture of the globe conveyed the absence of boundaries as a visual experience, electronic networking converts it into a communications (and air transport into a travel) experience. The constant high-volume, lightning-fast flow of bits of information around the globe achieves the abolition of distance as well as the compression of time; electronic space produces a spatio-temporally compact globe (Altvater and Mahnkopf, 1996).

The information highways may be compared to the railways: the digital network is to the rise of a global economy what the railway network was in the nineteenth century to the rise of a national economy (Lash and Urry, 1994). Just as the railway infrastructure became the backbone of the national economy (because falling transport costs enabled regional markets to fuse into a national market), so the digital infrastructure is the backbone of the global economy because falling transmission costs enable national markets to fuse into a global market. Distance is not, of course, truncated in the same way everywhere in the world. This results in a new hierarchy of space: the 'global cities' stand at the top of the pyramid, closely bound together across frontiers by high speed air and land links and by glass fibre cables, while at the bottom whole regions or even continents – Africa or Central Asia, for example – constitute 'black holes' in the informational universe (Castells, 1996), not connected to one another in any significant degree.

On closer examination, then, the networks of transnational interaction rarely assume configurations that stretch across the whole planet; they are not global but transnational, because they bind together only shifting segments of the earth. They are deterritorialized rather than globalized. Unlike earlier types of internationalization, this is particularly the case for the characteristic economic forms of the global age – geographically extended chains of value creation and global finance markets. Basing themselves upon an infrastructure of electronic and physical traffic, companies are now in a position to split up their value-creation process and locate individual parts in areas of the world with the most advantageous wage, skill or market environment. Thus, for a product taken at random, the early stages may take place in Russia, the further processing in Malaysia, the marketing in Hong Kong, the research in Switzerland, and the design in England. Instead of the traditional factory where products were largely manufactured from beginning to end, a network of partial locations makes it possible for previously unheard-of efficiency gains to be achieved. The textbook case of collapsing frontiers, however, is provided by the operations of finance markets. Shares, loans and currency stocks have long left 'paper' behind and become digitalized; their owners can be switched at the press of a key, regardless of borders or geographical distance. Nor is it an accident that the most extensively globalized market is the one that deals in the least physical of all commodities: money. Dependent only on an electronic impulse, it can move angel-like in real time anywhere within a homogeneous space. It seems as if the narrative of collapsing frontiers can best be translated into reality when it takes place within the incorporeality of cyberspace.

How economic globalization reduces the use of resources

For the protagonists of economic globalization, there is no greater thorn in the side than closed economic areas. Import restrictions and export regulations, product standards and social legislation, investment guidance and laws on the sharing of profits – in short, political provisions of any kind that establish a difference between one country's economic system and those of others – are perceived by the globalizers as so many obstacles to the free movement of the factors of production. They therefore seek to undermine, and gradually to break up altogether, the state-defined 'containers' of national markets, and to replace them with a transnational arena where economic actors are no longer prevented by special rules and regulations from carrying through the dynamic of competition. The multinational economic regimes – whether geared continentally to ASESN, NAFTA or the EU, or globally to GATT and the WTO – come down to the construction of homogeneous competitive areas stretching across nations.

The promise held out in these initiatives is one of a world that gets the utmost out of its limited means. A way has to be found of satisfying more and more people around the world, with more and more claims, and it is from this challenge that the friends of globalization derive their task – indeed, their mission – to subject the world's economic apparatuses to a course of efficiency-raising treatment. For the point of market liberalization is to ensure, through the selective power of competition, that capital, labour, intelligence and even natural resources are everywhere deployed in the most efficient manner. Only such treatment continually renewed, argue the globalizers, can lay the basis for the wealth of nations. True, companies do not act out of lofty motives but simply take advantage of opportunities for profits and competitive triumphs. Nevertheless, the 'invisible hand' of the market is expected in the end to produce greater prosperity for all, even at a world level. A dynamic must therefore be set in train that exposes every protected zone of low productivity to the bracing wind of international competition.

The main targets for such a strategy are the state-run economic complexes in the former Soviet Union and in many countries of the south. In fact, external protectionism and internal sclerosis often go hand in hand, for parasitical structures arise most easily where power elites can use their possession of the state to appropriate a country's wealth. Insulated from competition, whether internal or external, the power elite can get away with deploying capital and other resources in short-term operations that produce a maximum surplus – a considerable part of which is then stashed away in foreign bank accounts. Along with the state monopoly of economic activity, the pressure on workers and the underprovision of consumers, it is especially the frenzied exploitation of natural resources that here rakes in a quick profit. Growth soon becomes synonymous with expanded extraction from nature: oil in the Soviet Union, Nigeria or Mexico, coal in India and China, wood in the Ivory Coast and Indonesia, minerals in Zaire. Of course, it was no accident that the use of resources in the former communist countries was much higher than in the west, for natural treasures were seen as a cost-free (because state-owned) means of fuelling industrial developments – especially as growth pressures were directed to extensive rather than intensive ways of increasing production. The opening up of bureaucratically ossified economies to competition was thus to the benefit of resource efficiency. Almost as soon as the wall of restrictions and subsidies crumbled, new suppliers from outside appeared on the scene and placed the old wasteful economy in question. Globalization razes strongholds of mismanagement to the ground, and in such cases cuts down on the use of natural resources by enforcing at least economic rationality.

This efficiency effect does not operate only through expanded entry to the market. Trade and investment also increase access to technologies that, in comparison with domestic ones, often bring considerable gains in efficiency. This applies in particular to such sectors as mining, energy, transport and industry. Examples range from the export of more eco-nomical cars from Japan to the United States, through the introduction of new power station technology in Pakistan, to the savings in material and energy that came with new blast-furnaces in the Brazilian steel industry. There is strong evidence that more open national economies deploy more resource-efficient technologies at an earlier date, simply because they have better access to the most modern – which usually means more efficient – technological investment. Moreover, trans-national corporations tend to standardize technologies between coun-tries at a more advanced level, rather than expose themselves to all kinds of co-ordination costs. The connection is by no means necessary, of course, but it is probable – and it may be said that more flexible invest-ment rules generally favour entry to a higher technological trajectory (Johnstone, 1997). The efficiency effect of more open markets is visible not only in supply-side technology transfers but also on the demand side: commodity exports from the fast-developing countries to the post-industrial regions of the north have to stand the test of consumer preferences in the north, and since the market demand there often displays greater environmental awareness, production structures in the exporting country may have to adapt to those standards.

The justification for economic globalization, then, is supposed to be that it establishes an empire of economic efficiency, and that this effect often extends to the use of energy and raw materials (OECD, 1998). This is understood as a growth in microeconomic rationality, as a striving to deploy the factors of production in an optimal manner everywhere. Of course, the promoters of globalization have to play down the fact that this can equally well go together with a decline in macro-rationality as regards both political–social relations and the environment. For market rationalization may lower the use of particular resources – that is, input per unit of output – but the total use of resources will nevertheless grow if the volume of economic activity expands. Growth effects may all too easily eat up efficiency effects. In fact, so far in the history of industrial society, efficiency gains have quite consistently been converted into new opportunities for expansion. This, from an ecological point of view, is the Achilles' heel of globalization.

How economic globalization expands and accelerates the use of resources

In recent years globalization has been hailed, often with the full red-carpet treatment, as opening a new era for humanity. Yet its goals are surprisingly conventional: it serves on its own admission to spur world economic growth, and it involves – under changed historical conditions – such longstanding strategies as intensive development and growth through expansion. On the one hand, there is the shifting distribution of the value-creation chain across far-flung regions of the world, which enables companies – in their choice of the best location for each stage of production – to enjoy to the full benefits of rationalization that were simply not available before. The advancing digitalization of economic processes has also created new scope for productivity gains – for example, through flexible automation in manufacturing, simulation techniques in research, or perfectly timed logistics in networks of co-operation. With the restructuring of large parts of the world economy, it has thus become possible to wring further growth from long drawn-out productivity competition in OECD markets that were largely saturated at the end of the 1970s. On the other hand, growth has occurred through expansion – and, in particular, through the quest for new markets abroad. Many companies that might not have been able to make much further progress on local markets decided instead to tap demand in other OECD and fast-developing countries. The combined result of these two strategies may be seen in the fact that the world economy was well on its way to doubling between 1975 and 2000. Even if all GNP growth does not involve a parallel rise in the flow of resources, there can be no doubt that the biosphere is under ever greater pressure from the anthroposphere.

Direct foreign investment and the expansion effect

The utopian horizon of globalization is a permeable borderless world in which goods and capital can move around freely. Whereas the various GATT agreements expanded the exchange of goods over a period of decades, the further elimination of national barriers has in the last fifteen years mainly affected the mobility of private capital. Between 1980 and 1996 the cross-border exchange of goods increased by an annual average of 4.7 per cent, but foreign investment rose by 8.8 per cent per annum, international bank loans by 10 per cent, and the trade in currency and shares by 23.5 per cent (*The Economist*, 1997a). If one looks at the geographical distribution of these flows it becomes clear that, although the lion's share of the capital traffic remains as before within the USA–EU–Japan triad, transfers of private capital have sky-rocketed mainly in the ten 'emerging markets' of East Asia and South America. They rose from an annual $44 billion at the beginning of the 1990s to $244 billion in 1996, before settling down at some $170 billion after the 1997 financial crisis in Asia (French, 1998: 7). An important sub-category – accounting for one-half in the case of manufacturing, more than one-third in services, and 20 per cent in the primary sector – has been foreign investment to buy up existing firms or to found new ones. For the investing company, the point of this has been to control the further extraction of natural resources, to erect a platform within a transnational chain of production, or to gain access to export markets. For the host state, on the other hand, the aim has been to draw in investment capital and know-how, as part of a fervent desire to take off economically and to catch up with the rich countries at some point in the future.

With the migration of investment capital from the OECD countries, the fossil model of development has spread to the newly industrializing countries and even well beyond them; whether it is a question of factories in China, chemical plants in Mexico or industrial agriculture in the Philippines, the countries of the south are entering on a broad front the resource-intensive fossil stage of economic development. That fateful style of economics that consolidated itself in Europe in the late nineteenth century, resting to a large degree upon the transformation of unpaid natural values into commodity values, is now expanding to more parts of the world in the wake of foreign investment. Certainly, a good part of this development is also being driven by locally accumulated capital, but the gigantic influx of foreign investment has deepened and accelerated the spread of – environmentally speaking – robber economies. Everywhere there prevails an industrial-social mimetism, a copying of modes of production and consumption that, in view of the crisis of nature, may already be regarded as obsolete. For in the conventional path of development, monetary growth always goes together with material growth. A certain uncoupling of the two appears only in the transition to a post-industrial economy. The favoured targets for investment on the periphery are thus raw materials extraction or energy and transport infrastructure, which all push the use of natural resources up and up. Even if input per unit of output is lower than that at a corresponding stage in the development of the rich countries, the absolute volume of the flow of resources has been increasing prodigiously.

The removal of national obstacles to investment activity stands in an increasing contradiction to the earth's biophysical limitations. Thus the fast-industrializing countries recorded a steep rise in their CO_2 emissions (varying between 20 and 40 per cent in the 1990–5 period), while the industrialized countries – at a higher level, of course – increased theirs only slightly (Brown et al., 1998: 58). All in all, fossil fuel use will double in China and East Asia between 1990 and 2005, to reach a volume almost comparable to that of the United States. The motor car may serve as a symbol in this respect. In South Korea (before the crisis broke), car ownership was expanding by 20 per cent a year (Carley and Spapens, 1998: 35). On the streets of India, virtually the only car to be seen in 1980 was the venerable old Ambassador limousine – a real petrol-guzzler, of course, but limited in numbers and therefore discharging far less gas than the huge fleet of more efficient vehicles turned out by the nine automobile corporations now operating there. Thus, in countries where transport has until now been mainly a question of bicycles and public services, further development of their eco-friendly systems will be blocked and replaced by a structure dependent upon high fuel use. It is altogether consistent with the logic of fossil expansion that the World Bank, for all its lip-service to 'sustainable development', allocates two-thirds of its expenditure in the energy sector to the mobilization of fossil energy sources.

Another symbol of lifestyle widely regarded as modern, the Big Mac, may serve to illustrate the mounting pressure on biological resources. In little more than five years between 1990 and 1996, the number of MacDonald's restaurants in Asia and Latin America quadrupled (UNDP, 1998: 56), against a background of tripled meat consumption over the past 25 years. Such trends mean more and more water, cereals and grazing land for cattle, so it is hardly surprising that, in the 1980s alone, the countries of South-East and South Asia lost between 10 per cent and 30 per cent of their forests (Brown et al., 1998). The forest fires in Indonesia, whose dense clouds of smoke covered half of South-East Asia in 1997–8, originated in massive slash-and-burn clearances and were widely interpreted as a warning of the destructive power of the Asian economic miracle.

Deregulation and the competitive effect

The creation of a global competitive arena requires not only a quantitative expansion but also a qualitative restructuring. Alongside the geographical extension of the transnational economy, its internal reordering has also appeared on the agenda of the day, for new rules of economic competition are indispensable if there is to be a homogeneous space no longer riven by national economic idiosyncrasies. There is no other way for would-be globalizers except to dismantle the national regulatory apparatuses that have previously encompassed economic activity. These apparatuses, which generally reflect a country's historical experiences, social sets of interests and political ideals, combine the logic of economics with other social priorities, in both fragile comprom- ises and institutions built to last. At a later stage of the secular process that Karl Polanyi called 'disembedding', the dynamic of economic glob- alization is intended to release market relations from the web of na- tional norms and standards and to bring them under the law of worldwide competition. Whatever these norms cover – labour condi- tions, regional planning or environmental policy – they are neither wrong nor right but are seen as obstructing entry into the global com- petitive arena. In this view of things, norms might be acceptable at a global level – although the question does not really apply, of course, in the absence of a political authority. Deregulation is thus a catch-all term for attempts to further global competition by dissolving the links be- tween economic actors and a particular place or a particular community.

Like any regulation of economic activity in the name of the public interest, the protection of the environment is also coming under pressure in many countries. As the number of economic actors on the global market continues to grow, so too does the competition between them – which is why governments everywhere tend to attach a higher value to competitive strength than to protection of the environment or of natural resources. New ecological norms, often imposed by democratic public opinion after years of struggle and controversy, are perceived by com- panies as a hindrance to competition and in many cases fiercely resisted. As competitive interests gain the upper hand over protective interests, it becomes many times more difficult to halt deforestation in Canada or over-mining in the Philippines, to stop the building of more motorways in Germany, to introduce eco-taxes in the European Union, or to main- tain ecological product standards in Sweden. However, although govern- ments are often determined enough to make their country a more attractive site for footloose capital, it is doubtless an exaggeration to speak of a 'race to the bottom' in matters concerning environmental standards (Esty and Gerardin, 1998). Sometimes the protective interests are too strong, or it may be that environmental factors are not all that significant in a siting decision. It would be more accurate to say that environmental regulation has tended to get 'stuck in the mud' as a result of increased competition (Zarsky, 1997). True, world market integration has brought a certain convergence among national regulatory systems, but this has been happening too slowly and at too low a level. In many countries, the process of economic globalization has blocked any real progress in national environmental policy.

Not surprisingly, the ambition to standardize competitive conditions throughout the world – especially in the case of cross-border trade –

clashes with the right of individual countries to shape economic processes. Now that tariff barriers for industrial goods have been largely dismantled through the successive GATT rounds, should environmental reasons be allowed to put certain categories of import at a disadvantage? This question has been much disputed ever since the Uruguay Round, and it continues to give rise to controversy within the WTO and OECD over deregulation and protection interests. Under the trade rules currently in force, individual states are entitled to lay down environmental and health standards, so long as the same kinds of goods are subject to the same regulation regardless of whether they are imported or locally produced. Of course, this applies only to the composition of a product: a government might decide, for instance, to slap a special tax on all cars above a certain power threshold. Here, it seems, the principle of national sovereignty contradicts only the principle of the unregulated circulation of goods. What is forbidden in international trade, however, is to discriminate against goods whose production process does not conform to certain environmental standards. Which chemicals are used to produce an item of clothing, whether wooden products come from forest clearance areas, whether genetic engineering methods have been used to produce a plant – on none of these questions is a government allowed by WTO rules to express a collective preference. Thus, in the well-known tuna affair, the ban on dolphin fishing could not be maintained under NAFTA rules, and one of the present disputes between the USA and the EU is over whether governments have the right to keep hormone-intensive beef out of their markets. Moreover, since local production standards are also put under strain when importers are able to gain a competitive advantage by externalizing environmental costs, individual states lose the power to insist that production processes in their own country should be environmentally sustainable. The deregulation interest nullifies the protection interest. Through the competitive effect of free trade, even gentle course corrections towards a sustainable economy are soon brought to a standstill.

All the deregulation efforts are also meant to cleanse the economy of extraneous influences, thereby ensuring optimal deployment of the factors of production. Consumers are ostensibly the main ones to benefit, since deregulated operations encourage a more varied supply through easier market entry as well as lower prices through greater competition. Nevertheless, a regime of ruthless efficiency in environmentally significant sectors may lead to greater overall use of resources. If the price of heating oil, petrol, coal or water falls, then normally demand for them will rise and it will be even less worth introducing conservation technologies. Deregulation of the electricity market in the OECD countries, for example, certainly helped promoters of energy-efficient power stations to enter the market, but it also showed that lower prices may hinder a changeover to cleaner energy sources such as natural gas and, more important still, actually encourage higher electricity consumption (Jones and Youngman, 1997). Anyway, it is fairly easy to see that falling prices within a price system that does not accurately reflect environmental costs will accelerate the quarrying of resources. So long as prices do not tell the ecological truth, deregulation will only take the market further down the ecologically slippery slope – and it is not exactly rational to keep running more efficiently in the wrong direction. But the purer competition becomes as a result of deregulation, the less ecological rationality will be able to assert itself against economic rationality. Under the given price system, global competition will deepen the crisis of nature (Daly, 1996).

Currency crises and the sell-out effect

Nowhere has a global competitive space been raised so clear of national boundaries as in the case of the finance markets. Goods take time to be carried from one place to another, foreign investment requires factories to be built or dismantled, and even services such as insurance cannot be traded overseas without a network of branches and representatives. Only financial transfers in the form of shares, loans or currencies are scarcely subject any longer to restrictions of time and space. Every day, billions of dollars change hands online in virtual space through mere touches on VDU keyboards, irrespective of physical distance. Only on these electronic markets does capital finally attain its secret ideal of completely unfettered mobility. For the money markets have very largely shaken off the inertia not only of temporal duration and geographical distance, but also of material goods; less than 2 per cent of the currency trade is now covered by actual commodity flows (Zukunfts-kommission, 1998: 73). This virtual economy has been made possible technologically by electronic networking, and politically by the deregulation of international capital traffic in the industrialized countries in the 1970s and 1980s, as well as in major developing countries in the 1990s.

As we have seen, it was the collapse of the Bretton Woods system in 1971 that gave the impetus to this development. Currencies could become commodities, their price set by the laws of supply and demand on the capital markets. But the value of a currency is a matter of fateful significance for a country: it determines the purchasing power of the national economy in relation to other national economies around the world. In fact, the ups and downs of freely convertible currencies reflect the expectations of future growth and competitiveness that investors entertain about the respective economies. In a way, a country's whole economy thus becomes a commodity, whose relative value crystallizes through the return envisaged by investment fund managers. This gives the finance markets great power *vis-à-vis* economically weak countries, so great that fluctuations in the exchange rate can decide the fate of whole nations. Governments, whether democratic or authoritarian, often find themselves compelled to gear their economic, social and fiscal policies to the interests of investors, with the result that the interest of their own people in social and economic security all too easily goes by the board. It is as if investors cast a daily ballot by transferring huge sums of money from one country to another (Sassen, 1996); the global electorate of investors lines up, as it were, against a country's local electorate, and not infrequently the government allies itself with the investors against its own electors. At the same time, however, the currency crashes in Mexico in late 1994, in several East Asian countries in 1997, and in Russia and Brazil in 1998 made it plain that investors are as jumpy as a herd of wild horses that stampedes off now in one direction, now in another, as danger threatens. The collective optimism with which investors forget about risks during an upturn is matched by the collective panic with which they flee out of loans and currencies during a downturn. Investment-seeking capital storms into countries and back out again. On its way in, it gives rise to false dreams; on its way out, it leaves behind ruined human lives and a ravaged ecosystem (Cavanagh, 1998).

Currency crises are quite likely to threaten nature in the affected countries, for those that are rich in exportable natural resources come under intense pressure to exploit them more extensively and at a faster tempo. The falling value of the currency means that they have to throw larger quantities onto the world market in order to stop their export earnings falling through the floor. An exchange-rate crisis thus intensifies the already chronic hunger of indebted states for foreign currency, so that they will be able to repay loans and to import at least the minimum of food, goods and capital. But often the only option left is to use freely available nature as a currency earner – as one can see from the current boom in the export of oil, gas, metals, wood, animal feed and agricultural produce from countries in the south hit by the financial crisis. Fishing rights are being sold by Senegal, for example, to fleets of vessels from Asia, Canada and Europe; tree-felling rights by Chile to US timber corporations; and exploration rights by Nigeria to the oil multi-nationals (French, 1998: 23). In times of need, desperate countries have to sell even their 'family silver'. So it is that valuable forest land is sold off stretch by stretch under the pressure of the debt burden. Mexico, for instance, after the peso collapse of 1994, rescinded its laws protecting national forests – and the people living in them – in order to promote a stronger export orientation. Brazil launched an action plan to make the export of wood, minerals and energy financially more attractive through massive infrastructural investment in Amazonia. Indonesia, after another currency crash, was compelled in talks with the International Monetary Fund to change its land ownership legislation so that foreign cellulose and paper corporations could move in on the forest (Menotti, 1998b). One might even, as Menotti acerbically suggests, speak of a causal link between falling currencies and falling trees.

Measures to rectify the economy after a currency and debt crisis – measures imposed under the often blackmailing care of the IMF structural adjustment programmes – also usually lead to forced selling of natural assets on the world market, for the aim of the numerous structural adjustment programmes in both the south and the east is to bring the balance of payments back into equilibrium through an increase in exports, and thus to entice investors back into the country. A glance at the history of these programmes shows, however, that – alongside the weaker sections of society – the environment is supposed to make all the sacrifices for an export upturn. True, the removal of environmentally damaging subsidies and the liberalization of markets do generally promote a more efficient use of resources. But the rate of exploitation soon increases with the mobilization of raw materials and agricultural produce for export; land demand and pesticide use rise together with the switch-over to cash crops; and tourism and transport also experience major growth (Reed, 1996). Furthermore, the new exporters' rights to natural resources collide with the hereditary rights of less endowed sections of the population to use forests, water and land; the poor are pushed to the sidelines, and compelled by rising prices to plunder marginal ecosystems for their survival. In this connection, a number of studies have concluded that the negative environmental effects of structural adjustment programmes far outweigh the positive benefits (Kessler and Van Dorp, 1998).

It is not uncommon, however, for the law of supply and demand to cancel out the fruits of the export drive. Prices often fall as demand increases on the commodity markets, and once more the lower earnings have to be offset by greater export volumes. Should the recipient countries also be hit by a financial crisis, both demand and commodity prices come under renewed pressure. This is precisely what happened after the Asian financial crisis of 1997. Commodity prices on the world market slid lower and lower – by more than 25 per cent within a year (*Die Zeit*, 24 September 1998). And since the crisis also depressed demand in countries such as Japan, South Korea and Malaysia, the price spiral kept moving downward and forcing dependent countries to intensify the exploitation of raw materials for export. Thus money flows overshadow commodity flows in quite a special way during periods of economic downturn.

Vanishing distance and the transport effect

The sudden awareness of living in a shrinking world may well be the fundamental human experience in the age of globalization. The satellite image of the blue planet visually presents what things are tending towards in reality: all places appear present at the same time. While distance between places becomes insignificant, the same time comes to prevail everywhere: space vanishes, time standardizes. For currency traders and news editors, company buyers and tourists, managers and scientists, less and less importance attaches to distance and, of course, more and more to time. It hardly matters any longer where on the globe something happens; what counts is when it happens – at the right time, too late, or not at all. Globalization, in all its facets, rests upon the rapid overcoming of space, rendering the present ubiquitous without delay. Computers, after all, count seconds, but not kilometres. How the earth is shrinking under the sway of time, how near everything is and how fast everything goes – it is in such experiences that the growing spatio-temporal compactness of the globe becomes discernible (Altvater and Mahnkopf, 1996).

Spatial compression requires transport, whether along physical or electronic channels. Electronic networking is the first constitutive element in the process of globalization. Without online data transfers there would not be the nervous system of signal communication that, in lightning-quick reactions, binds together events on the globe without consideration of space. If one thinks, however, that in 1995 there were 43.6 computers and 4.8 Internet users per thousand of the world's population (UNDP, 1998: 167), four-fifths of whom lived in the industrialized countries, then it is all too clear that one can speak of globalization only in a geographical, and certainly not a social, sense. No more than 1–4 per cent of the world's population are electronically linked to one another, and no more than 5 per cent have even sat in an aeroplane.

From an ecological point of view, electronic communication is assuredly less wasteful of resources than is physical transport. Yet one should not underestimate the additional strain that the construction and maintenance of a digital infrastructure place upon the earth's resources. High-quality materials used in hardware and peripherals are obtained through numerous refining processes that impose a large (and often toxic) extra burden on the environment, cables of all kinds use a lot of material, and satellites and relay stations also cannot be had without a drain on the environment. Finally, whatever the many prophets of the information age merrily predict, electronic networking will in the long term probably generate more physical travel than it replaces. Anyone who has established close contact with distant places via electronic media will sooner or later want to seal the contact face to face. In any event, the main effect is a positive feedback between electronic and physical transport and still more transport.

All forms of economic globalization, outside the international finance markets, rely heavily upon physical transport. Everywhere distances are springing up – on both the consumption and factor markets, they are growing longer and more numerous. T-shirts come from China to Germany and tomatoes from Ecuador to the United States; machinery from Europe stands in Shanghai harbour; the global class of 'symbol analysts' (Castells, 1996) keep bumping into one another in the airports of OECD countries. After all, the value of world trade has been rising by more than 6 per cent a year, roughly twice as fast as the world economy itself. Foreign products – from meat to precision machines – play a more prominent role in many countries, and even small firms seek their fortune on overseas markets. And yet the term 'international trade' has a number of false associations. It no longer means that nations exchange goods that they themselves do not produce – as in the classical exchange of raw material for industrial goods – but that foreign suppliers appear alongside local ones in largely OECD-centred trade. They no longer make up for gaps in the local supply, but try to oust the local supply either through undercutting or through the use of different symbols (Pastowski, 1997). Korean cars for Carland America, Mexican beer for Beerland Germany: roughly a half of world trade takes place within industrial branches, that is, the same commodities are being imported and exported at the same time (Daly, 1996: 5). The main purpose of international goods transport is thus to ensure the competitive presence of many suppliers in as many places as possible.

Distance-chopping and rapid transport for high-quality goods and people are mainly provided by the international air system. Passenger transport, if it continues growing at its present annual rate of 5 per cent, will double every 15 years, and although by now roughly half of air travel is for leisure purposes, the geography of economic globalization is reflected in the increased flow. Between 1985 and 1996, the income of airline companies grew sevenfold on routes within China and threefold within South-East Asia and between Europe or North America and North-East Asia, whereas on other routes there was at most a twofold increase or sometimes, as in the case of Africa, stagnation (Boeing, 1998). Air freight has been rising still faster: after annual growth of 7–12 per cent in the mid-1990s (ibid.), the assumption is that it will now average 6.6 per cent and add up to a tripling of revenue by the year 2015 – figures naturally surpassed by the anticipated growth rate for international express services, where DHL and similar firms reckon on an annual increase of 18 per cent.

Without rapidly declining freight costs, the expansion of global markets would not have been possible. For such costs must not be a decisive factor, if the dynamic of supply and demand is to develop independently of geographical location. The more freight costs weigh in the balance, the less worthwhile it becomes to use price and innovation to gain an advantage over far-flung competitors; lower marginal costs in production would soon be eaten up by greater outlays on transport. Only if the costs of overcoming space tend towards insignificance can corporate strategies alone determine the choice of location. A number of reasons have been given for the relative cheapening of freight. First, it is precisely on global markets that transport volume is being constantly reduced in relation to a given value of trade. For a computer producer in Texas, for example, it matters little whether his hard disks come from Singapore or California; as transport costs become less significant, the more the economic value of a transported good is independent from its size or weight. In fact, those branches of the economy that go in most for 'global sourcing' – computers, motor vehicles, consumer electronics, textiles – are often not the largest-volume traders (Sprenger, 1997: 344). Second, containerization and easier transfers between modes of transport have greatly increased efficiency (*The Economist* 1997b). But the third and main reason why distance has been losing its resistance is that the price of fuel oil, used in nearly all forms of transport, has fallen dramatically since 1980. As a matter of fact, that price is far from reflecting the full ecological costs of the production and consumption of oil. For all the efficiency gains, transport in the OECD countries is the only sector in which CO_2 emissions have continued to increase in recent years. Transport also requires various facilities: vehicles, highways, harbours and airports, a whole infrastructure which uses a considerable amount of materials and land. Yet most of these costs are passed on to society and do not show up in the freight bills. It becomes easy to overlook the extent to which the overcoming of geographical distance and temporal duration is paid for through the spoliation of nature.

How economic globalization fosters a new colonization of nature

The results of the GATT Uruguay Round, which ended in 1993 with a package of trade agreements and the founding of the WTO, included an accord on intellectual property rights. In contrast to the main preoccupation, which had been to dismantle national controls on cross-border trade, it was here a question of introducing a new level of regulation. Yet both strategies – deregulation as well as reregulation – were pursued in the name of freedom of trade. The contradiction disappears as soon as one realizes that the aim in both cases was to create uniform legal foundations for a global economic space. While a plethora of national obstacles to the circulation of goods and capital had to be dismantled, it was also necessary to establish an international legal framework that would give such circulation a powerful helping hand. Factor mobility can be obstructed by a mass of laws, but it can also be left hanging in mid-air if there are no laws at all. Especially relevant in this respect was the case of property rights in goods based on genetic engineering – a case in which legal security had been defective in most countries around the world. This was the gap that the agreement on 'trade-related intellectual property rights' (TRIPS) was designed to close, for without it the exploitation of newly available raw materials – the genetic material of forms of life – would not have much of a commercial future.

Under the TRIPS agreement, all countries are required to provide legal protection for patented inventions of both products and processes, in all fields of technology. Industrial patents, of course, have long assured their owners an exclusive income from inventions for a certain length of time, but a similar system has only slowly come to apply to biological products and processes. The protection of a patent is nevertheless indispensable for the commercialization of research-intensive products, since only proprietary rights give them a commodity status – otherwise they would just be useful objects freely available in the public domain. For this reason, a guaranteed property system is the legal–social corset of a market economy, just as the more or less forcible enclosure and appropriation of common territory (fields, pasture, forest, fishing grounds) was the historical prerequisite for the lift-off of agrarian capitalism. If the research-intensive products are organisms such as seeds or plants, this raises the additional marketing problem that they easily reproduce themselves (Flitner, 1998). Seeds, for example, bring forth plants, which in turn bear the seeds for the next sowing. The commodity character of a living organism does not last long, therefore; the second generation no longer needs to be bought. But this is bad news for any investor, since if commodities can reproduce themselves, it means that the reproduction of capital is on shaky ground. That leaves just two possibilities. Either their reproducibility is curtailed (for example, through the insertion of 'terminator genes'), or patents allow fees to be charged for the use of a technologically modified living process.

Patents to genetic innovations ensure the economic control of 'life industries' over modified organisms and their offspring. Only through the establishment of proprietary rights over cells, micro-organisms and organisms does the genetic material of the living world become available to be marketed. Patents empower firms to take ownership of parts of the natural realm, to turn it into an economic resource, and as far as possible to monopolize it so that no one can use it unless they pay for an approved purpose. Life patents thus play for 'life industries' the same role that land deeds played for emergent agrarian capitalism. They define ownership, keep other users away, and establish to whom the benefits of use should accrue. Activities such as planting, animal-raising or curative treatment, which used to be part of the public domain, thus come increasingly under the control of corporations. Whereas colonialists used to appropriate mineral or land resources by physically controlling a territory, the genetic engineering firms exploit genetic resources through world-recognized patents over DNA sequences.

The consequences for plant diversity, however, are likely to be similar. There is no need to consider the numerous dangers bound up with an uncontrollable spread of transgenic species; even the accident-free introduction of genetic technology into the agriculture of the south would cause a whole range of plants to disappear from the evolutionary picture. Whereas agrarian capitalism led in many places to monoculture of natural plant varieties, the life industries might force specialization in a few genetically optimized, and economically useful, plants (rather along the lines of the 'Green Revolution' of the 1960s and 1970s) (Lapp and Bailey, 1998). In the fierce competition for markets that is likely to ensue, non-industrial and local strains would fall by the wayside – which would undermine food security, especially for poorer people without the means to purchase industrial produce. All plants other than a few strains capable of large-scale cultivation would be lost. A global system of legal patents for genetic inventions, which incorporated and irrevocably modified parts of the human biological heritage for commercial ends, would threaten to result in nothing less than a simplification of the biosphere.

How economic globalization changes the geography of environmental stress

In recent years, more and more salmon dishes – fresh, smoked or grilled – have been appearing on German menus, almost as if it were a fish from local waters. By now Germans consume nearly 70 million kilograms a year of the favoured fish, which is brought from farms in Norway or Scotland to supermarket displays (Oppel, 1999). But as in the mass farming of any other creature, large quantities of feed have to be supplied – to be precise, five kilograms of wild deep-water fish have to be processed into one kilogram of fishmeal, which is then used to feed salmon for consumption. This raw material is mostly caught off the Pacific coast of South America, where catches are declining because of overfishing, and it is then turned into meal in Peruvian harbour towns that are in danger of suffocating in the gaseous, liquid and solid waste matter that results from the process. While German consumers can feast themselves on fresh low-calorie (and rather expensive) fish, people in Peru are left with pillaged seas and filthy towns.

This example shows how a lengthening of the supply chain can shift the ecological division of labour between countries of the south (and east) and those of the north. For economic globalization does not mean that the costs and benefits of economic activity are globalized. On the contrary, it is more likely that extension of the value-creation chain to different locations around the world will bring a new allocation of advantage and disadvantage. When a production process is divided up among different countries and regions, a tendency soon appears to separate costs and benefits by redistributing them up and down the chain. Anyway it would be wrong to imagine that the worldwide networking of offices, factories, farms and banks is accompanied by a decentralization of all functions from production and planning to finance, not to speak of the collection of profits (Sassen, 1996). Despite many attempts to increase the autonomy of sub-units, the opposite is generally the case: that is, the diversification of economic activities leads to a concentration of control and profit at the nodal points of the network economy (Castells, 1996). The flux of investment into distant countries is offset by a reflux of power and profits to the originating country, or more precisely, to the 'global cities' of the north. As special export zones multiply in Bangladesh, Egypt or Mexico, where cheap labour, tax breaks and lax environmental norms considerably reduce production costs, the sky is the limit for the towers of banks and company offices in Hong Kong, Frankfurt or London.

The changed distribution of economic power goes together with a change in how the pressure on the environment is distributed across geographical space. If power, in an ecological sense, is defined as the capacity to internalize environmental advantages while externalizing environmental costs, then it may be supposed that the lengthening of economic chains will start a process that concentrates advantages at the upper end and disadvantages at the lower end. In other words, the environmental costs incurred within the transnational value-creation chains will become especially high in the countries of the south and east, while the post-industrial economies will become ever more environmentally friendly. Or to use an analogy (with the salmon example in mind), the rich countries will increasingly occupy the upper positions in the food chain (where larger volumes of low-value inputs have step-by-step been converted into smaller volumes of high-value food), while the developing or poorer countries will occupy the middle and lower positions. In fact, along with numerous individual examples, a series of highly aggregated data on international flows of materials lend credence to this interpretation. Thus, 35 per cent of total resource consumption is incurred abroad in the case of Germany, 50 per cent in Japan, 70 per cent in the Netherlands, and so on (Adriaanse et al., 1997: 13). The smaller the area of an industrialized country, the greater seems to be the geographical separation between the sites of pressure on the environment and the sites of consumption benefit. In all these countries, there has been a tendency over the past fifteen years for a growing proportion of environmental consumption to take place abroad involving not so much raw materials as semi-finished products.

In agriculture, southern regions of the world no longer supply only agrarian mass produce as in the days of colonialism, but also supply goods with a high dollar value per unit of weight for affluent consumers in the north. Highly perishable items such as tomatoes, lettuce, fruit, vegetables and flowers come as air freight to Europe from Senegal or Morocco, to Japan from the Philippines, or to the United States from Colombia or Costa Rica (Thrupp, 1995). As in the case of salmon, health-conscious shoppers with an average-to-high income are only too pleased to have a supply that does not depend on the season, while plantations and glasshouses in the areas of origin impose irrigation, pesticide use and the repression of local farmers. Nor are things much different with shrimp or meat production. The breeding of shrimps and prawns in Thailand or India for the Japanese and European markets means that people have to wade through toxic residue to catch them and that many a mangrove forest has to disappear from the scene. More refined consumption in the north occurs at the price of the environment and subsistence economics in the south. This pattern has rooted itself deeply in the food-produce market since the 1970s. The raising of cattle and pigs in Europe draws in manioc or soya both from the United States and from countries such as Brazil, Paraguay, Argentina, Indonesia, Malaysia or Thailand. The old law that the market puts purchasing power before human need asserts itself still more powerfully in a world economy beyond frontiers.

Of course, the expansion of the fossil development model into one or two dozen aspiring economies in the south and east has done most to change the geography of environmental stress. As the newly industrialized nations entered the age fuelled by fossil resources, the possibility presented itself of stretching the industrial production chains beyond the OECD countries. The south's share of world output has thus been growing (and the OECD's slowly declining) in primary industry, metalworking and chemicals (Sprenger, 1997: 337; Mason, 1997), rising in the last of these from 17 per cent in 1990 to 25 per cent in 1996 (French, 1998: 27). What is happening is not so much migration for environmental reasons as a redistribution of functions within the world economy. The stages of an international production chain that put most pressure on the environment are usually in less-developed regions, while the cleaner and less material stages tend to be in the G7 countries. In the aluminium industry, for instance, the quarrying of bauxite takes place in Guyana, Brazil, Jamaica and Guinea (along with Australia). The actual smelting of the aluminium, which is the next stage along, moved more and more in the 1980s from the north to countries such as Brazil, Venezuela, Indonesia or Bahrain, while the research and development stage remained chiefly located in the OECD area (Heerings and Zeldenrust, 1995: 33). Despite higher use overall, the production of aluminium grew strongly in Japan and weakly in Europe; imports from the south filled the gap (Mason, 1997).

A look at the computer branch further along shows just how much high-tech industry lives off the new ecological division of labour. In the case of 22 computer companies in the industrialized countries, more than half of their (mostly toxic) microchip production is located in developing countries (French, 1998: 280). Does this not show in outline the future restructuring of the world economy? The software economies of the north will pride themselves on their plans for a cleaner environment, while the newly industrialized economies will do the manufacturing and contend with classical forms of water, air and soil pollution, and the poorer primary economies will do the extracting and undermine the subsistence basis of the third of humanity that lives directly from nature.

Which and whose globalization?

Globalization is not a monopoly of the neoliberals: the most varied actors, with the most varied philosophies, are also caught up in the transnationalization of social relations; indeed the ecological movement is one of the most important agents of global thinking. Accordingly, the image of the blue planet – that symbol of globalization – conveys more than just one message. The imperial message of collapsing frontiers always found itself confronted with the holistic message of the planet's finite unity. A clear line can be drawn from Earth Day 1970 (often seen as the beginning of the American ecological movement) to the United Nations conference on world climate held in Kyoto in 1997. In the squares where people assembled on that first Earth Day, speakers and demonstrators underpinned their demands for comprehensive environmental protection with photographs of the earth taken less than a year before from the surface of the moon. And nearly thirty years later, the emblem of the planet was prominently displayed on the front of the conference hall where, for the first time, the world's governments entered into legally binding commitments to limit pollution levels. That picture shows the earth as a single natural body binding human beings and other forms of life to a common destiny; it globalizes our perception both of nature and of the human story. Only with that image did it become possible to speak of 'one earth' or 'one world' in the true sense of the term. For neither the name of the environmental association Friends of the Earth, nor the title of the Brundtland Report, *Our Common Future* (WCED, 1987), would have meant much without that photo of the planet.

But the 'blue planet effect' and its message of finitude go deeper still: they produce a way of seeing that places local action within a global framework. The picture shows the outer limits of the living space of everyone who looks at it. Does not everyone know that, if only the image were sufficiently enlarged, he or she would be able to find himself or herself on it? For the observing subject cannot be separated there from the observed object; in scarcely any other example is self-reference so inextricably woven into the image. This virtual superimposition of global and individual existence has shifted the cognitive and moral co-ordinates of our perception of ourselves. The consequences of an action, it suggests, may extend to the edges of the earth – and everyone is responsible for them. All of a sudden, car drivers and meat buyers are linked to the greenhouse effect, and even a hairspray or an air ticket is seen as having overstepped the global boundaries. 'Think globally, act locally': this electoral slogan of the ecological movement has played its part in creating a 'global citizen' who internalizes the earth's limits within his or her own thinking and action. The narrative of limitation derives its moral force from this association of planet and subject in a common drama. The ecological experience is thus undoubtedly one dimension of the experience of globalization, because it overturns people's conventional notion that they live and act in national, political and social spaces that are clearly demarcated and separated from one another (Beck, 1997: 44).

Yet the ecological movement cannot escape the fact that, however provisionally, the imperial message has won through. One sign of this is the way in which multinational corporations have almost completely seized for themselves the image of the blue planet. The perception of the world as a homogeneous space, visible and accessible all the way across, has everywhere become hegemonic. This vision is imperial, because it claims the right to roam the world unhindered and to grab whatever it fancies – exactly as if there were no places, no communities, no nations. The mechanisms of GATT, NAFTA and the WTO were born in the spirit of frontier demolition. They codify the world as a freely accessible economic arena, in which economics enjoys the right of way. The newly established rules are designed to proclaim transnational corporations as sovereign subjects within global space, exempt from any obligation to regions or national governments. State protectionism is thereby abolished, only to be replaced by a new protectionism that favours corporations. Transnational partnerships are entitled to claim all sorts of freedoms and rights, while territorial states – not to mention citizens or civic associations – have to take second place.

When people look back on the last century of this millennium, they will be forced to conclude that Rio de Janeiro was pretty good on rhetoric, but Marrakesh was taken in real earnest. Here the UN conference on the environment held in Rio in 1992 stands for a long series of international agreements – notably the conventions on climate and biodiversity – that were supposed to steer the world economy in less ecologically harmful directions. Marrakesh stands for the founding of the World Trade Organization after the end of the GATT Uruguay Round, and for the growing importance of the IMF as a shadow government in many countries. There the basis was laid for an economic regime in which the investment activity of transnational actors would be free of regulation anywhere on the globe. These transnational regimes – the environmental and the economic – are attempts to give a political–legal foundation to transnational economic society, but the two stand in marked contradiction to each other. The environmental regime is concerned with protection of the natural heritage, the economic regime with equal rights to exploit it; the environmental agreements are based on respect for natural limits; the economic agreements on the right to carry through economic expansion successfully. Paradoxically, moreover, they wager on different systems of responsibility and accountability. On the one hand, the environmental agreements appeal to sovereign states as responsible entities that are supposed to uphold the public good in their territory. On the other hand, the economic agreements assume sovereign, transnationally active corporations that belong to no territory and are therefore responsible to no state. Already today the world's hundred largest economies comprise 49 countries and 51 corporations (Anderson and Cavanagh, 1997: 37).

It is therefore not clear how the conflicting messages that appropriate the image of the blue planet can be reconciled with each other. Even transnational civil society has succeeded only on specific occasions in confronting corporations with their responsibility towards nature and the overwhelming majority of the world's citizens. If the holistic message stands for 'sustainability' and the imperial message for 'economic globalization', then it would seem necessary to suppose that, however great the synergies at a micro-level, the chasm between the two is continuing to widen. But that is the greatness of a symbol: it can hold together divergent truths within a single visual form.

Bibliography

Adriaanse, A. et al. (1997) *Resource Flows: the Material Basis of Industrial Economies*, Washington: World Resources Institute.

Altvater, E. and Mahnkopf, B. (1996) *Grenzen der Globalisierung*, Münster: Westflisches Dampfboot.

Anderson, S. and Cavanagh, J. (1997) 'The Rise of Global Corporate Power', *Third World Resurgence*, 1/97, pp. 37–9.

Beck, U. (1997) *Was ist Globalisierung?*, Frankfurt: Suhrkamp.

Boeing (the Boeing Company) (1998) www.boeing.com/commercial.

Brown, L. et al. (1998) *Vital Signs 1998*, Washington: Norton.

Carley, M. and Spapens, P. (1998) *Sharing the World: Sustainable Living and Global Equity in the 21st Century*, London: Earthscan.

Castells, M. (1996) *The Rise of the Network Society. The Information Age: Economy, Society and Culture*, vol. I, Oxford: Blackwell.

Cavanagh, J. (1998) *Background to the Global Financial Crisis*, Manuscript, San Francisco: International Forum on Globalization.

Daly, H. (1996) *Free Trade, Capital Mobility and Growth versus Environment and Community*, Public Lecture on 26 September 1996, The Hague: Institute of Social Studies.

Esty, D. C. and Gerardin, D. (1998) 'Environmental Protection and International Competitiveness: a Conceptual Framework', *Journal of World Trade*, 32, 3, pp. 5–46.

Flitner, M. (1998) 'Biodiversity: Of Local Commons and Global Commodities', in M.Goldman (ed.), *Privatizing Nature: Political Struggles for the Global Commons*, London: Pluto Press, pp. 144–66.

French, H. (1998) *Investing in the Future: Harnessing Private Capital Flows for Environmentally Sustainable Development*, Worldwatch Paper 139, Washington: Worldwatch Institute.

Garrod, B. (1998) 'Are Economic Globalization and Sustainable Development Compatible? Business Strategy and the Role of the Multinational Enterprise', *International Journal of Sustainable Development*, 1, pp. 43–62.

Heerings, H. and Zeldenrust, I. (1995) *Elusive Saviours. Transnational Corporations and Sustainable Development*, Utrecht: International Books.

Johnstone, N. (1997) 'Globalisation, Technology, and Environment', in OECD Proceedings, *Globalisation and Environment*, Paris: OECD, pp. 227–67.

Jones, T. and Youngman, R. (1997) 'Globalisation and Environment: Sectoral Perspectives', in OECD Proceedings, *Globalisation and Environment*, Paris: OECD, pp. 199–221.

Kessler, J. J. and Van Dorp, M. (1998) 'Structural Adjustment and the Environment: the Need for an Analytical Methodology', *Ecological Economics*, 27, pp. 267–81.

Lapp, J. M. and Bailey, B. (1998) *Against the Grain: the Genetic Transformation of Global Agriculture*, London: Earthscan.

Lash, S. and Urry, J. (1994) *Economies of Signs and Space*, London: Sage.

Mason, M. (1997) 'A Look Behind Trend Data in Industrialization: the Role of Transnational Corporations and Environmental Impacts', *Global Environmental Change*, 7, pp. 113–27.

McCormark, G. (1996) *The Emptiness of Japanese Affluence*, St. Leonards: Allen & Unwin.

Menotti, V. (1998a) *The Environmental Impacts of Economic Globalization*, San Francisco: International Forum on Globalization.

Menotti, V. (1998b) 'Globalization and the Acceleration of Forest Destruction since Rio', *The Ecologist*, 28, pp. 354–62.

OECD (1998) *Kein Wohlstand ohne offene Märkte. Vorteile der Liberalisierung von Handel und Investitionen*, Paris.

Oppel, N. V. (1999) 'Aus fünf Kilo Fisch wird ein Kilo Zuchtlachs', *Greenpeace Magazin*, 1/99, pp. 40–1.

Pastowski, A. (1997) *Decoupling Economic Development and Freight for Reducing its Negative Impacts*, Wuppertal Paper 79, Wuppertal: Wuppertal Institute for Climate, Environment and Energy.

Reed, D. (ed.) (1996) *Structural Adjustment, the Environment and Sustainable Development*, London: Earthscan.

Sassen, S. (1996) *Losing Control?* New York: Columbia University Press.

Sprenger, R. U. (1997) 'Globalisation, Employment, and Environment', in OECD Proceedings, *Globalisation and Environment*, Paris: OECD, pp. 315–66.

The Economist (1997a) *Schools Brief: One World?*, 18 October, pp. 134–5.

The Economist (1997b) *Schools Brief: Delivering the Goods*, 15 November, pp. 89–90.

Thrupp, L. A. (1995) *Bittersweet Harvests for Global Supermarkets: Challenges in Latin America's Agricultural Export Boom*, Washington: World Resources Institute.

United Nations Development Programme (UNDP) (1998) *Human Development Report 1998*, New York: Oxford University Press.

World Commission on Environment and Development, (1987) *Our Common Future*, Oxford: Oxford University Press.

Zarsky, L. (1997) 'Stuck in the Mud? Nation-States, Globalisation, and the Environment', in OECD Proceedings, *Globalisation and Environment*, Paris: OECD, pp. 27–51.

Zukunftskommission der Friedrich-Ebert-Stiftung (1998) *Wirtschaftliche Leistungsfahigkeit, sozialer Zusammenhalt, 'kologische Nachhaltigkeit, Drei Ziele – ein Weg*, Bonn: Dietz.

5
The Peaceful Settlement of Disputes between States and the Problem of Globalization

Ian Brownlie

My theme is the peaceful settlement of disputes between states, and the problem of globalization. The peaceful settlement of disputes is arguably as important as the promotion of human rights. The alternatives to peaceful settlement in practice include economic reprisals and armed conflict. Armed conflict results in harm to civilians, economic devastation, refugee flows and sometimes civil war and ethnic cleansing.

Before approaching this particular theme, some perspective needs to be established. Globalization as a concept is too protean and amorphous to be of instant utility. For example, it can refer to both a tendency and a completed process, and it can refer to processes of politics, finance, development economics, public order and so forth. It is now offered in some quarters as a proper subject of study. Thus a respectable European university has established an Institute of Globalization, International Economic Law and Dispute Settlement. None of this matters too much, as long as normal forms of historical and legal analysis are not jettisoned in favour of fashionable verbiage like governance or globalization, and used as banners to attract the unwary. In all this it is necessary to avoid the anachronism that tendencies towards globalization are of recent formation. The people of British East Africa who in the late nineteenth century were required to pay hut tax and poll tax in order to force them into a money-based economy and thus to make them enter the labour market, must indeed have been impressed by the local effects of globalization in their time. With this mild plea for a historical perspective, I move to consider international public order.

What are the key elements of globalization within this perspective? The first key element is the existence since 1945 of a global security system based upon the United Nations Charter and in particular chapter 7 of the Charter which is the enforcement chapter dealing with threats to peace. This system can be very efficacious but is contingent upon the solidarity or otherwise of the permanent members of the Security Council. The results are variable. Some violators of Security Council resolutions face the disproportionate use of force, while others do not even face economic sanctions. There are other flaws in the system. Regional collective defence organizations may engage in operations which in practice are not adequately constrained by the Security Council and which have more in common with hegemonial intervention than the maintenance of international peace and security. The important special department of international public order is, of course, arms control and the non-proliferation of weapons of mass destruction. This programme is clearly in the public interest but in practice has taken the form of a programme more designed to produce a policy of selective proliferation than that of non-proliferation. So much for the global security system.

The second key element of public order is the promotion and enforcement of universal standards of human rights and of the humanitarian law of armed conflict. By a sort of paradox, the more successful legal structures concerned with the maintenance of human rights standards are those based not upon universal bodies but upon regional organizations such as the Council of Europe and the OSCE. What are the connections between the standards of human rights and the peaceful settlement of disputes between states? This is a very complex subject and a few points may be made in passing. It is sometimes asserted that the main, or even exclusive, cause of disputes between states is the violation of human rights within states. In my submission there is very little evidence to support that proposition. The nature of inter-state disputes, and especially classical territorial disputes, is unconnected with regimes and survives the process of decolonization and other radical internal political change. For example, the various disputes between Pakistan and India in the post-independence era have been resolved without either the provenance of the dispute or the mode of its resolution depending upon the character of the political systems in the sub-continent. There is, however, at least one sphere in which human rights and inter-state disputes overlap, and that concerns the difficult legal and moral question of whether the principle of self-determination of peoples enshrined in Article 1 of the UN Charter can justify a right of secession in the case of minorities which have a discrete territorial base. Academic opinion tends to be divided and the practice of states inconsistent. Kurds appear to have a right of self-determination within Iraq but not apparently within Turkey. Similarly, Croats and other ethnic groups within Yugoslavia have a right of self-determination according to some opinions but not the Chechens or other nationalities within Russia.

The other key elements of globalization in the context of international public order can be reviewed more succinctly. The third element is the determinist principle that the means of protecting the environment are *ex hypothesi* global given that the environment is evidently global. Uncontroversial as this may sound there are difficult problems to be faced when the question is raised: who is to pay for environmental programmes? The Brundtland Commission and the World Bank among others have made proposals involving institutional financial commitments in respect of the protection of the environment under the title the Global Environmental Trust Fund. There is a certain overlap between the programme of objectives for the protection of the environment (and the prevention of threats to the environment) and the settlement of disputes between states. Damage caused to the environment of another state including its territory, air space and shared water resources such as boundary rivers may give rise to classical disputes governed by international law. Such disputes may, and sometimes do, end up in front of courts of arbitration or the International Court of Justice. In practice, however, the compensation-based adversarial approach is simply not an appropriate way of dealing with environmental threats. Such an approach is *ex post facto* when the best approach is anticipatory and preventive.

Cumulative sources of harm to the atmosphere are difficult to relate to the normal system of state responsibility in public international law. Moreover, in practice, states are reluctant to present claims which may create unpleasant precedents and may not lead to receipt of substantial compensation. Thus the Chernobyl disaster affected a surprising number of European states but none presented a claim against the former Soviet Union.

The fourth key element in globalisation for present purposes is the effectiveness of the electronic information system, the use of transistor radios and satellites, and the resulting scope for global propaganda. Such global propaganda has played a major role in several recent crises and frequently succeeds in presenting the consequences of a problem as the cause itself. Thus there is reason to believe that the cause of suffering in the Sudan is not famine but the civil war, exacerbated by outside interference, and the resulting displacement of many refugees.

The fifth key element in the system of international public order is the element of effective global surveillance based upon military satellites, local use of radar systems and night sensors. Such technology can of course be used to enhance security and to service peace-keeping operations. It can be used to monitor threats to the peace and regimes of arms control. Once in place, and its existence publicized, it can produce both benefits and on occasion embarrassment. Thus, when in 1976 South African forces invaded Angola, the media reported that it was impossible to identify the origins of the invasion. This was not easy to believe. In the same context, during the conflict between the Sandinista government in Nicaragua and US-backed Contra rebels, the US alleged that Nicaragua was providing military assistance to left-wing rebels in El Salvador. Such assistance would have been monitored by the extensive surveillance systems available to the US. No evidence of such movements across the Gulf of Fonseca was ever produced.

The sixth element of public order is the worldwide mobility of weapons systems. This element, of course, is not particularly new and it is not in all respects global. If the potential of such weapon systems and the logistical accompaniments are placed at the disposal of the organs of the United Nations then the technology obviously serves global purposes. It can also serve effective unilateral action unsanctioned either by the Security Council or by regional collective self-defence organizations.

Two other factors remain. The first of these presents a paradox. International linguistic understanding is not the necessary consequence of the global electronic information system. Linguistic problems obviously remain. They sometimes affect the effective functioning of multinational bodies. Simultaneous translation is usually available and most inter-governmental bodies have the necessary facilities and funding. However, severe problems may affect bodies which are multinational and which must handle substantial quantities of documentary evidence. Such decision-making bodies include courts of arbitration and the International Court of Justice. Courts of arbitration usually have adequate funding and fairly limited linguistic problems, but this is not true of the International Court. This consists of fifteen judges of different nationalities, all of whom take a role as individuals in the process of deliberation. If adequate translation facilities are not available the court cannot operate as quickly as it should, given the nature of its functions. Unfortunately, budgetary constraints imposed (in effect) by the US Congress, have created serious problems for the Court by limiting its resources and reducing the capacity for expeditious translation of documents. Not much globalism is in evidence in this neck of the woods.

So, finally we reach the global system providing for the settlement of international disputes. At the outset, it is necessary to offer some definition of the concept of a dispute. Neither lawyers nor international relations experts have produced a useful typology. The international lawyers tend to segregate legal disputes and move on from there and are quite content simply to do that. For present purposes it will suffice if the sheer variety of types of dispute is recalled. The classical type of dispute concerns territorial sovereignty, that is to say, title to territory. Such disputes have a discrete subject matter and are fairly often submitted to the International Court or to ad hoc courts of arbitration. Similar in character are boundary disputes, including maritime delimitation, for example, the partition of areas of continental shelf or fishing zones.

A second type of dispute involves the determination of legal responsibility for some types of damage. In the *Corfu Channel Case* in 1949, before the International Court, the issue was the responsibility of Albania for damage to two British warships and the loss of life caused by mines laid in the territorial waters of Albania, for which Albania was eventually held to be responsible. In the *Phosphate Lands in Nauru* case in 1992, the issue was whether or not Australia, as the co-administrator of a UN trusteeship, was responsible for the rehabilitation of worked-out phosphate lands on the Pacific island state of Nauru, the homeland of 8000 Nauruans. Disputes falling within these two categories have a distinct subject matter and are readily identified as having a primarily legal character.

Another category of dispute is the frozen dispute which is, quite often, the long, unsettled issue lying behind other questions. The Taiwan question is often seen as a question of political status and self-determination. In fact the origin of the question was the intervention of the US in China's civil war long ago in order to prevent communist forces occupying Taiwan. The legitimate government of China (that is big China, the Peking government), always regarded this as an illegal intervention in China's internal affairs. Some difficult disputes are ramifications of situations which themselves cannot easily be classified as disputes at all. The disintegration of Yugoslavia which began in 1991 involved a complex situation containing elements of spontaneous political action, foreign covert action and a three-way civil war in Bosnia. This situation has produced a series of special issues and disputes which do have legal dimensions and are quantifiable, that is to say, issues of state succession as between Yugoslavia and the former units, such as Croatia; disputes about boundaries between the former federal units; and disputes concerning the responsibility for acts of genocide. The issue of genocide resulted in an ongoing case brought by Bosnia against Yugoslavia in the International Court and also a counter-claim by Yugoslavia.

Another major category of disputes can be classified as disputes involving the legal status of one or more of the parties. The Taiwan case also falls within this category. Other examples include the status of the Palestinians as a unit of self-determination, the creation of puppet states by aggressors, and the problems of deciding on the legitimacy of governments produced as a consequence of foreign intervention. Such disputes relating to status are as much political as legal and are inherently difficult to settle. Ordinary legal resolution is impossible precisely because each party does not accept the status or the equality of status of the other.

The last category worth mentioning derives from hegemonial issues involving competition between political groupings of states by way of surrogates. One form of analysis of the political warfare directed against Nicaragua by the US after the overthrow of the Somoza government was to the effect that the US saw the Sandinistas as a source of Soviet and, therefore, Cuban intervention. Such forms of political warfare may give rise to recognizable legal disputes. Foreign vessels in Nicaraguan waters were damaged by mines laid by agents of the US. As a result five European states protested to Washington. Nicaragua itself brought successful proceedings against the US in the International Court of Justice in 1984.

It is sometimes said with some justification that international lawyers do not take enough interest in the solution of political disputes. The fact remains that certain types of dispute are more appropriate for legal resolution than others. Both lawyers and non-lawyers thus rely upon a distinction between legal and political disputes. Formulating this distinction is fairly difficult. The object is to identify issues which can be characterized sufficiently in legal terms, and can therefore be submitted to a procedure of legal settlement involving arbitration or the International Court. It is at least clear that, whilst certain issues are exclusively political, the same question may be both partly legal and partly political. The claim that a certain area of the high seas should be demilitarized as a zone of peace is a purely political proposal. The problems of Central America were a mixture of hegemonial or political issues and of discrete legal issues concerning the legality of mining the waters of a state with which the US was not at war, and with which it still maintained diplomatic relations. After this effort of examining the characterization of disputes it may be helpful to offer the standard definition of a legal dispute. It is very simple: the disagreement on a point of law or fact, the conflict of legal views, or of interests between two states.

The next task is to provide some indication of the concept of peaceful settlement of a dispute. No doubt the basic polarity is obvious enough. A peaceful settlement involves recourse to negotiation, third-party conciliation or mediation, arbitration or judicial settlement. Non-peaceful settlement involves invasion, forceful occupation, or aerial or naval bombardment or threat of any of these to achieve a particular demand or political aim. Iraq's attempt to annex Kuwait is a good example. Once this simple polarity is left behind a grey area is to be seen. There are various episodes of peaceful settlement in recent history in which coercion has played a role. Peace settlements commonly rely on implicit institutional coercion as the political lever. The Japanese peace treaty and the Geneva agreements concerning Indochina of 1954 provide two examples of many. The Dayton agreements of 1995 were the consequence, I am told, of 3500 aerial sorties against targets in the Serbian-held areas of Bosnia. The degree of free negotiation at Dayton was problematical to say the least.

In such situations, some form of legitimacy may be conferred, usually by one of two methods. In the first place the international community may provide multilateral approval of the outcome of the coercion, either by means of a Security Council resolution, or by multiple acts of individual recognition or acquiescence in the result on the part of states. The hostage crisis of 1979 involving Iran and the US resulted in an agreement brokered with the assistance of Algeria, which dealt with the freeing of the US diplomats and arrangements concerning $7.8 billion worth of US property claims. No doubt, on the release of the hostages, the US could have repudiated the agreement on the grounds of coercion. However, because the arrangements for the settlement of disputes for the future were deemed to be satisfactory, the US chose to waive the illegality.

Having considered the more flawed and eccentric forms of dispute settlement it is now time to examine the main aspects of the system of peaceful settlement available to states generally. The system in its essentials has not changed since 1921. Its characteristics are as follows. First, the system is focused on the peaceful settlement of legal disputes between states. Individuals and other non-state actors do not normally have access to the system. Secondly, the system depends upon the consent of states. Thirdly, there is a duty, according to the Charter of the United Nations, to settle disputes peacefully, but there is no duty to settle disputes. Indeed the United Nations Charter in its relevant chapter, chapter 6, has only very weak provisions on dispute settlement, going no further than giving permissive powers to the Security Council to recommend recourse by the parties to a dispute to the International Court of Justice or other forms of pacific settlement.

The system of dispute settlement consists of a spectrum of different methods. There are five methods in all and these do not involve either arbitration or adjudication. They are negotiation, mediation, conciliation, and the use of the political organs of the United Nations. There is also a rarely used mechanism known as commissions of enquiry which simply investigate the points of fact which lie behind disputes. The irony is that negotiation, mediation, conciliation and so forth, have been the standard forms of dispute settlement in international law for a very long time. Nowadays, they are terribly fashionable. We suddenly discover that they are in fact 'alternative dispute settlement' and so exactly what in International Law was the norm (with adjudication being the more radical development) is regarded in terms of municipal law as the reverse, with adjudication the norm, and alternative dispute settlement as something which is seen as a recent development.

In fact, the methods which do not involve arbitration or adjudication are of the first importance, because negotiation, which of course is hardly an original method of dispute settlement, has the magnificent quality of flexibility. Courts and courts of arbitration are good at, as it were, property disputes. They are good at saying that the item in issue belongs to state A or state B. They are good at attributing responsibility for harm. They are no good at dealing with complex situations on frontiers, involving conflict between states, where what is needed is structuring, and an outcome other than the rather simplistic methods which courts use to attribute responsibility or to attribute rights to territory or property. One of the more subtle methods of settlement which does involve third-party settlement by negotiation is the method of mediation. This is one of a series of methods of third-party dispute settlement including conciliation. Mediation is fairly unusual. There have been some very spectacular exercises in mediation which do not usually find their way into the law books. Such a mediation was the one between Chile and Argentina in 1979 which, in fact, lasted five years. In December 1979 there was a very severe crisis in the relations between Chile and Argentina. The US government had knowledge of the intention of the Argentine navy to invade some disputed islands on the southern tip of Chile. It takes some time for the navy vessels to go from the Plate estuary southwards, and this delay was used by the US government to involve the Vatican in a mediation process. The Vatican ordered Cardinal Samore to go to Buenos Aires. He apparently sat at a table opposite the military men and spoke, very frankly, and induced them to sign a small piece of paper. He then flew over the Andes, faced the military men in Santiago, got them to sign a counterpart piece of paper, and these two letters were the constitutional basis for the papal mediation, which did in fact result in a very complex treaty of peace and friendship in 1985. This has been described by people on the inside as one of the most successful exercises in peaceful settlement since 1945.

So we have an orchestra, a spectrum of varied methods of settlement. Is it possible to call this spectrum of methods of settlement a system? Probably not. The picture is simply one of a series of options. There is, in particular, no hierarchy. There is, generally speaking, no appeal from decisions of courts of arbitration or decisions of the International Court of Justice. The reasons for this peremptory element in international justice are somewhat obscure. The emphasis on the settlement of disputes as a substitute for forcible self-help may provide some explanation. After all, if a definitive resolution of a dispute is postponed, threats to the peace may recur. The principal characteristic of the system is that it depends upon the agreement of states. The exercise of jurisdiction by international tribunals is always based on the prior consent to such jurisdiction by the parties to the dispute. This is true of the institution of arbitration, the International Court of Justice, and the World Bank system of dispute settlement. With few exceptions the system depends on agreement and good faith and not upon *ab extra* enforcement by third parties or the Security Council. Such a system causes disquiet among legal theorists in universities, but I am afraid it is the way things are done in the world outside. In this context the universal system of voluntary arbitration provides a long established and clearly global institution. The paradigm is commercial arbitration, but arbitration took place between the Greek city states and in the nineteenth century there were several major state arbitrations.

Arbitration was made fashionable by three major arbitrations of the nineteenth century. The most striking of these was the *Alabama Claims Arbitration*. In 1862, during the American Civil War, the attention of the British government was drawn by the government of the US to the fact that a vessel for warlike purposes was being built in England to the order of the insurgents. This vessel, afterwards called the *Alabama*, left Liverpool in July 1862 unarmed but was met at the Azores by three other vessels also coming from England which supplied guns and ammunition so that she could at once begin to prey upon the merchantmen of the north. On the conclusion of the Civil War, the US claimed damages from Great Britain for the enormous losses sustained through the operations of the *Alabama* and other raiding vessels. Negotiations went on for several years, and finally in 1871 the parties entered into the Treaty of Washington for the purpose of having their difference settled by arbitration. Great Britain, the US, Brazil, Italy and Switzerland each chose one arbitrator. The arbitrators met at Geneva in 1871 and held 32 meetings, giving their award on 14 September 1872, and, in accordance with the award, Great Britain paid $15.5 million in damages to the US.

A more recent major arbitration involved a territorial dispute over islands in the Red Sea between Eritrea and Yemen. The background was an armed conflict, luckily not of great intensity, in November 1995. There was very constructive mediation, by the US and French governments. The outcome in October 1996 was an arbitration agreement. The arbitration agreement mandated the tribunal to provide rulings in accordance with international law in two stages. The first stage was to deal with the attribution of title to the islands themselves, and the second stage was to deal with the subsequent issues of maritime delimitation once the question of title to the islands had been settled. The award in the first stage was given in 1998. The major islands went to Yemen and it has to be said that the government of Eritrea implemented the award without delay. An award determining issues of maritime delimitation was rendered in 1999.

Not all arbitrations have a successful outcome. In the relations between Chile and Argentina which were eventually the subject of papal mediation to which reference has already been made, the first effort to settle the dispute about the islands in the south was the result of a special agreement negotiated with the assistance of the British government in July 1971. This is the famous *Beagle Channel Arbitration*. A distinguished court of arbitration (which included several judges of the International Court) gave an award in 1977. This involved three islands, and it is an awkward fact of life that islands are very difficult to divide up. In mountain areas, everybody gets something. These three islands were awarded to Chile. There was a change of government in Argentina and the result was that Argentina reneged on the award. In a situation like that, if one of the parties reneges, it is difficult to do anything effective to deal with the situation. There was a great deal of subsequent diplomacy and, after a further crisis in 1979, there was the exercise in third-party mediation.

The most radical, and perhaps the most global, of institutions of peaceful settlement is the International Court of Justice. This was first created in 1921. It is a standing international court. It was recreated in 1945 and it remains today a very radical institution. The more conservative governments in the world, whether of the left or the right, tend to regard it with caution. It is not concerned with criminal responsibility, it deals with ordinary disputes between states. It has three principal bases of jurisdiction: special clauses in standard-setting treaties like the Chicago Convention dealing with civil aviation; special agreements rather like arbitration agreements by which two states decide to take the particular dispute to the International Court, where the Court is being used almost in the same way as one uses a court of arbitration to settle a particular dispute; and lastly, there is a system which is called the compulsory jurisdiction, which is compulsory in the sense that once states have made declarations accepting the jurisdiction of the court, they are bound by the consent they have given for the future. Sixty-one states at the moment have accepted this type of jurisdiction. The court has a secondary role, which is the giving of advisory opinions on legal matters in response to requests from political organs of the UN and the specialized agencies.

The general performance of the court is good. Its purpose is to settle disputes and since 1945 it has handled 73 cases. Of course, compared with the doings of the European Court of Justice, that is a terribly small score, but I think it is necessary to look at the stakes involved. Is the Court able to prevent wars? Well, yes and no. No, because of course the activities of a single institution are unlikely to stave off something as complex as the Second World War. But, yes, in certain respects. It removes difficult questions between states and one of the characteristics of state behaviour is that even well-run states find it difficult to negotiate about territory.

The in-house lawyers and diplomats do not want to go down in the historical record as the ones 'who gave the islands away'. The alternative, then, is either a war, which may not be decisive, or third-party settlement. The best form of definitive third-party settlement is to be obtained from the International Court of Justice. So it does remove some very thorny disputes from the agenda which could well produce wars. Its last role is that of law-making. That is important but it is certainly not its primary purpose.

So, how global is the system of peaceful settlement in practice? It is certainly global in terms of accessibility, and availability. It is more or less global in other terms but there are cultural exceptions. Communist states have always combined nationalism with strong isolationist tendencies, and they tend to be very loath to use third-party settlement. This was true of the Soviet Union and it is true of present-day China. Such states tend to make exceptions in the case of commercial arbitration, but in respect of inter-state arbitration or resort to the

International Court, they are very conservative. The US is a mixed case. It does use peaceful settlement machinery, it has a respectable history in that respect, but in the more modern period in the light of the Nicaragua case it has become more cautious and reluctant. It has ceased to be a party to the compulsory jurisdiction of the International Court.

Generally speaking, resort to the International Court and arbitration is universal. With whatever exceptions there may be, the states resorting to the International Court in the last twenty years have come from every region in the world. There is no pattern. The only general feature is the absence of pattern. Disputes are not resolved in ways that conform with standard assumptions about the behaviour of states and the rule of law in international affairs. Since 1945 only a few states have refused to implement decisions of the International Court. The few states have included Albania and the US. Libya, a state often characterized as a pariah state has, in fact, been in front of the International Court in eight cases. These included a case concerning a major territorial dispute with Chad, the so-called Aouzou strip, although in fact the area in issue was much bigger. Following the decision (which was wholly unfavourable to the Libyan claims), Libya, under supervision, withdrew its administration from the disputed area. The media did not think that was at all interesting and it was not reported. That is one of the difficulties of being an international lawyer.

6
The Security of International Finance[1]

Valpy FitzGerald

> (The inter-war experience suggests that without controls on capital movements)... 'loose funds may sweep round the world disorganizing all steady business' (John Maynard Keynes 'The Post-War Currency Policy', *The Collected Writing of John Maynard Keynes*, Vol XXV)

Introduction

Half a century after Keynes' dictum, the security of international finance has clearly become a cause for acute concern far beyond Wall Street and Canary Wharf.[2] 'Steady business' – and thus the livelihoods of almost all the world's population ranging from British pensioners to Indian peasants – is apparently threatened by the volatility of paper assets, the very existence of which they are unaware. Daily news headlines tell us of yet another financial crisis in some far-flung corner of the globe; while world leaders gathered in Davos or Hong Kong seem to regard currency instability as the critical threat to western civilization at the close of the twentieth century – in sharp contrast to the threat of socialist revolution with which it opened. A significant and even symbolic characteristic of current global financial insecurity is the uneasy combination of the speed and sophistication of computerized trading systems with the faltering economies of 'emerging markets'. Sudden exchange rate collapses lead not only to steep income declines for millions of poor people but also to major bank and stock market losses in advanced industrial countries. For the first time, economic events in the developing world are affecting the financial security of developed countries.[3] The G7 has mobilized some US$300 billion as lender of last resort to major economies such as Mexico, Korea, Indonesia,

Russia and Brazil because of the threat to the international market system.[4]

This concern reflects in turn the fact that although 28 advanced industrial countries still dominate the international financial and trading system, 48 per cent of global production and 55 per cent of world investment now takes place *outside* this group of rich countries.[5] Discussions on 'global financial architecture' thus necessarily involve the two-fifths of the world population living in countries who until recently were seen only as clients for development assistance. The debate on the security of the international financial system thus extends beyond technical economic issues to encounter problems derived from the problematic nature of globalization itself.

Here, I shall try to explain the origins of inherent instability in international capital flows, and why this requires public institutions to maintain an orderly market. I shall then argue that despite widespread recognition of this problem, the necessary institutions do not exist due to the mismatch between intergovernmental power and the requirements of a global market. Lastly, I shall sketch some of the implications of this dilemma for belief in the efficiency of markets, the establishment of international property rights, and ultimately for global citizenship itself.

The inherent instability of international financial markets: sources of systemic volatility

Global capital markets are characterized by asymmetric and incomplete information derived from the fact that all financial assets are promises to pay in an uncertain future. The increasing international exposure of bank balance sheets and equity funds in industrial countries to the financial systems in emerging market economies has not been accompanied by a corresponding depth of information about the true value of the assets and liabilities. The speed and scale of shock transmission between markets has increased enormously due to technological advances in trading and settlement, which forces traders to act without knowledge of wider price movements, exacerbating random fluctuations into serious instability. There are also substantial agency problems for bank lenders and portfolio investors. Unlike multinational corporations involved in direct foreign investment, they can exercise little direct control over the asset acquired and thus cannot protect its market value. To the extent that banks and funds cannot count upon their own governments or the international financial institutions to ensure payment of their loans or maintenance of asset value, their logical response is to avoid assets which cannot be rapidly sold if things go wrong. These information and agency problems explain the two main characteristics of so-called 'portfolio' investment in emerging markets. First, international portfolio investors and bank lenders seek liquidity and use rapid exit as a means of containing downside risk by buying quoted securities or rolling over short loans. In consequence, indicators such as the 'quick ratio' of a country's short-term foreign liabilities to central bank reserves become critical to market stability, and can easily trigger self-fulfilling runs on a currency. Second, fund managers control risk not by seeking more information or control, but by portfolio diversification based on an assumed lack of co-variance between emerging market indices. The competition between funds for clients[6] drives them towards high-yield, high-risk assets; and by the same token obliges them to make frequent marginal adjustments to their portfolios in response not only to changes within these emerging markets but also in anticipation of what all other fund managers are likely to do next.[7]

The effect of these behavioural characteristics is exacerbated by the way in which financial markets clear. It is now well established in theory and practice that financial markets are in permanent disequilibrium in the sense that demand for funds always exceeds supply at the equilibrium interest rate.[8] In consequence, asset prices and interest prices do not fully reflect risk: lenders use portfolio allocation rules – and thus rationing – to reduce uncertainty. Domestic banks and securities firms are closely regulated to make sure they do this prudently and always have sufficient collateral and adequate reserves. In this way an 'orderly market' is established.

In contrast, international investment flows – which often enjoy neither legal collateral nor prudential regulation – react sharply to changing perceptions of country solvency rather than to variations in underlying asset value. Even if information on the return (or risk) on a particular asset can be acquired at a cost, the value of this knowledge declines as the opportunities for diversification increase, so investors have no incentive to search for information. Herding behaviour becomes endemic as the observed asset prices, exchange rates and reserve levels send the same signal to all participants but they all attempt to anticipate the same trend in order to make a capital gain.

Emerging market assets form a relatively small part of savers' portfolios in developed countries, but a large part of firms' and banks' liabilities in developing countries. Because of this asymmetry between borrowers and lenders, marginal shifts in lenders' positions tend to destabilize borrowers.[9] These surges are then worsened by herding behaviour because as opportunities for diversification increase the impact of news on the allocation of funds in a single country relative to initial allocations grows without bounds, resulting in massive flows, further threatening financial stability.[10]

Why the security of international finance matters

The international financial system is vulnerable to emerging market volatility; rather like banking in the US and the UK in the nineteenth century, when huge fluctuations in the real economy were associated with banking booms and busts.[11] There is often a high degree of leverage in short-term flows; banks making loans to hedge funds and similar intermediaries based in largely unregulated offshore international banking markets. In other cases they are on-selling risky securities to their clients, or extending short-term loans which are renewed every six months. Banks and other financial intermediaries have financial assets far larger than their own capital, so that the loss of only a small part of their loans threatens their survival. This is why they are restricted in the loans they can make by regulators. In consequence, when such losses do occur, they must sell other assets in order to recover the liquidity necessary to maintain their own capital. This exacerbates market fluctuations, leading to collapses more rapid and more deep than the preceding boom, for two reasons.

The first is a process known as 'rolling margin calls' where other assets (many of which are not owned, but rather obligations or options to buy or sell at some future date) have to be quickly sold, depressing their price and forcing other investors to sell further assets and so on. Thus the selling wave moves through the market far more rapidly than the original buying surge. When this results in a reduction of credit to firms in the 'real' economy, firms which have relied on the renewal of bank credit to finance operations are forced into bankruptcy.

The second reason is the effect that losses have upon the reputation of banks and funds, in a process known as 'contagion'. In the absence of reliable information as to the value of the assets held by a particular bank or fund, depositors withdraw their funds rapidly from this and related institutions – thus bringing about the very situation they fear and panic spreads – affecting firms in the same sector or country indiscriminately independently of their solvency. It is this situation which usually obliges central banks to intervene by supplying sufficient liquidity for banks to meet their short-term obligations without becoming bankrupt.

Financial markets are thus inherently unstable, which is why at a domestic level they are so closely regulated. At the international level, it is precisely at the interstices between regulatory authorities that the largest short-term profits are to be made and the greatest risks of systemic collapse are to be found.[12] Emerging markets are particularly vulnerable[13] to this instability, not only because they have weak and inexperienced financial regulators. Developing countries have shallow and narrow capital markets, where relatively small flows of foreign capital can have a large effect on prices, particularly those of government bonds and privatization issues which tend to make up the bulk of traded securities. Their firms tend to be highly geared and dependent on borrowed funds, so that credit restrictions have a disproportionate effect upon production. Their populations in turn are vulnerable because much of their population lives near the poverty line, unprotected by modern welfare systems; so that macroeconomic fluctuations – particularly large deteriorations in the exchange rate – can have serious social consequences.

Despite this vulnerability, rapid financial liberalization has been pressed by both international agencies and local modernizing elites in emerging market countries. As a result, large international liabilities have been built up by the private firms and households to finance both investment and consumption. The currency risk was perceived as low by foreign lenders due to the strong growth record and nominal exchange rate stability underpinned by the same capital inflows.

The volatility of short-term capital flows (or 'capital surges') is now recognized as a major problem for macroeconomic management in developing countries, which subsequently translates into investment, growth, employment and welfare.[14] Government expenditure cannot be efficiently allocated to the satisfaction of social priorities when both the borrowing ability and the cost of funds varies so sharply.[15] The impact of short flows on output and investment by firms through the availability of bank credit is also large, reducing private investment. Employment levels and real wage rates are affected by the influence of capital surges on real exchange rates and domestic demand levels.

Missing institutions

In response to these problems, special institutional arrangements have emerged historically in industrial countries as part of the process of constructing orderly financial markets. It would seem logical, therefore, to expect that an orderly global capital market would require similar institutions at an intergovernmental level.

These would be four:[16]

1. The core central banking functions of providing liquidity to the market, including last-resort lending under distress conditions in order to support otherwise sound banks and prevent contagion; this is the putative function of the IMF – although at present it has insufficient funds and is only empowered to lend to governments (or their central banks) and cannot deal directly with global or local private banks.

2. The prudential regulation of financial intermediaries, in order to prevent not only fraud but also unsafe lending with wider consequences; to some extent this service is provided by the Bank for International Settlements, but it leaves the greater part of global financial intermediaries still unregulated.

3. The existence of private financial institutions ('market makers') who stand ready to buy and sell assets at the current price – creating 'depth' and thus stability in the market – and to take over insolvent financial intermediaries when necessary; such co-operation is notable by its absence – particularly in international rescue operations.

4. Possibly most significantly, a sound and transparent legal system that secures contracts and provides for efficient dispute settlement between contracting parties and between financial intermediaries and the regulators; such a 'multilateral framework for investment' which could stabilize expectations and thus asset values, does not yet exist.

The political economy of global financial reform

The effectiveness of international financial institutions

The existing international institutional 'architecture' to cope with these problems in emerging markets is based on the agencies founded at Bretton Woods in 1944, the International Monetary Fund in particular. As intergovernmental institutions, the IFIs are essentially lenders of last resort, against which facility they can impose policy conditionality designed to restore long-term solvency in return for the provision of liquidity. Whatever the effectiveness of this approach in the sovereign debt crises of the 1980s, or to the chronic economic problems of the least developed countries, it is not appropriate for the emerging market crises of the 1990s. The recent Latin American and East Asian crises are essentially related to private sector asset deflation and illiquidity, not state failure.

The root causes of the breakdown were not prevented (and possibly have been exacerbated) by Bretton Woods policies of accelerated financial liberalization, exchange rate anchoring and encouragement of private portfolio investment as a substitute for sovereign borrowing.[17] The IFIs appear to have taken the pre-crisis position that because the external deficits reflect private investment-savings gaps rather than fiscal deficits, they must reflect rational market decisions and thus be respected. However, even had they wished to prevent such inflows, their ex-ante influence over lenders is limited to issuing negative macroeconomic evaluations with the consequent danger of market collapse.[18]

Ex-post, their insistence on large devaluations, high interest rates, credit restrictions and fiscal retrenchment have tended to further undermine both corporations and banks, worsening the crises they attempt to resolve. The failure of recent IMF interventions in East Asia and Mexico essentially derive from the failure to recognize and correct private debt problems. In the commercial world, of course, insolvent companies are placed under new management and the unserviceable debt is written off by the creditors. There is, however, no equivalent in international debt crises.[19]

Of course, global surveillance is not only carried out by the IFIs. In principle, if the issue were one of information as such, the ratings agency should be able to invest in better information on country risk than any one investor and then provide what is effectively a public good for a modest fee. However, the failure of the leading private ratings agencies to predict collapse in Mexico and East Asia is notorious. The way in which information is used by ratings agencies seems to be deficient – an issue of economic interpretation rather than economic statistics.[20] There are various reasons for this, including the methodology used to construct ratings (which is largely backward- rather than forward-looking) and the natural desire not to destabilize already fragile markets.[21]

One of the key reasons for the volatility of capital flows is doubts about the solvency of particular developing countries. The existence of a large international public debt overhang represents a major constraint on further long-term foreign investment on any significant scale – due to the uncertainty caused by the prospect of severe stabilization measures in order to meet debt service, or the sovereign risk inherent in debt default. This debt overhang is also a major disincentive to private domestic investors, for the same reason.

In effect, the process of financial intervention in developing countries by the Bretton Woods institutions has led to the transfer of sovereign debt from commercial creditors to the IFIs themselves. Once so refinanced, it has become almost impossible to write off. The main reason given for not cancelling this debt is one of 'moral hazard'[22] – the belief that if developing country sovereign debt is cancelled, then their governments – freed from the external constraint – will return to 'irresponsible' policies. Unfortunately, the current HIPC initiative[23] is both insufficient in scale and too lengthy in process to make a substantive contribution to the reduction of investor uncertainty.

Global financial architecture

The recurrent financial crises since Mexico in 1995 have naturally tested policy-makers' enthusiasm for deregulation; but no lasting lessons were drawn from Mexico: it was only the East Asian collapse of 1997 followed by the Russian and Brazilian collapses of 1998 that forced discussion of institutional reform. All four required the US Treasury to engage in large support operations[24] through the IMF with somewhat reluctant assistance from Europe and Japan and without the consent of Congress. Indeed, Republican legislators remain unconvinced of the need to strengthen the capacity of the IMF to intervene in such crises, believing that losses should be fully borne by investors. It can be argued that it was only the collapse of Long Term Capital Management and its bail-out by the Federal Reserve Bank of New York in order to prevent systemic collapse of Wall Street, that finally made the case for reform.[25]

It is generally agreed that reform is needed but there is little evidence of tangible progress. One problem is the lack of a clear idea as to what to do; but more crucial is the unwillingness of major states to act together. Even a minimal measure such as restoring the previous reserve requirements on international bank lending and doing so effectively would require concerted G10 action and vigilance of offshore operations. However, the US financial services industry has sufficient lobbying strength to block even this limited measure. Indeed similar supervision is required to combat the narcotics trade and has not yet been implemented.[26]

The two proposals on the table at present are relatively timid and yet the source of considerable disagreement:

1. The 'G22 proposal' supported by Washington, is for the ad hoc grouping of leading industrial and emerging market countries convened by the US Treasury for the first time in 1998 to become more formalized.

This is the only existing forum containing financial authorities from both developed and developing countries. The idea is to both strengthen financial supervision in emerging markets and maintain US control of the process. Washington believes that Europe is over-represented in the G7, the G10 and even the IMF, although abolition or restructuring of the IMF seems unlikely.

2. The UK proposal is for an international standing committee of the IMF, the World Bank, the Bank for International Settlements and key national regulators to monitor international capital markets and report on the cross-border activities of major financial institutions. Supervisory authority would remain with national regulators, but the standing committee would ensure exchange of information; their work would be based on the Basle Committee's 'Core Principles for Effective Banking Supervision', and the IMF's 'Framework for Financial Stability' which is derived from it.[27]

Nonetheless, regulators in industrial countries are responding to the increasing consolidation of the financial services sector itself. In the US, cross-sectoral mergers are accelerating in anticipation of the repeal of legislation which prohibits linkages between banks and securities houses and insurance companies.[28] Transborder banking consolidation in Europe is being accelerated by the introduction of the Euro and thus riskless cross-border transactions. The ECB may be forced to take a more active part in bank regulation and act as lender of last resort like the Federal Reserve.

Finally, the reinstatement of capital controls are being reconsidered by a number of emerging market governments in the wake of the East Asian crisis.[29] Although administrative controls are unlikely to return, financial liberalization is likely to be much more cautious in future. Taxes and reserve requirements on short-term capital flows based on the Chilean model are likely to become more common; while greater emphasis will be placed on encouraging FDI as a more stable form of external finance.[30]

Triad co-ordination

The provision of an orderly international capital market clearly requires not only improved banking regulation but also a reasonable degree of co-ordination between the three major currencies in order to reduce uncertainty and encourage longer-term lending. Indeed this was the aim – and achievement – of the postwar Bretton Woods system, although this was based on the US dollar as a single world currency.

After the successful launch of the Euro, the dollar is no longer the only key trading and asset currency. Moreover, encouraged by this opening, the Japanese government is pressing for a currency grid system between the three currencies, supported by their respective central banks. In addition, the Hong Kong Monetary Authority has suggested that an 'Asian monetary area' be established with cross-asset holdings by central banks in the region (rather than holding reserves in dollar assets) and eventually a common currency for trading purposes. These notions are strongly opposed by Washington which fears the decline of the dollar as the leading world currency. Moreover, the Federal Reserve is tasked to maintain low inflation and steady economic expansion in the United States. It is not responsible for the parity of the dollar, and traditional policy has been one of 'benign neglect' of the exchange rate. On the one hand, international financial affairs are the concern of the US Treasury. Indeed, finance has become the principal instrument of US foreign policy since the end of the Cold War. On the other hand, Congress is wary of international monetary commitments, and has effectively prevented monetary co-ordination even with Canada and Mexico within the NAFTA – despite this being one of the contributory causes of the Mexican crisis in 1995.

The European Central Bank has an even narrower brief – to maintain low rates of inflation. Frankfurt has no responsibility for Euro parity, and there is no provision for a central treasury function in Brussels either. Although there is every expectation that the Euro will steadily strengthen against the dollar, this is not the result of a considered policy but rather due to demand for the Euro as a reserve currency and the growing US trade deficit. The Bank of Japan is subject to the Ministry of Finance, which does attempt to intervene to stabilize the yen, but its effective powers are limited by the domestic banking crisis and thus the need to keep its own banks solvent and accommodate the reflationary fiscal initiatives of the government.

These are more than conjunctural limitations. In the case of the Federal Reserve and the European Central Bank they derive from a political axiom that monetary policy should be removed from elected governments and entrusted to 'independent experts' with strictly limited responsibilities. In addition, the difficulty of co-ordinating three asynchronous economic cycles is often given as a reason why nothing further can be done; despite the successful experience of the Bretton Woods system in the 1950s and 1960s.

This stalemate can be characterized in two ways. On the one hand, it can be regarded as a classic problem of collective action, where there is a need for pooled sovereignty in order to increase the welfare of all three participants – and by extension the rest of the world.[31] Failure to agree essentially reflects misguided nationalism and a 'lack of leadership' in this explanation. On the other hand, the stalemate can be seen as a classic problem in international relations, with the declining hegemon – that is, the US driven by strategic objectives and bank lobbyists – unwilling to cede global economic dominance to rising regional powers.[32] Meanwhile, international financial crises will probably become more frequent.

Financial security, market rationality and global democracy

The rationality of markets

Global policy-makers share the orthodox doctrine that the liberalization of trade and investment will increase efficiency, raise human productivity and eventually eliminate world poverty.[33] In political terms this has been reinforced by the widespread belief that governments are inherently self-seeking and inefficient, or at best hostages to populist pressures from their electorates. In contrast, markets provide a superior and in some sense more equitable rationality upon which social organization can be based. This view of the market as an objective standard is not fully shared by business people even though they naturally prefer as few regulatory restrictions as possible,[34] but it is a doctrine which appears to be received wisdom for most senior politicians and civil servants. This has a number of corollaries. One is the tendency to entrust economic management to 'independent' and 'technical' bodies such as autonomous central banks,[35] independent of the control of the legislature or elected government. The fact that such institutions inevitably derive their autonomy as much from their coalition with leading banks (or in the case of emerging markets, multilateral agencies) as from their constitutional mandates is often overlooked. Another such corollary is the frequent argument that 'there is no alternative' (TINA) to conservative economic policies such as welfare restrictions and employment flexibility at the national level, because acceptable standards of conduct are set by international capital markets. Any other policy will be 'punished' by capital flight.[36]

In consequence, to admit that international capital markets are inherently unstable – as I have been arguing explicitly and the proposals for a new financial architecture do implicitly – is to undermine a central *political* doctrine and one, moreover, which is not confined to the realm of ideas. The shift away from occupational and state pension funds on the one hand, and away from bank deposits and fixed-rate mortgages on the other, towards greater involvement of ordinary households (and voters) in financial markets also has profound political implications. The exposure of voters' sense of well-being to financial asset values (the 'wealth effect') has obvious benefits when stock markets are booming and interest rates are low; but any reversal (despite the small print) has equivalent political costs.

In the specific context of the security of internal finance, the neoliberal trend has been reflected in the gradual move of regulatory practice away from the traditional prescriptive approach based on rules and prohibitions towards designing incentives for private financial institutions to behave in socially optimal ways. After determined lobbying from international banks, 'risk modelling' has been permitted by regulators in order to determine the capital reserve requirements of banks. As a result of the 1996 modification to the Basle Capital Accord, leading securities authorities announced in May 1998 that IOSCO members could permit the use of statistical models for regulatory purposes. However, these models have performed so poorly in the recent financial turmoil that it has become clear that the assumptions upon which these models were based were incompatible with extreme market stress.

This has revealed a fundamental problem in the dominant view of market rationality. While it is clear that asset markets are volatile by their nature, banks argued that the volatility involved could be estimated from past performance and certain 'fundamentals'. The measurable risk involved could be priced (in much the same ways as insurance premiums are calculated from actuarial tables) and compared to the yield on a safe asset (such as US Treasury Bills) in a portfolio constructed so as to offset the risk in one asset against another. However, this was to confuse risk with uncertainty and it is now clear that future outcomes were not effectively priced into asset values – which reflect subjective enthusiasms (and fears) rather than rational expectations of predictable outcomes.

The problem has been worsened by a lack of clarity as to what 'fundamentals' actually are. Once gross fiscal imbalances have been overcome and market deregulation is under way, the main indicators can become confusing signals for investors. Thus large current account deficits are seen by some as a sign of success in attracting foreign investment and by others as a sign of an overvalued currency; while growing corporate foreign debt is seen by some to reflect efficient financial diversification, and by others as dangerous exchange rate exposure by unhedged corporate treasurers. This means that the notion that markets would be more stable if more information were available is probably misguided. If the way in which probabilities should be constructed from available data is in doubt, then more data will not necessarily help and may even confuse. Unlike risk, uncertainty cannot be insured against and arguably is the main reason why institutions exist in the first place. Thus, despite the neoliberal paradigm still being firmly entrenched, it is not surprising that there is a discernible change of mood back towards a desire for stronger international market rules, even in some business circles.[37]

Global property rules

Although over the past decade all countries have embarked on an unprecedented liberalization of their financial regimes, international investment agreements – such as bilateral investment treaties, double taxation treaties, regional trade agreements and certain WTO provisions have all multiplied. These trends reflect a move away from national rights to control foreign investment and norms for corporate conduct; and play a key role in building investor confidence by locking in policy commitments over time.[38] They are usually based on general standards of treatment; coupled with norms on specific matters such as expropriation, compensation and the transfer of funds, as well as mechanisms for the international settlement of disputes. In consequence, the twenty-nine OECD members launched negotiations in 1995 on the world's first multilateral agreement establishing comprehensive and binding rules for investment providing market access, legal security and a 'level playing field' for international investment flows.[39] Negotiation was between OECD members only, although the Multilateral Agreement on Investment was intended to be eventually open to accession by non-member countries who could reach the required regulatory standards.

This non-inclusive negotiating format had a precedent in the early GATT rounds, but it was clearly a fundamental weakness insofar as emerging market interests could not be directly reflected. Moreover, a number of non-governmental organizations became concerned by the apparent exclusion of strict safeguards on labour standards and environmental protection from the MAI. Nonetheless, the eventual breakdown of the Paris negotiations in 1998 arose from the nature of the exceptions claimed by OECD members (particularly the USA and France) rather than the development issue as such. It now appears that negotiations on a 'Multilateral Framework for Investment' were transferred to Geneva in 1999, not least because of the many investment-related trade issues already built into the WTO framework. France, Canada and the United Kingdom all support this approach, and the European Commission included investment in its proposed list of agenda items for the comprehensive 'Millennium Round' of multilateral trade talks which it wanted to see launched in 1999.

Effective multilateral taxation of corporate profits and asset incomes has also become a topic of increasing concern to industrial countries. There are current moves towards tax harmonization and to establish withholding taxes in the EU in order to reduce the tax loss on the profits generated there. In order to strengthen this process of fiscal capture, it will become necessary to eliminate tax havens – or at the very least deny the benefits of international investor protection to firms registered there. Such an agreement would not only improve the fiscal revenues of participating countries[40] but would also strengthen the effort to combat money laundering and financial fraud – again, stabilizing financial flows.

If such a multilateral tax treaty were to include developing countries it would confer a number of advantages. First, it would prevent wasteful tax competition between developing countries in order to attract foreign investors. Second, as all tax paid in developing countries is deductible against tax liability in (developed) home countries, increased effectiveness in tax collection by developing countries would be a net transfer between the treasuries of home and host country – far more effective than the present system of development assistance. Third, this would provide a stable source of long-term funding for the public investment in education, health and infrastructure that developing countries require. Fourth, it would permit effective taxation of their own nationals with considerable overseas assets; and reverse the trend towards national tax systems being forced to tax their main immobile factor of production – labour.

Such an approach would be superior to proposals for a so-called 'Tobin' tax on short-term financial transactions.[41] Such a turnover tax would have little effect on speculative flows, because at any feasible rate it would imply a penalty of marginal importance compared to the prospective losses from maintaining asset holdings in a currency under attack. In addition the Tobin tax would be impossible to collect in view of the complexity, speed and substitutability of cross-border currency transactions – leaving aside the problem of offshore transactions.

In contrast, multilateral corporate taxation can be based on the statutory requirement to present accounts in some jurisdiction, and only requires the effective co-ordination of the vast web of existing bilateral tax treaties. It would also deliver resources to developing country governments rather than to an international body and not require – in principle – a new international bureaucracy to administer it.

Global citizenship?

The difficulty in establishing international rules as the basis for global financial security underlines the fact that no system of international commercial law exists. There does exist a system of international public law which regulates – albeit under some strain at times – the relations between states.[42] However, there is no equivalent in the fields of trade and investment, beyond the treaty obligations of governments under – say – the World Trade Organization.

In consequence, international commercial cases are arbitrated either in the national jurisdiction of the contracting parties' choice[43] or at private tribunals. Indeed the only persons traditionally recognized under international law are pirates, and more recently perpetrators of genocide. The right of foreign investors to make claims against states on their own behalf has, however, been established recently for the first time in a major plurilateral treaty in the North American Free Trade Agreement (NAFTA); a precedent which generated considerable disquiet when it was included in the draft of the Multilateral Agreement an Investment (MAI).[44]

The recognition of firms ('juridical persons') in international law as the basis for international property rights, would have considerable implications for global citizenship – although what these implications might be is far from clear. Many critics of globalization would argue that the consequences of such a development would be to further strengthen the hand of multinational corporations free to move around the world and hold governments to ransom, as against local labour forces confined to their national territory and forced to reduce wages and work conditions in order to find employment.[45]

This would seem to be an argument for stricter *international* regulation of investment, rather than attempts at national withdrawal from the global economy. Equitable negotiations of international investment and taxation rules, along the lines discussed above, would seem to be a first step towards this. What is more, the recognition of firms under international law would make the recognition of persons almost inevitable – thus strengthening the subsequent development of international human rights. A historical precedent is the way in which property rights formed the basis for civil law in England, and subsequently for civil and thus human rights.

It is true that the growing mobility of capital contrasts markedly with the increasing immobility of labour.[46] However, this would reflect a serious challenge to the notion of citizenship even if an equitable financial architecture were in place and multinational corporations all behaved in an irreproachable manner. As modern economic theory has shown, it is not just financial capital, management skills, modern technology and skilled labour – all of which are internationally mobile in principle – which determine productivity growth and living standards at the national level. Rather it is the 'social overhead capital' of infrastructure, institutions and even culture which account for the larger part of international income differences. These common assets are built up historically through social investment (and tax payments) of previous generations, and thus are specific to nations (or cities) and not internationally mobile. This form of capital is 'owned' by the nationals of the country in question; and in essence means that their passport is the principal asset which citizens of rich countries possess. Their incomes depend upon the 'dividend' from joint ownership of their country's social overhead capital – an equity which they mainly inherit through birth and deny to other members of the global community by prohibiting immigration.[47]

In the strict sense of liberal political philosophy set out by Rawls, this arrangement is clearly unjust. All parents in poor countries would doubtless prefer that their children be born citizens of a rich nation, independently of where they were eventually to reside.[48] Once behind the 'veil of ignorance' and not knowing which passport their children would receive in a lottery system, future parents from both poor *and* rich countries would logically vote for the free movement of labour around the globe. In Rawls' rigorous sense, the 'indifference test' demonstrates that the current situation is manifestly unfair and unacceptable.[49]

It can be argued, of course, that the citizens of individual countries do not belong to a single political community and can only be represented internationally by their respective states. This is a realistic interpretation, but leads logically towards more equitable representation in international organizations charged with the regulation of the international economic system. Specifically, this implies that the United Nations should be the forum in which investment issues are settled through the equal representation of states,[50] or possibly by the creation of an 'economic security council' reflecting regional economic interests.[51]

Nonetheless, it is worth considering the implications for the Hegelian moral imperative of the debates on international financial security outlined in this lecture, however hypothetical these may be. All human beings *are already* members of a single political community by virtue of their participation in a global market; a participation in which they were not consulted. If financial assets become internationally recognized as they must be if they are to be effectively regulated, and if a multilateral property (and tax) system emerges, then this eventually means the recognition of natural persons as subjects of international law. Finally, such recognition opens the door to the redistribution of the global income from capital towards the labouring poor and the eventual elimination of global poverty in the form of social transfers rather than 'aid' in the twenty-first century, in much the same way in which social citizenship replaced charity in modern Europe during the twentieth.[52]

Conclusions

This argument has progressed from economic theory to political economy and then on towards political philosophy – a somewhat perilous inter-disciplinary expedition which I trust has been worthwhile.

To recap, my three main points have been:

1. Financial markets are inherently unstable because they deal in expectations; they require strong regulation to underpin contracts and prevent systemic collapse; so that global financial markets require global regulation – not as a means of protecting consumers or small investors, but just so that they can function at all – particularly for the three-quarters of the world population outside the OECD.

2. It has taken repeated international crises to convince global policy-makers that the Bretton Woods institutions are wholly inadequate to provide the required international security; but the implementation of the required regulatory framework faces the opposition of both the major global economic powers and private financial intermediaries; resolution of this impasse may only come about through the geopolitical balance between new currency areas.

3. The process by which a new intergovernmental financial architecture is established will be slow and driven by successive crises; but it will entail a more critical approach to market 'rationality' as a substitute for political process, to the nature of international property rights, and possibly ultimately towards the concept of global citizenship itself.

My argument has thus *not* been against global financial integration – which in any event is an inevitable trend – but rather a case *for* the construction of an appropriate international framework which an orderly market requires. The construction of that framework will be slow and driven by national interest, but I believe that it just might contain an opportunity for global emancipation.

Postscript

A key theme of this chapter has been that the nature of finance is necessarily volatile and essentially unpredictable. This is why capital markets cannot reach equilibrium, and thus cannot be considered as 'rational' in the technical sense; and why a complex institutional underpinning of both supervisory rules and discretionary intervention is necessary at the national level. By extension, similar underpinning is just as necessary – or even more so – at the international level, but the present degree of intergovernmental co-operation, let alone supranational organization, is clearly insufficient to achieve an orderly market.

In consequence, it is hardly surprising that since the Wolfson College lecture on which this chapter is based was delivered in January 1999, major events have occurred in international capital markets. However, I have decided not to update the text, for two reasons. First, further financial upsets will presumably take place between now and the date of publication, let alone that of reading. Second, recent events, particularly the collapse of Brazil and the recovery of Korea, have tended to strengthen my argument rather than invalidate it. In this postscript I focus, therefore, on the principal institutional changes that have taken place at the intergovernmental level since early 1999 in response to the continuing crisis.

The G7 countries have responded to the serious financial crises in emerging markets between 1994 and 1999, by embarking on an agreed series of measures to ensure a more resilient international financial system. Pilot programmes are under way in information transparency, the assessment of standards and codes, and the identification of financial sector vulnerability. This work involves both the development of better analytical tools and more accurate, relevant and timely data; and has made some progress through the vehicle of IMF surveillance. Less progress has been made in ensuring private sector involvement in crisis prevention and resolution.

A range of international institutions are involved in efforts to strengthen the international financial architecture, including the Bank for International Settlements (BIS), the OECD, the World Bank and the new Financial Stability Forum – which for the first time involves leading emerging market authorities. Standard-setting bodies such as the IOSCO, IAIS, the various accounting bodies and the UNCITRAL have become involved in the assessment of financial stability and the setting and observance of standards. While adherence to such standards would undoubtedly benefit all developing countries, the cost and difficulty of doing so for low-income or small countries may make this very difficult for the foreseeable future. It is probably necessary, therefore, to establish simpler and more robust standards if they are not to be denied access to international capital markets.

Attempts to draw in the private sector in crisis prevention and resolution have involved consultations on the modification of sovereign bond contracts in order to facilitate debt negotiations through the inclusion of collective action clauses. IMF lending into sovereign and non-sovereign arrears to private bondholders has been initiated, as has the elimination of regulatory bias towards short-term inter-bank credit lines and the establishment of market-based contingent credit lines to provide liquidity in time of crisis. However, progress has been slow, despite the potential benefits to both debtors and creditors of such initiatives.

The support of aid donors is essential if developing countries are to achieve access to international capital markets on stable and acceptable terms. The role of the development banks in the process of intermediation between savers in developed countries and investors in developing countries has come under critical scrutiny, with two aspects causing concern. The first is the apparent overlap between the regional development banks and the World Bank, in Latin America and Asia in particular. The second is the continued weight of middle-income countries in development bank lending, despite the access of both their public and private sectors to international capital markets. However, there has been little progress as yet in adapting the international financial institutions (established at Bretton Woods more than half a century ago) to the global capital markets of the twentieth century.

The burden of external debt continues to impede the access by many developing countries to international capital markets. While the burden of debt service has been contained by successive restructurings and cancellation of bilateral debt, the difficulty of writing down the multilateral institutions' own debt has meant that the nominal debt overhang remains very high and inconsistent with long-run solvency. This overhang represents a risk factor for private investment that probably outweighs any potential benefit from the enforcement by donors of macroeconomic discipline. Further debt cancellation, possibly conditional upon adherence to the emerging international financial codes, would be necessary in order to encourage investment. However, the main barrier to long-term private capital flows to low-income countries is investor risk in its various forms. Developed countries can play a significant role in overcoming risk by providing export and investment insurance in order to support large infrastructure projects, and technical assistance to developing countries wishing to modernize their regulatory systems.

Finally, at the turn of the millennium it has become clearer (and more broadly accepted) that current international taxation arrangements for foreign investment – and the role of offshore financial centres in particular – pose peculiar problems for developing countries. They require a fair share of potential fiscal resources generated by transborder firms (both foreign and domestic) to service debt and supply basic social services, but capital mobility makes this increasingly difficult. Socially inefficient tax competition between developing countries in order to attract foreign investment leads to declining fiscal revenues. Difficulties in taxing income from overseas assets held by domestic residents stimulate capital flight and further reduce resources available for development. Existing double taxation treaties could be refined to ensure that they promote development; particularly the tax credit system and information exchange. Such an initiative could start with those countries with sound administrative and economic systems, and involve an extension to developing countries of the 1988 Multilateral Convention on Mutual Administrative Assistance in Tax Matters. Support could also be given to international efforts to reduce harmful tax competition between developing countries as well as the current OECD initiatives. The extension of current UK and OECD efforts to regulate offshore financial centres, aimed at preventing such centres acting as tax havens and reducing poor countries' legitimate fiscal revenues from both their own residents and foreign investors, would also be desirable.

Notes

1. I would like to thank the MacArthur Foundation for support to the research programme at the Finance and Trade Policy Research Centre from which this paper is derived. This chapter was also presented as a paper at the Jornadas de Economía Crítica, Albacete, February 2000.
2. According to the *OED* the use of the word 'security' in a financial sense is at least as old as that of personal safety, and that the latter originally implied carelessness: **Security: I.** The condition of being secure. 1. The condition of

being protected from or not exposed to danger; safety. 2. Freedom from doubt. Now chiefly, well founded confidence, certainty 1597. 3. Freedom from care, anxiety or apprehension; a feeling of safety. *arch.* Formerly often culpable absence of anxiety, carelessness 1555 ('Security Is Mortals cheefest Enemie' Shaks) **II.** A means of being secure. 1. Something which makes safe; a protection, guard, defence 1586. 2. Ground for regarding something as secure, safe or certain; an assurance, guarantee 1623. 3. Property deposited or made over, or bonds, recognizances, or the like entered into by, or on behalf of a person in order to secure his fulfilment of an obligation, forfeitable in the event of non-fulfilment 1450. 4. One who pledges himself (or is pledged) for another, a surety 1597. 5. A document held by a creditor as guarantee of his right to payment. Hence, any form of investment guaranteed by such documents. Chiefly *pl.* 1690 ('Liquid Securities, or in other words, those easily convertible into cash when necessity arises' 1879). The sense of 'state security' first appears in the 1965 *Addenda*.

3. The oil crisis did of course cause serious problems for industrial countries, and was accompanied by calls for a 'New International Economic Order' from critics of the Bretton Woods system; but it did not lead to any change in the way the OECD countries viewed the world or arranged their institutions.

4. It is to say the least ironic that in an attempt to broaden the membership of the OECD to include industrializing powers, Mexico and Korea were admitted in 1994, while the candidates in 1997 were Russia, Indonesia, India, Brazil and China. Five of these 'big seven' have since suffered financial collapse.

5. Calculated from IMF, *World Economic Outlook*, Washington DC: International Monetary Fund (October 1998). As is frequently pointed out, these countries account for only 16 per cent of the world population.

6. Because depositors in (say) pension funds cannot know the eventual value of the asset acquired when they retire, they can only rely on the *current* return on the fund in question as an indicator of the fund manager's capability. This encourages short-term maximization of returns by fund managers in order to gain market share; a bias which is exacerbated by the system of quarterly bonuses as a form of remuneration.

7. Just as good driving consists in correctly anticipating the actions of pedestrians and other motorists rather than efficient use of the vehicle as such.

8. 'Global Saving and Interest Rate Behaviour: Why Don't International Capital Markets Clear?' in S. Sharma (ed.), *John Maynard Keynes: Keynesianism into the Twenty-first Century*, London: Elgar, 1998, pp. 223–9.

9. In addition, financial liberalization means that in an economy such as Mexico, the entire domestic money supply is – in effect – a contingent foreign exchange claim on the central bank because bank deposits can be converted into dollars on demand.

10. See IMF, *Toward a Framework for Financial Stability*, Washington DC: International Monetary Fund, 1998.

11. C. P. Kindelberger, *Manias, Panics and Crashes: a History of Financial Crises* (3rd edn), Basingstoke: Macmillan, 1996.

12. BIS, *Sixty-eighth Annual Report*, Basle: Bank for International Settlements, 1998. The BCCI and Barings cases are two of the best known examples.

13. There is an interesting parallel with the epidemiological concept of vulnerability to (say) tuberculosis, which combines exposure to a particular environment and the resilience of the victim.

14. E. V. K. FitzGerald, 'International Capital Markets and Open-economy Macroeconomics: a Keynesian View', *International Review of Applied Economics*, 10, 1 (1996), pp. 141–56.

15. See E. V. K. FitzGerald, 'Capital Surges and Sustainable Macroeconomic Policy', *Adjustment and Beyond: the Reform Experience in South East Asia*, International Economic Association, Basingstoke: Macmillan, 1999.

16. For further details, see E. V. K. FitzGerald, 'Coping with Uncertainty: Global Capital Market Volatility and the Developing Countries', paper presented to the North–South Roundtable Seminar at Easton MD, 26 June 1998.

17. E. V. K. FitzGerald, 'Global Capital Market Volatility and the Developing Countries: Lessons from the East Asian Crisis', *IDS Bulletin*, 29, 4, 1998.

18. E. V. K. FitzGerald 'Intervention vs Regulation: the Role of the IMF in Crisis Prevention and Management', *Unctad Review 1996*, pp. 35–53.

19. B. Eichengreen and R. Portes, *Crisis? What Crisis? Orderly Workouts for Sovereign Debtors*, London: Centre for Economic Policy Research, 1995.

20. The assessment over whether the current account deficit of a particular country reflects longer-term debt solvency, and thus the evaluation of the exchange rate risk and the probability of a policy shift which could affect asset values, depends not only on knowing what the current payments and debt situation is, but also the expected rate of growth, the expected world interest rate and what investors will regard as an acceptable debt ratio. These are all matters of economic (and political) judgement rather than statistical information.

21. It is sometimes suggested that these agencies have emerging market governments as clients for the rating of new issues. They are reluctant to downgrade them – but there is no reliable evidence of this.

22. The concept of moral hazard originates in accident insurance, where car owners once insured may be careless of damage to their vehicle unless there is a minimum claim or no-claims bonus. Whether this notion can be rigorously applied to major macroeconomic crises where the outcome (i.e. a bail-out) is uncertain, seems very doubtful – it is not applicable to life insurance after all. The other justification – that cancellation would reduce the IFIs' credit ratings and thus ability to mobilize further development resources – is wholly implausible because the ratings depend not on the quality of lending but underwriting provided by the member governments. In other words, IFI borrowing on international capital markets is secured against fiscal receipts in *developed* rather than developing countries.

23. DAC, *Development Assistance Report 1998*, Paris: OECD/Development Assistance Committee, 1998.

24. Each of these has required funds of the same order of magnitude as the entire annual aid budget to all developing countries.

25. Ironically it had two Nobel laureates in economics on its board. It should be noted that although LTCM was a hedge fund registered in Bermuda and thus unregulated, it was speculating in US Treasury bill futures at the time.

26. The argument that offshore financial centres are autonomous states and thus cannot be forced to co-operate is of course nonsense – their very existence depends on the protection of a G7 member.

27. IMF, *Toward a Framework for Financial Stability*.
28. Specifically, the 1933 Banking ('Glass-Steagall') Act and the 1956 Companies Holding Companies Act.
29. E. V. K. FitzGerald, *'Caveat Creditor*: the Implications of the Asian Crisis for International Investment Regulation', paper presented to the UNCTAD Seminar on 'The Asian Financial Crisis', 1 May 1998, Geneva.
30. S. Griffith-Jones, M. Montes and A. Nasution (eds), *Managing Capital Flows in Developing Countries*, Oxford: Oxford University Press (forthcoming).
31. See P. Krugman and M. Obstfeld, *International Economics: Theory and Policy*, London: Scott, Foresman, 1988.
32. See A. Wyatt-Walter, *World Power and World Money: the Role of Hegemeony and Monetary Order*, Hassocks: Harvester Wheatsheaf, 1993.
33. This is the perspective set out by the OECD countries: OECD, *Open Markets Matter: the Benefits of Trade and Investment Liberalization*, Paris: Organization for Economic Cooperation and Development, 1998. See also World Bank, *Private Capital Flows to Developing Countries: the Road to Financial Integration*, Washington DC: World Bank, 1997.
34. See the lecture by John Kay in this series 'Global Business in Search of Security'.
35. Sometimes referred to as 'institutions of restraint' – a significant choice of words.
36. See World Bank, *World Development Report 1997*, Washington DC: World Bank, 1997.
37. 'We have this false theory that markets, left to their own devices, tend towards equilibrium ... To argue that financial markets in general, and international lending in particular, need to be regulated is likely to outrage the financial community: yet the evidence for just that is overwhelming' (George Soros, *Financial Times*, 31 Dec 1997).
38. *World Investment Report, 1997*, Geneva: United Nations Conference on Trade and Development, 1997; and WTO, *World Trade Report, 1997*, Geneva: World Trade Organization, 1998.
39. See E. Fitzgerald, R. Cubero-Brierly and A. Lehmann, *The Implications for Developing Countries of the Multilateral Agreement on Investment*, London: Department for International Development, Paris: OECD, 1998.
40. From the point of view of individual countries, corporate profits are difficult to tax for two reasons. First, because capital is mobile it can be driven abroad by high tax rates or deterred from investing in the first place. This leads to downward fiscal competition between developing countries and a lower average tax rate. Second, by arranging their international transactions appropriately, companies can accrue profits in the lowest tax jurisdictions – which are often 'tax havens' – and thus further reduce the tax burden on capital. In both cases there is a clear loss in global welfare to the extent that the tax revenue would have been used for social infrastructure investment or effective poverty relief.
41. The case for such a tax is set out in M. U. Haq, I. Kaul and I. Grunberg (eds), *The Tobin Tax: Coping with Financial Volatility*, Oxford: Oxford University Press, 1996. The reasons why it would not in fact reduce volatility are set out in P. Arestis and M. Sawyer, 'What Role for the Tobin Tax in Global Governance' [mimeo], University of East London and University of Leeds,

1998. The other apparent attraction of the Tobin tax is to provide resources for international development assistance in general and for the UN in particular. However, aside from the fact that there are easier forms of raising international taxation (such as a tax on international airline tickets) the major barrier is clearly political – the unwillingness of national legislatures to devote more funds to aid, or *a fortiori* to the United Nations.

42. This contrasts with advances in international public law, though even here the 'right to development' established by the UN is not effective. See I. Brownlie, *Public International Law*, 4th edn, Oxford: Clarendon Press, 1990, and also his lecture in this series 'The Peaceful Settlement of Disputes between States and the Problem of Globalisation'.

43. Frequently the New York courts, which are reputedly collapsing under the strain.

44. See FitzGerald, Cubero and Lehmann, op cit. Interestingly, the MAI draft also includes a proposal that the senior executives of foreign firms should be granted exemption from migration controls.

45. UNRISD, *States of Disarray: the Social Effects of Globalization*, Geneva: UN Research Institute for Social Development, 1995.

46. The reasons, of course, are largely political. Nonetheless, it is striking how few (if any) libertarian advocates of an unregulated global economy are willing to mention (let alone propose) the free movement of labour. See also Robin Cohen, this volume, 'Labour in an Age of Global Insecurity'.

47. For a formal model of this notion of 'the asset value of citizenship' and a preliminary approximation of its financial valuation, see E. V. K. FitzGerald and J. Cuesta-Leiva, 'The Asset Value of a Passport: a Model of Citizenship and Income Determination in a Global Economy', *Working Papers Series QEHWPSxx* on <http://www.qeh.ox.ac.uk>, 1998.

48. Indeed many Latin American mothers – both rich and poor – strive to give birth in the USA for just this reason.

49. This argument is developed in E. V. K. FitzGerald, 'Rethinking Development Assistance: the Implications of Social Citizenship in a Global Economy', Geneva: UN Research Institute for Social Development, 1997 (also as *Working Papers Series QEHWPS01* on <http://www.qeh.ox.ac.uk>).

50. N. Schreiber, *Sovereignty over Natural Resources: Balancing Rights and Duties*, Cambridge: Cambridge University Press, 1997.

51. F. Stewart, 'The Governance and Mandates of the International Financial Institutions', *IDS Bulletin*, 26, 4, 1995, pp. 28–34.

52. To reach the target agreed by OECD members of halving the proportion of developing country population living in poverty by 2020 would require a doubling of per capita income over the next 20 years, and thus a sustained GDP growth rate of over 5 per cent per annum (DAC, *Development Assistance Report 1998*). This is far beyond the track record of poor countries and similar to that of East Asia between 1970 and 1990. In contrast, since the poor receive only 1 per cent of world income, a transfer of 1 per cent of the income of industrial countries (i.e. 0.5 per cent of world income) would halve the number of poor immediately.

7
Global Business in Search of Security

John Kay

My aim is to explore the connection between a range of economic environments, the insecurities facing business, and economic perform-ance. We can start by considering a commodity: the Ford Mondeo, a characteristic product of what we think of as global business, hence its name. The Mondeo is Ford's 'world car'. It epitomizes the conventional wisdom of business economics about globalization. Manufacturing is dominated by large firms, products are increasingly homogeneous, and, as a result of the globalization of business, products, firms and their international managers gradually and steadily lose their nationality and become bland. A new breed of international manager is created whose loyalty is owed not to their country of origin but instead to the company for which they work.

There is some truth in that, as the example of the Mondeo shows. Ford is indeed a very large company. The Mondeo is a car which is on sale around the world. While Ford of the United States is a quintessentially American company, Ford of Europe is, in many ways, one of the most international of companies. In ignoring national boundaries within Europe, Ford of Europe is also perhaps a more effectively European organization than is any explicitly European company. The Mondeo is a bland product. It is designed not to offend people in any culture or in any part of the world. It is sold in very similar guises, in very similar shapes all round the world and it is also sourced internationally: the bodywork made in Brentwood, the engine made in Spain, the gearbox made in France.

But this conventional wisdom is at best superficial and at worst quite substantially wrong. It can be argued that the Mondeo is not, in fact, the quintessential phenomenon of globalization and of the development of international business. Instead, a less illustrious company called Hilti is a more appropriate example of global business. Hilti is the largest company in Liechtenstein, founded in 1941 and employing 1400 people in Liechtenstein and a total of 12 000 people around the world. Hilti is a world leader in the manufacture of industrial fasteners.

I will suggest that Hilti is the more important phenomenon of the globalization of business and of the development of international business than is the Ford Mondeo. As a result of the simultaneous development on the one hand of Mondeo-like products, but on the other of the international growth of firms like Hilti, the aggregate effect of industrial concentration on the role which large firms play in the world economy, of their globalization, is actually ambiguous. As markets become more global both products and national economic structures become heterogeneous. Furthermore, nationality and geography become more rather than less important in determining the products we buy.

The key feature of the globalization of business is that industries which were previously organized around scale and historic (national) market share are restructured in ways based primarily on the competitive advantages of individual firms. This is the change exemplified by Hilti, a firm which cannot rely on the market for industrial fasteners in Liechtenstein. The firm exists because it works on a world scale. Hilti is as important a part of globalization as Ford. Hilti exemplifies an industry previously organized around scale and market share, dominated historically, both in production and consumption, by the United States.

We can even see this ambiguity in the conventional example of automobiles. In the 1950s, the world car industry was dominated by three firms: General Motors, Ford and Chrysler. Studebaker, the smallest American manufacturer of cars had just gone bankrupt. Kaiser, a steel firm in the United States which had flourished during the Second World War, had attempted to enter the automobile industry and had failed. The process of steadily increasing concentration in the world automobile industry was widely predicted as inevitable. Further entrants into the world car industry were inconceivable. In fact, the share of the three largest firms in the world market has fallen steadily and the degree of concentration in the global automobile industry has likewise diminished. About thirty major new firms have succeeded in entering the world car industry. The best-selling car in the history of the world is not the Ford Mondeo but the Toyota Corolla, the product of a Japanese company that made textile machinery in the early 1950s.

Similar trends occurred within individual countries such as Britain. In 1967, in the heyday of industrial strategy the whole of what remained of the British car industry was merged into one company (British Leyland) in order to create an organization sufficiently large to compete in the world markets. 1967 was also the year in which Honda Motors made their first car. Twenty years later, the only way that British Leyland could survive was as a result of inputs of cash and technology from Honda.

In this process of falling concentration and rising entry, weak national players have disappeared. The number of British car firms fell from ten to zero. All British car producers today are subsidiaries of foreign-owned companies. While some of the new entrants have come from countries like Japan, with large domestic markets for automobiles, they also come from countries which have very small domestic markets: in effect, the Hilti phenomenon. Far from it being the case that globalization required large scale in the automobile industry, it has encouraged small firms with strong international competitive advantages. Neither Proton, the leading Malaysian producer of cars, or Hyundai, the top Korean producer, could be in business at all if they had to rely on either the Malaysian or the Korean market.

Furthermore, the world car market has become more differentiated. As incomes have risen, the range of products that people want to buy has increased. Rather than firms relying on cheap products based on economies of scale, it is firms which are able to compete globally in particular niche markets that have proliferated. We consider BMW as being one of the great successes of the world automobile industry, but BMW was not always successful. BMW was founded during the First World War to manufacture aero-engines. Aero-engines were indeed that company's business until 1945, when being Germany's leading manufacturer of aero-engines was not a very strong market position to have. And it was made worse by the fact that BMW's largest plant was sited in the Soviet occupation zone. Throughout the 1950s BMW was a company stumbling in search of a niche. It was no longer able to make aero-engines; it made motorbikes; it also made bubble cars and limousines which were rather inferior to those built by Mercedes. By 1959, in fact, BMW was a company on the verge of bankruptcy – thought lucky to be taken over by Mercedes. After some rather tortuous corporate politics, it found a supportive external shareholder who refocused the company on what were then the BMW 1500 and 1600, first-ever designs for up-market production saloons. What BMW succeeded in doing in the early 1960s combined mass production with a quality of engineering without precedent in such a product. That enabled BMW to establish a niche with a price premium at the top of the global mass-produced automobile industry. BMW went on to develop that niche and, of course, built a brand and a reputation that is recognized today.

BMW, along the lines of the Hilti model, is as equally a product of the globalization of the world car market as is Ford. It is the balance between these two kinds of global manufacturing which describes the evolution of this or any other industry. On the one hand, large economies of scale can be derived by organizing production on a worldwide basis. On the other hand, firms with very specific competitive advantages are now able to make use of these advantages on a global platform; but the outcomes, in terms of concentration, diversity, and the structure of these industries depends on the balance between these two forces. Even in the case of automobiles, which is one of the industries most strongly characterized by scale economies, the global exploitation of advantage has proved to be a more important factor in the development of markets than the creation of large companies centred round economies of scale.

The trends exemplified by the evolution of the automobile industry are actually characteristic of the way in which many other markets and industries have developed. Take the washing machine industry for example, often cited in the business literature of the past as one of the creations of international marketing and international business. Indeed, for a couple of decades, the washing machine industry was the Harvard Business School's favourite case study of European industry. The European washing machine industry was one of the early creations of the Treaty of Rome which destroyed tariff barriers across the EC. The European industry started with twin tub machines and then moved to automatics with one drum. In the 1950s and 1960s the European market was swept by Italian manufacturers who derived large-scale economies from producing very long model runs of particular models from factories in northern Italy. In the 1970s, three or four Italian producers with motors manufactured by Fiat came to dominate the whole European washing machine industry. So, the early development of washing machines displayed the Mondeo phenomenon, with homogeneous products produced in north Italy. But since the 1970s, the washing machine industry has changed. In the early 1980s, two of the leading Italian producers who had previously dominated the European market actually went bankrupt. The washing machine market has become renationalized. If you are German you are more likely to buy a German machine than an Italian machine.

There are two reasons for renationalization. First, economies of scale have become less important because demand is less sensitive to price. When people first purchased washing machines, they occupied a much larger proportion of household income than they do today. So washing machines are much more affordable than they were, and economies of production are much less significant. Second, at the same time, the growth of flexible computer aided design and computerized manufacturing processes make it easier to produce a wide range of machines. People want rather different products. An Italian purchaser is content with a machine that has a rather slow spin speed, because in Italy one can hang washing out to dry and Italians frequently do. One can't do this in Denmark, with the result that the machines sold there have very fast spin speeds. Germans like to buy the types of machines that can be dropped from the sixth floor of an apartment block and still work when you pick them up. The French prefer machines that, instead of loading from the front, are loaded from the top. Washing machines reflect social habits. So France alone has substantial sales of top-loading machines and international companies make these machines for French markets. Bosch and Miele make distinctively indestructible machines for the German market, and the British buy machines made by British companies that lie somewhere in between.

Once again, there are the two factors at work: there are the economies of scale that come from being able to produce and manufacture on a global basis and there is increased demand for differentiation. In the washing machine industry, as in the automobile industry, it is differentiation that has dominated development. These two different factors work in most global industries. In order to understand more clearly what this implies for the structure of global manufacturing industry, we need to examine how industries whose structure was once based on scale and on history, are finding that scale and history matter less whilst competitive advantage matters more.

The structure of competitive advantage changed radically in the course of the twentieth century. If we examine the twelve largest companies in the world in 1912 (Table 7.1), the company we know today as USX was known as US Steel, and was not only the biggest steel company, but the biggest company of any kind. The need for concentration and rationalization in the industry, the inevitability of increasing globalization, and the greater role for larger firms were factors stressed at the start of the century. It was indeed such arguments that led to the creation – by amalgamation – of US Steel. Today, USX, although it bought an oil company twice its size in the early 1980s, is not only no longer the largest industrial company in the world, it is not even the largest steel company (Table 7.2). USX today has a market capitalization which is 5 per cent of the size of today's largest company, interestingly one which was further down the list of large companies in 1912 – General Electric.

Table 7.1   Top twelve global industrials by market capitalization at the beginning of the century (1912)

Rank	Company	Industry	HQ country	Equity capitalization ($m)
1	USX	steel	US	741
2	Exxon	oil	US	390
3	J. & P. Coats	textiles	UK	287
4	Pullman	railcars	US	200
5	Royal Dutch Shell	oil	UK/N	187
6	Anaconda	copper	US	178
7	General Electric	electricals	US	174
8	Singer	machinery	US	173
9	American Brands	cigarettes	UK	159
10	Navistar	machinery	US	160
11	BAT Industries	cigarettes	UK	159
12	De Beers	diamonds	SA	158

Table 7.2   Top twelve global industrials by market capitalization at the end of the century (1995)

Rank	Company	Industry	HQ country	Equity capitalization ($bn)
1	General Electric	electricals	US	223
2	Royal Dutch Shell	oil	UK/N	191
3	Exxon	oil	US	158
4	Coca-Cola	brands	US	151
5	Intel	chips	US	151
6	Merck	pharmaceuticals	US	121
7	Toyota Motor	cars	J	117
8	Novartis	pharmaceuticals	Sw	104
9	IBM	computers	US	104
10	Philip Morris	brands	US	101
11	Proctor & Gamble	brands	US	93
12	British Petroleum	oil	UK	86

Comparing these two lists, the largest companies in 1912 were: USX, or US Steel; Exxon, an oil company still going today; J. & P. Coats, astonishingly Britain's largest company in 1912, today a small part of Coats Viyella which is today a small company by any standards in the UK; Pullman which was the largest manufacturer of rolling stock for railroads in 1912, no longer around; Royal Dutch Shell, very much around today; Anaconda Copper, gone; General Electric now moved to number one; Singer, absorbed by another company; American Brands, in 1912 the largest manufacturers of cigarettes in the world and the ninth largest company in the world, it exited the tobacco industry in 1995 and is now much smaller; Navistar, then known as International Harvester, is the largest manufacturer of farm machinery. The list today includes three companies which were there in 1912, with a whole raft of others, which were either then insignificant in size, like Philip Morris, or like Intel, yet to be created. Coca-Cola, founded by an Atlanta pharmacist back in the 1890s, had not reached anywhere remotely their contemporary size.

One remarkable feature of this comparison of ranks is that the products made by the largest firms in 1995 are mostly smaller than the things which the 1912 firms made. The 1912 firms made farm machinery, railroad cars and shipped goods around the world. Fully half the companies on the later list: Coca-Cola, Intel, Merck, Novartis, Philip Morris, possibly Proctor and Gamble, make things that you can actually put in your pocket. If success is measured by size, there has been a shift in the distribution of value added away from the production of raw materials and of intermediate goods. The competitive advantages of firms today are based on the transformation of raw materials. Competitive advantages based on size and scale have yielded to competitive advantage based on brands, reputation and knowledge (as in Coca-Cola or a leading accountancy or law firm) or innovations and standards (as in Glaxo or Microsoft). Or they are based on the structures of relationships, as with the competitive advantages for firms that are at the centre of complicated networks like Toyota or Marks & Spencer and Benetton. Another source of competitive advantage comes from strategic assets, of enjoying a monopoly, mostly with the aid of a supportive government. So the sources of firms' competitive advantage have migrated from market power and scale and market position to these kinds of knowledge-based advantages coming from brands and reputations, innovations and standards, or the ways in which information is processed and managed in networks. That is the fundamental change in the nature of competitive advantage that has occurred across the century. What the globalization of markets has done is to enable the firms that have these kinds of advantages to reap their benefits worldwide irrespective of their scale.

If you go to Brescia in Northern Italy, you will discover quite an extraordinary valley and quite an extraordinary industry, one based on small-scale metalworking. Almost every house or group of houses in that particular valley appears to have a small workshop attached to it. Small metal components are made for high-precision manufacturers. This kind of cottage industry, almost literally a cottage industry, might be thought to be the relic of some bygone age of international business. Firms like those in Brescia, if they haven't been swept away already, might be expected to be swept away by the growing forces of large firms and international business. This prediction is wrong. That valley has enjoyed unparalleled prosperity and today it is one of the richest parts of Europe. The tiny firms that characterize that valley have increased their output, production, profits and wealth. They have reinvested heavily in sophisticated but small-scale, computer-aided machinery. That is simply one of the spectacular examples of the phenomenon of clusters of small firms which operate in a co-operative mode and which specialize in the production of quite narrowly defined commodities. If you are wearing a silk tie, you will probably find that it is made in Italy and if it is made in Italy it is almost certainly made in a small area around Lake Cuomo which is where the majority of Italian tie manufacturing actually takes place. In the same way Italian shoes are likely to come from Lumezzane or the area around there.

There firms are developing along the same principles as Hilti or BMW. In this case they are extremely small firms. The competitive advantages of these particular businesses in these particular regions can be developed worldwide. While the cluster of collaborating firms seems to be almost unique to the structure of Italian industry, networks and clusters have been identified elsewhere. So another set of questions is raised concerning the evolution of world business. Do competitive advantages exist for *countries* as well as *firms*? Companies like Coca-Cola and Microsoft and Intel have developed knowledge-based competitive advantages which they have exploited around the world. Are there national competitive advantages in the same way? There is a very high probability that cameras are either made in Japan or manufactured under licence or supervision of a Japanese company somewhere else in the Far East. Perfumes are probably French. If you have software, there is a very high probability that it is American. A high quality kitchen is probably German. Clothing at the top end of the fashion market is likely to be Italian. And financial services are disproportionately availed of from the United Kingdom. The point about all of these industries is that there appears to be a national competitive advantage to them, in the specific sense that the international competitive advantages are enjoyed by firms from a particular country. However, in all of these industries there are many firms within that country which specialize in the production of the particular product. There are many French perfumiers, several Japanese camera manufacturers, a plethora of American software companies and a whole range of British financial companies. There appears to be competitive advantage that relates to countries as well as to individual firms. If we look at the roots of these competitive advantages we see that they are of a rather similar type as the ones described for individual firms. Brands and reputation are one kind of competitive advantage: for example, Coca-Cola. If we examine successful international brands – Coca-Cola, Marlboro, MacDonald's – the vast majority turn out to be American in origin. And Japan, in what is one of the most extraordinary achievements of the last thirty or forty years, has transformed itself from having an historic reputation for shoddy products to having one that is such that we tend to believe that any Japanese product, regardless of its manufacture or nature, is likely to be more reliable than a product from elsewhere. There is quite a lot of evidence to support that expectation. If we look at innovation-based competitive advantages, we discover that an extraordinary proportion of them are enjoyed by American firms. The United States is quite simply, and by a large margin, the most innovative economy the world has ever seen. But if Microsoft's competitive advantage is based around a standard which it enjoys in MS-DOS and in Windows, Britain has a competitive advantage in areas like education and the audio-visual industries. The competitive advantage comes from having the linguistic equivalent of a world operating system: the English language.

There are also countries that have competitive advantages based around structures of relationships. The Italian networks give their industries the advantages of creativity and motivation in small-scale organization together with many of the marketing advantages that would otherwise only accrue to larger firms. Finally, there are advantages of monopoly or incumbency. Some industries have incumbent advantages which persist long after the reason for the incumbency has disappeared. Hollywood is a good example, because the reason film manufacturers and producers went to Hollywood in the 1920s, when making movies was rather hard, was to exploit the excellent light in southern California. Films are no longer set solely in California but Hollywood became the largest marketplace and then the centre of the world film industry. It has remained as such even though the historic reason for this location has long since disappeared. Britain's position in marine insurance and shipbroking has exactly the same origin. It dates from when Britain had by far the largest merchant navy in the world which is no longer the case. An established position in the provision of market services means position may be retained even though the underlying rationale for it has disappeared.

So individual countries have competitive advantages just as individual firms do. And, once we have understood that, we can see some implications of globalization and the way in which trade in manufactured goods and services between countries has actually been developing. Countries are able to derive and develop these kinds of competitive advantages on a global scale.

National advantages and firm level competitive advantages may combine in a range of nationally based competitive advantages. Japanese business culture is based essentially on a structure of trust relationships. Toyota makes nearly as many cars as General Motors but it does so with less than a fifth of the employees that General Motors has. That is partly because Toyota is more efficient than General Motors, but it is largely because most of the things that go into a General Motors car are made by a General Motors employee while most of the things that go into a Toyota car are made by employees of surrounding firms. And the form of organization which Japan enabled Toyota to bring to the car industry, was one in which production took place in a co-operating group of much smaller sub-contractors. The result of that in turn was that Toyota achieved both more rapid model cycles and higher levels of component reliability than General Motors has been able to do. General Motors had to own their suppliers in order to stop opportunistic behaviour by them and to try and supervise – not very successfully – their production quality. By embedding their production system in the structure of trust relationships, Toyota did not need to do this. The business culture of Japan based on trust is reinforced by a structure of social relationships that binds together a working environment and a social environment and thus raises the penalties for opportunistic behaviour.

So Japan is characterized by very low levels of opportunistic behaviour and the United States by very high levels. The latter actually accompanies the very high levels of innovation which are characteristic of American society. That is why American competitive advantages are based on innovations and brands, which are the very public statement of commitment to trust relationships which the US has produced in response to that different business culture and the society in which it is embedded.

So there are sources of national competitive advantage that are rather similar to those of competitive advantage at the level of the individual firm. These national competitive advantages in some cases are based on elements of path-dependency: historical accidents that took film-makers to California or brought marine insurers to London. Almost all of them are then reinforced by a social embeddedness that means the different business cultures we observe are both varied and depend on other aspects of the social and political context. In my view the key benefit of globalization has been to allow us to enjoy the full benefits from that variety of business cultures. It enables us to buy cameras made in Japan which has a business culture in a supportive social structure conducive to the manufacturing of cameras, and to buy our software from the United States which is a business culture and a supportive social system designed to achieve that. We need to understand that the effect of globalization on world business is not going to be to produce a single product, a single system, or a single identikit manager who can do what he likes anywhere round the world. It is not going to produce a bland convergence of global products. Rather, it is going to remind us that there is no 'best' system of social and economic organization. There are many different and incommensurable components of an effective business and commercial organization. And there are many different business cultures that are part of a successful global economy.

Bibliography

Hannah, Leslie (1996) 'Marshall's "Trees" and the Global "Forest": Were "Giant Redwoods" Different?', London, Centre for Economic Performance, LSE.

Kay, John (1995) *Foundations of Corporate Success*, Oxford: Oxford University Press.

Kay, John (1999), 'Is there a Competitive Advantage of Nations?' *ESRC Lecture no. 5*, ESRC, Swindon.

Mönnich, Horst (1991) *The BMW Story: a Company in its Time*, translated from the German by Anthony Bastow and William Henson, London: Sidgwick and Jackson.

8
Globalization and the Means of Destruction: Physical Insecurity and the Weapons Industry at the Turn of the Millennium

Susan Willett

Introduction

For much of the 1990s globalization was proclaimed a panacea for all economic ills and a force for global political stability as societies around the world became integrated into the global capitalist system.[1] The argument was premised upon two suppositions: firstly, that free trade and unfettered markets encourages economic growth which in turn enhances the living standards of the poor, and in so doing reduces the tensions and conflict about the distribution of resources; secondly, economic interdependence renders war unprofitable, because if a country's main markets risk being destroyed, war is unlikely to be initiated for reasons of vested economic interests.[2] In this manner economic interdependence was thought to reduce the previous lack of altruism of the dominant nation-states and encourage greater co-operative behaviour on a global scale through a process of collective self-interest.

These assumptions have been subject to intense scrutiny since the unfolding events of 1997. In the space of a few months the East Asian financial crisis reversed many of the development gains that had been achieved within the region over the previous two decades. The socio-economic hardship and in some cases (Indonesia) violent conflict which accompanied the market adjustments, provided evidence of the potentially destabilizing nature of unregulated global markets.

In the autumn of 1999 in Seattle a broad coalition of protesters from NGOs, labour organizations, church groups, and human rights organizations took the World Trade Organization to task about the negative effects of indiscriminate trade liberalization. Similarly, in March 2000 protesters demonstrated against the policies of the IMF and World Bank in Washington, highlighting the social and economic hardships imposed upon the poor as a result of the debt crisis and structural adjustment programmes. These groups have drawn attention to the ways in which globalization has marginalized the poor and concentrated wealth into the hands of an already privileged global elite. In a world of finite resources the polarization of wealth and power has its corollary in the growing levels of poverty, human insecurity and violent conflict in the periphery of the global economy.

Strengthening the protesters' arguments are a growing number of analysts who have begun to question whether globalization in its present guise has gone too far. Deep challenges were made about the distributional inequity of the current global economic system, and major reforms of the multilateral institutions which manage the global economy were called for at the UNCTAD Ten meeting held in Bangkok in February 2000. At this conference the UNCTAD Secretary General called for the construction of a new international order founded on real reciprocity that takes into account the underlying asymmetries in the economic structures of the countries of the north and south.

The underlying asymmetries of the global economic system are beginning to be recognized as inherently destabilizing, as poverty and marginalization contribute to the growing sense of human insecurity in the periphery of the global economy.

Rather than reform the economic principles which are generating instability, the dominant world powers, in particular the United States, have responded to the growing world disorder through a process of rearmament, which is in itself destabilizing. Breaking out of this vicious cycle of insecurity requires a new approach to global development and security which addresses the underlying asymmetries and inequities in the global economic structure.

In tackling these issues this chapter is divided into five discrete sections. The first briefly explores the concept of globalization, the second looks at effects of globalization on human security, the third looks at the trend between globalization and patterns of weapons proliferation and the fourth part analyses the strategic responses of the dominant military powers to the new security challenges. The final section suggests an alternative approach to global development, which is aimed at enhancing rather than diminishing security and stability.

Globalization

Globalization has come to have many meanings and has been widely utilized to explain the cause, effect and justification of many aspects of life at the end of the twentieth century. In the economic sense globalization has been closely associated with post-industrial modes of production and service delivery that are increasingly organized into worldwide production and marketing structures via global technology networks.

Two major forces are driving the contemporary process of globalization: information technology and market liberalization. Technical innovations in communication systems (telecommunications and computers) have allowed for global interactions which are instantaneous, virtually reducing the traditional space and time barriers which previously operated in international commercial transactions. Space–time compression is one of the most distinctive features of the globalized economy and facilitates the creation of socio-economic communities and institutions in diverse and scattered locations. Cheaper and efficient communication networks allow firms to site different parts of their production processes in diverse locations around the world while remaining in close contact in near real time. At the same time, information technology reduces the need for physical contact between producers and consumers and therefore allows some previously untradable services to be traded on a global scale.

The second factor driving globalization is economic liberalization. Economic liberalization draws its inspiration from neoliberal economic doctrine which places strong emphasis on private property, market relations and individualism. In policy terms it translates into trade and financial market liberalization, the opening up of domestic markets to foreign investment and competition, the privatization of state assets and the deregulation of markets. Liberalization has proceeded at different speeds in different countries, but the trend has been worldwide, with only a handful of isolated countries resisting the process. As a result of WTO negotiations and multilateral pressure from the World Bank and IMF, almost all countries have lowered their barriers to foreign trade and capital flows. As a result, the volume of trade has increased twice as fast as output, foreign direct investment has increased threefold and cross-border trade in shares has increased ten times as fast in the last decade than in previous decades. These remarkable achievements underlie the strong support for globalization amongst the major trading nations who have reaped the lion's share of the rewards and benefits of globalization.

A notable feature of the recent phase of globalization has been the extension and liberalization of financial markets which has facilitated unprecedented flows of private capital around the world. A decade ago official capital flows to developing countries were much greater than private capital flows, but by 1996 annual private flows of capital to developing countries around the world were more than seven times larger than official flows. For instance in 1996 more than $250bn in private capital flowed to emerging markets, compared to roughly $20 billion ten years ago.

The broadening and deepening of global financial linkages has been hastened in recent times by the connectivity facilitated by advanced communication systems capable of beaming events around the world in near real time. While there are considerable advantages from scale economies from unified global markets, mistakes or imperfections within the system are transmitted on a global stage in a matter of seconds. This is one of the reasons why financial crises have become more frequent and more severe in recent times. However, although the pace of transactions has increased, the mechanisms and institutional structures designed to deal with the mistakes and imperfections within global financial markets remain unchanging, despite major calls for reform of the international financial architecture since the East Asian financial crisis.

Before the liberalization of capital movements in the early 1980s national governments maintained real power over financial markets through exchange controls which limited external dealings. But under international pressure to liberalize, central banks can no longer dictate exchange rates and control foreign exchange markets. Interest rates and levels of inflation cannot differ greatly from those considered pertinent by the financial markets and states are no longer privileged borrowers in domestic capital markets. Governments are regarded by global markets in the same way as local governments and companies are, in terms of their ability to service debt. In consequence a significant degree of autonomy in macroeconomic policy has been lost and states can no longer control certain important economic variables. State policies have been obliged to adapt themselves in order to attract foreign direct investment and other capital flows. As a writer for the *Economist* has noted: 'The financial markets now sit as judge, if they deem that a new national health-care scheme or a massive education reform will prove too costly, they will punish the country with higher interest rates or a collapsing economy. In this way global market forces not only rule out the kind of compensation to losers that would make globalization easier to live with, they also seem to challenge democracy itself.' In this very real sense economic and political sovereignty is being eroded, particularly in the weaker states at the periphery of the global economic system.

Susan Strange in her book *The Retreat of the State* notes that this contemporary shift of power from the state to the market is having the profound effect of restructuring the global order from a world system based on states to one based on powerful non-state actors such as the international financial institutions (IFIs) and international banks. This systematic weakening of the state in the periphery of the global economy is a major factor contributing to the growing levels of insecurity being experienced in the emerging market economies of Eastern and Central Europe and the developing world.

Those who are linked to core economic activities of the global economic system are doing well, but the promise of shared prosperity and global peace that was envisioned at the beginning of the 1990s from the global spread of capitalism has failed to materialize in many parts of the developing world. Many communities on the periphery of the global economy (whether in the rich countries of the north or in the poor countries of the south) have suffered a decline in their living standards and many are excluded altogether from formal economic activity. Some stark UNDP figures summarize the balance of poverty towards the end of the twentieth century:

- More than a quarter of the developing world's people still live in poverty as measured by the UNDPs human poverty index (HPI). About a third (1.3 billion people), live on incomes of less than $1 a day.
- Sub-Saharan Africa has the highest proportion of people in human poverty. Some 220 million people are poverty stricken and it is estimated that by 2000 half the people in sub-Saharan Africa will live in poverty.
- Eastern Europe and the countries of the Commonwealth of Independent States (CIS) have seen the greatest deterioration in their living standards in the past decade. Poverty has spread from a small proportion of the population to about a third (120 million people live on less than $4 a day).
- Certain groups of people are particularly vulnerable to poverty – these include children, women and the aged. An estimated 160 million children are moderately or severely malnourished. And some 110 million children receive no education. Women are disproportion-

ately poor and often disempowered. Their lack of access to land, credit and better employment opportunities inhibits their ability to improve their economic circumstances. The aged often live their final years in acute poverty and neglect.

The current neoliberal preoccupation with the benefits of globalization, which have been hailed as the great panacea for all the world's economic problems, has done little for the 1.3 billion people whose economic circumstances have deteriorated in the last ten years. The neoliberal idea that somehow the benefits of global economic growth will 'trickle down' to the world's poor, has been challenged by the stark reality of the experience in the world's poorest societies. John Kenneth Galbraith once described trickle-down theory using a less than elegant metaphor, when he said that 'if you feed a horse with enough oats some will pass through to the road for the sparrows'. The empirical evidence gathered by the UNDP in its annual *Human Development Reports* strongly indicates that globalization has resulted in a severe fissure between the 'winners and the losers' in unfettered global markets.

Widespread economic collapse in the periphery has undermined the social cohesion of many societies exposing the fragility of developing states and their inability to extend basic security to their citizens. Tragically, the plight of the poor, the marginalized and the displaced are only taken seriously when they become a *threat* to the perceived global order. The resources required to eradicate poverty are a mere fraction of the resources available in the global economy. Nevertheless the rich countries of the north appear increasingly reluctant to respond constructively to the plight of many in the developing world. The Special Adviser to the UNDP has warned 'The cost of accelerated action must be measured against the cost of allowing poverty to grow – that is against continuing political conflict and instability, poverty and disease and affronts to human sensibilities.'

The economics of conflict

The deep polarization of wealth that has become a structural feature of the global economy has been identified as one of the major threats to future peace and security in the coming millennium. Conflict theorists have for some time been at pains to point out that the unequal distribution of wealth and the failure to meet basic human needs constitute a source of structural violence that lies at the heart of the many conflicts.

Distributional inequalities are of course not the only trigger of violent conflict.

The French writer Alain Minc in his book *Le Nouveau Moyen Age*[3] has noted that the collapse of bipolarity, the weakening of the developmental state and the shift of power from the weaker to stronger states have resulted in a loss of security in a growing number of regions around the world, referred to as *zones grises*. The latter are characterized as regions where state legitimacy and the rule of law have broken down. Collapsing states are defined by William Zartman as 'a situation where the structure, authority (legitimate power), law, and political order have fallen apart'. Minc's *zones grises* are on the increase with the greatest concentration in sub-Saharan Africa and the former Soviet Union. In such regions authority and power are increasingly divided between what is left of the formal institutions of the state (which are invariably corrupt), local warlords and gang or mafia leaders.

Minc's *zones grises* are largely composed of states where economic collapse poses a serious threat to basic human security. Human security is here defined as freedom from fear and freedom from want. Poverty, the basic factor undermining human security, not only leaves basic needs unmet, but creates the conditions for conflict and violence, as groups compete for access to scarce and often diminishing resources. The relationship between poverty and conflict is evident when one examines the list of impoverished countries at war or emerging from conflict situations. At the time of writing in March 2000, of the 34 poorest counties in the world, nine were engaged in conflict (Angola, Afghanistan, Eritrea, Ethiopia, Cambodia, Democratic Republic of Congo, Rwanda, Sierra Leone and Somalia), while twelve (Burundi, Central African Republic, Chad, Djibouti, Haiti, Liberia, Mali, Mozambique, Niger, Nigeria, Uganda and Yemen) are currently undergoing the fragile process of transition from conflict to peace.

The majority of countries engaged in conflict are based in sub-Saharan Africa where development has failed to take hold. According to the World Bank, the minimum requirement for a basic standard of living is an annual income of $370. In 1998 the average per capita income in sub-Saharan Africa (excluding South Africa) was $316 per annum, life expectancy at birth was 50 years, infant mortality was 92 per 1000 live births and illiteracy was 40 per cent of the population over the age of 15. The average annual growth of real gross domestic product has fallen from 2.5 per cent between 1985 and 1989 to 1.9 per cent between 1990 and 1997 (Table 8.1).

Table 8.1   Average annual percentage rate of growth in selected sub-Saharan African countries

Country	1975–84	1985–9	1990–7
Angola	–	4.7	−1.6
Burundi	3.8	5.1	−2.8
Cameroon	8.5	−0.1	−0.9
Congo, Democratic Republic	−0.3	1.7	−6.7
Ethiopia	–	4.1	3.5
Gambia	4.3	3.3	2.4
Kenya	4.7	5.9	2.1
Liberia	0.1	−1.2	–
Mozambique	–	6.0	4.2
Rwanda	6.8	2.9	−5.5
Sierra Leone	2.0	0.8	−3.3
Sudan	2.6	0.9	–
Zambia	0.2	2.3	−0.4

Source: World Bank Data 1998.

Facing extremes of economic deprivation and threats to basic human security (life, food, shelter, income) the widespread resort to arms within sub-Saharan Africa can be understood as a 'Darwinian' bid for survival. In the absence of a state that is able to provide basic safety-nets or basic security individuals or communities will resort to their own solutions. Survival takes a variety of forms from sporadic and localized banditry, as in Mozambique where ex-combatants have failed to secure employment in civilian life and returned to the use of the gun as a means of survival, to the violent and organized crime of South Africa, where mugging, car hijacking and burglary are popularly referred to as 'distribution by other means'. Alternatively it has taken on a more structured form, as in the case of warlordism in Somalia, representing as it does an alternative structure of economic and political power, in the absence of a state.

In some cases these new centres of authority have adopted organizational forms that represent alternative forms of government. Although they engage in activities declared illegal by the formal state, many of their functions imitate the characteristics of formal state activities. Authority is exercised through established power structures and obedience is rewarded and disobedience punished often with the use of violence. The pervading culture of violence undermines attempts at conflict resolution and peace-building. Under such circumstances the risks to life and property have grown substantially. This situation is compounded by the ready availability and abundant flows of small arms.

The spread of warlordism is widespread within sub-Saharan Africa where warlords are often engaged in a struggle for control over strategic assets such as mines or oil (Sierra Leone, DRC, Liberia, Angola). In this pursuit, warlords often secure support from multinational companies that have a vested interest in maintaining access to profitable natural resources. Multinational companies operating in regions of conflict are also known to hire the services of mercenary groups such as Executive Outcomes and Sandline who often secure payment in lucrative mining concessions. In this manner international capital rewards and reinforces the indigenous structures of violence, enhancing militarized solutions to resource disputes and often inadvertently undermining legitimate state or international resolutions to conflict. Mercenary groups which profit well out of such disputes have few incentives to seek a peaceful resolution to conflict.

The resort to violence, while benefiting certain militarized actors, interrupts normal economic activity, inhibits inward investors and increases the sense of personal insecurity and tension within these societies and regions. But far from being the irrational responses as some liberal scholars would have us believe, these 'postmodern' forms of violence are in fact highly rational in a situation of economic scarcity where there are few choices in terms of survival.

As these organizations become established and flourish they have developed their own trade and communications networks that operate outside the formal global economy but have become an enduring feature of globalization. The economic activities of warlords and organizations such as the Russian Mafia and the Colombian drug cartels have rapidly developed into powerful and clandestine transnational networks with operations in the international drugs trade, prostitution and illicit arms business. The international linkages between powerful criminal groups are as much a feature of the current structures of globalization as are the formal linkages through which legal economic transactions take place.

The means of destruction in the periphery

One of the factors contributing to the intensity of violence and to the growing levels of physical insecurity in the growing number of *zones grises* around the world is the increased availability of arms, particularly small arms.

As a result of the downsizing of military forces since the end of the Cold War there has been a cascading of surplus or second-hand weapons on to the global market much of which has found its way into intra-state conflicts, especially in those situations where the state has ceased to exert control. The widespread proliferation of small arms is particularly alarming, as they are responsible for most of the deaths in contemporary intra-state conflicts. Huge numbers of small arms were supplied by the superpowers into conflict zones around the world during the Cold War.

Small arms typically weigh less, cost less, are more portable and less visible than major conventional weapons. Weapons in this class do not require extensive logistical and maintenance capability, and are capable of being carried by a combatant or by a light vehicle. This category includes assault rifles, hand grenades, rocket launchers, landmines and explosives. The mobility and ruggedness of these arms ensure their constant circulation and supply into new conflict situations, which in turn contributes to the duration and intensity of hostilities. Often small arms transfers affect the balance of power between warring factions and are therefore identified as one of the 'triggers' to internal conflict by spreading fear and insecurity – conditions which in turn are largely responsible for the existence of millions of refugees and internally displaced people.

Much of the supply of small arms is legal, but there has been a dramatic rise in illicit trade in weapons. As United Nations embargoes have increased and a growing number of conflicts involve non-state actors, black market suppliers have become important sources of supply. Other sources of illicit supply have been through theft from government arsenals, ambushes designed to seize arms and sub-national groups conducting arms deals with each other. Apart from being used in armed conflict these weapons are increasingly used in armed robberies, hijacking, terrorism, the stealing of livestock, drug trading and smuggling.

Where light weapons are widely distributed in a society, development organizations and humanitarian agencies have found it increasingly difficult to conduct their work which has led to a decrease in donor aid in regions of violence. More generally it has encouraged a general process of disengagement by the major military powers from regions of violent conflict, or to new military strategies that emphasize over-the-horizon engagement which reduces the threat of engagement on the ground.

Globalization and defence production

Although it is predominately small arms which are used in the intra-state conflicts which are proliferating in sub-Saharan Africa, the Balkans and Central Asia, there is also a worrying trend in the proliferation of more conventional weapon systems.

In the past the major military powers considered the unilateral command of high technology weapon systems as a crucial strategic asset. However, with the end of the Cold War budgetary constraints have grown and military technology has rapidly been turned into export commodities. Krause's history of the diffusion of military technology demonstrates that the leading edge in military technology has never been maintained for long periods and that the arms trade has been instrumental in the proliferation of military technology. Periods of qualitative innovation have always been followed by export-driven proliferation. The current situation bears all the hallmarks of a new age of export-driven proliferation, for despite calls for multilateral controls on the arms trade and 'dual-use' technologies, the major military powers are engaged in intensive arms export drives in order to maintain defence industrial capacities.

As competition has become more cut-throat and buyers' power has been enhanced, there has been a qualitative escalation in the transfer of arms and related technologies. Buyers have become increasingly adept at extracting concessions from suppliers eager to secure sales. The more industrially advanced buyers have insisted on the transfer of technological know-how in order to build up their indigenous defence industrial capacity. A number of mechanisms have been developed to facilitate the transfer of technology such as direct industrial offsets, buy-back programmes, joint production and joint development. Through such mechanisms the defence companies in the developing world have become integrated into the growing web of transnational production, supply and service of advanced military technology. At the same time, some of the large defence companies from the major military powers have begun to relocate sub-component production to the more industrialized developing countries in order to take advantage of cheaper factor inputs and better access to local and regional markets. These trends indicate early stages in the globalization of defence production and have raised fears about the security implications of the diffusion of military technology.

At the centre of the current phase of the globalization of the defence sector is the importance of technology as a factor of defence industrial competitiveness and the emergence of civil innovation as the driver of technological change. During the 1970s and 1980s technological advances in IT being driven by commercial market demand began to outstrip military sector innovations. This resulted in the diffusion of civilian technology into defence products rather than vice versa, a trajectory characterized as spin-on, rather than spin-off.

As a result of the adoption of value for money procurement systems military products increasingly rely on a pool of technology deriving from civil industries. With the growing importance of civil or dual use technologies, the traditional demarcation between civil and military production has become increasingly blurred. Commercial rather than military market forces are increasingly determining the geospatial structure of the arms industry. Global restructuring on these lines makes attempts to stem global weapons proliferation ever more complex and challenging.

The paradox of contributing to a more liberal and permissive arms market is that the main military powers have resorted to developing ever more sophisticated military technology in order to maintain a leading edge against the military equipment that they are exporting around the world. This technologically driven arms race has ensured the survival of the armaments culture which was previously nurtured during the Cold War.

The means of destruction at the leading edge

The problems stemming from intra-state conflicts and the proliferation of weapon systems has helped to undermine the general mood of optimism that lay behind US foreign and security policy at the beginning of the 1990s. The ignoble defeat of US peace enforcement operations in Somalia in 1994, the genocide in Rwanda and the unremitting nature of ethnic cleansing in the Balkans has produced a more pessimistic view of the 'new global order' in the late 1990s. Such events have resulted in waning support for humanitarian intervention to halt massive human rights abuses or even genocide. In its place there is growing advocacy for 'conflict management' which appears to be corresponding with an increasingly selective and conditional approach to western powers' funding of interventionist activity.

Academically the mood of pessimism about the deteriorating post-Cold War order has been reflected in the work of scholars such as Robert Kaplan, Matthew Connelly, Paul Kennedy and Samuel Huntington who have collectively painted a grim picture of a future world embroiled in chaos, full of malevolent hordes, intent on destabilizing global law and order and undermining and destroying 'civilized' society. In essence the 'new pessimists' have returned to a pure Hobbesian view of global politics in which the international system is viewed as a state of anarchy where the strong dominate the weak, and only self-protection can guarantee security. Much follows politically, diplomatically and militarily if one accepts such precepts.

Since the routing of US troops from Somalia in 1994 the US public has displayed a deep-seated reluctance to tolerate casualties in overseas operations. In avoiding direct military intervention, much effort and resources have been put into military technologies that enable 'over-the-horizon intervention' which allows military reprisals without committing soldiers to the battlefield. The use of such strategies was exemplified by the cruise missile attacks on Sudan in 1998 and the NATO use of Tomahawk missiles against the Serbs in 1999.

This strategic shift to reliance on over-the-horizon high-tech weaponry is reflected most graphically in the so-called revolution in military affairs (RMA). RMA involves the use of a number of advanced technologies like overhead surveillance, global mapping, instant video-feeds, satellite link-ups, interactive fibre-optic networks, computer simulations, etc. that create the technical ability to fight war with minimum casualties and at arm's length. The power of RMA (at least in theory), lies in its ability to collapse distance by bringing the 'there' here in near real time and with near-verisimilitude – what the US army refers to as the 'fifth dimension' in global warfare.

In theory at least, RMA is designed to create a strategic as well as comparative advantage in the production and utilization of the means of destruction. But it also creates huge military technological asymmetries which may encourage more developing states to resort to weapons of mass destruction as the only guarantor of deterrence against the overwhelming technological superiority of an increasingly isolationist and belligerent United States.

This incongruity has not been lost on certain US politicians. In November 1997 William Cohen, Secretary of Defence, warned: 'Indeed, a paradox of the new strategic environment is that American military superiority actually increases the threat of nuclear, biological and chemical attacks against us by creating incentives for adversaries to challenge us asymmetrically. These weapons may be used as a tool of terrorism against the American people.' In this sense the RMA may create its own 'security dilemma', reducing rather than enhancing national and global security. The perception of threat from the weapons of mass destruction has encouraged US military planners to redefine US nuclear deterrence. The conclusion of a review of the US nuclear posture conducted in 1994 and the reiteration of a Presidential Directive (PD) in 1997 commits the US to maintain a robust triad of strategic forces based on leading edge technologies and in sufficient numbers to double the size of the START 11 force as a hedge against political reversals in the Russian Federation or elsewhere. Such trends indicate a deeply entrenched reluctance to contemplate significantly reduced reliance on nuclear weapons.

With conventional weapons US military planners persist in their preoccupation with long-range precision bombing capabilities, intercontinental ballistic missiles and missile defences, amphibious operations and the use of carrier-based air power, satellites, automated battlefields and cyberwarfare. Such technologies come at a price. As a consequence, the US administration is seeking a substantial increase in military expenditures of $12.6 billion for the financial year 2000, which will take US military expenditure up to $280.8 billion. Some $1.3 billion is for the National Missile Defence (NMD) programme.

If these recent developments in strategic planning are any indication, the coming years may indicate a deepening isolationism and a tendency to grant less importance to arms control and diplomacy in favour of the use of military instruments and sovereign defence. The US fixation with technological solutions to meet the uncertainties of the global security environment seems to provide evidence that the more collective sentiments expressed in the early 1990s are giving way to more traditionalist approaches to international relations.

Resorting to a strategy of rearmament in response to an increasingly insecure and unstable world is unlikely to enhance either global security or indeed the security of the United States itself. While the structural violence of the global systems persists such responses can only exacerbate tensions and instability around the world. What is needed is a radically different approach to both economics and security.

An alternative vision

In the *Human Development Report 1994*[4] the UNDP warned that 'it is not possible for the community of nations to achieve any of its major goals – not peace, not environmental protection, not human rights or democratisation, not fertility reduction nor social integration – except in the context of sustainable development that leads to human security.' The emphasis placed on sustainable development rather than more orthodox economic growth strategies derives from a realization that neoliberal policies of development based on material enrichment as measured by GNP per capita, have not necessarily improved the conditions of the vast majority of the populations of the developing countries of the world. In fact, as this chapter has attempted to show, despite growth in GDP, poverty and deprivation have been on the increase and with them a growing sense of insecurity and violence.

The paradigm of sustainable human development values human life for itself. It does not value life simply because people can produce or consume material goods. Nor does it value one person's life over another. No human being should be condemned to a short life just because they are born in a certain region or country, are a certain race or sex. Development should allow individuals the choice to explore their human potential to the full and to put these capabilities to the best use in the economic, social, cultural and political life of their societies.

The universal right to life is the link which binds the needs of human development today to the development needs of the future, especially the need for environmental preservation and regeneration. The strongest argument for protecting the environment is the ethical need to guarantee to future generations opportunities similar to the ones earlier generations have enjoyed.

The universal right to life is also the common thread which binds the notion of sustainable human development with that of human security. The fear of want and fear from threat are the major factors that contribute to the overwhelming sense of insecurity for the poor and marginalized in the developing world. For far too long the concept of security has been tied to the idea of territorial security or the protection of national interests in foreign policy or as global security from the threat of a nuclear holocaust. These concepts overlooked the fact that for many millions of people the greatest threats to their security come from disease, hunger, unemployment, crime, social conflict, political repression and environmental hazards. In contrast to traditional notions of security which are preoccupied with weapon systems and balance of power politics, human security is concerned with the basic right to life and human dignity.

The elements of human security include economic security, food security, health security, environmental security, personal security, community security and political security, all of which are interdependent. When the security of people is endangered anywhere in the world many other nations are drawn into their predicament. This is because the problems of famine, disease, drug trafficking, terrorism, ethnic disputes and social disintegration know no borders. Their consequences traverse the globe. Thus providing guarantees for human security to those most threatened in their daily lives ensures greater security for all people around the world. Replacing a global economic system which marginalizes and impoverishes people with one that provides sustainable livelihoods is a starting point for guaranteeing human security for all.

As an alternative to the neoliberal model, sustainable human development is intrinsically related to the creation of social stability by virtue of the fact that it seeks to remove discriminatory factors within an economy (sources of conflict) by providing opportunities for all members of society to attain their socio-economic potential. In this sense sustainable human development provides an ethical and normative framework that conforms with certain fundamental universal moral values about the right to life and freedom of choice. It can be viewed as a tool both for economic well-being and for conflict prevention and local, regional and global security.

Sustainable human development fundamentally departs from the neoliberal growth strategies promoted by the Washington institutions. Although there is a clear correlation between material wealth and human well-being, this relationship is noticeably absent in many developing societies which have adopted classical economic growth strategies. The ruthless pursuit of growth for growth's sake has in all too many cases led to increasing levels of income inequality with its attendant low levels of life expectancy, poor levels of literacy and high levels of infant mortality. A virtuous cycle of economic growth and human development arises only when growth is employment generating and when human skills and health improve. In tackling the deprivation of the Third World, the UNDP argues that in future the world must move away from concern with economic growth as an end in itself to one which promotes 'pro-poor growth' through credit for small businesses, access to land and education and better opportunities for those presently marginalized from mainstream economic life.

In the sense in which sustainable human development provides an ethical and normative framework that conforms with certain fundamental universal moral values about the right to life and freedom of choice, it can also be viewed as a tool for conflict prevention and local and regional security. This view is supported by the UNDP's observation that states that spend very little on defence and much more on human development have been more successful at defending their national sovereignty than those spending heavily on arms. By way of illustration, the relatively peaceful experiences of low defence spenders such as Botswana, Costa Rica and Mauritius can be compared with the conflicts afflicting high military spenders such as Iraq, Myanmar and Somalia.

Long-term sustainable development is required not just to alleviate the grinding poverty of the poor, but as a key strategy for conflict

prevention and political stabilization. But current and future development potential is hindered by trade disadvantages, the debt crisis, environmental exploitation and political instability. If these issues are to be
addressed head on, the international community needs to build a more
integrated approach towards the issues of economics, security and development and one that is grounded in a new culture of peace and
security.

Attempts to articulate an alternative value system for the global political economy are to be found in the *Alternative Declaration* produced by
the NGO Forum at the Copenhagen Summit. It lays stress on equity,
participation, self-reliance and sustainable human development. And in
so doing it rejects the economic liberalism accepted by the governments
of the north and south, seeing it as a path to aggravation rather than the
alleviation of the global social crisis.

The recognition of the need to manage economic reforms in such a
way as to enhance rather than undermine political stability has been
forced rather reluctantly on to the agendas of the Washington institutions by the experience of the East Asian crisis. It has opened the
way to an acknowledgement that governments must be fully involved
in defining the reform process and that programmes must be tailored to
a country's particular political and economic circumstances. But if economic inequality as a source of structural violence is to be effectively
challenged, the international institutions need to do far more than
simply tinker with reforms. There needs to be a fundamental transformation of the ideological foundations upon which these institutions
legitimize themselves. Global security will not be enhanced until such
time as the existing economic orthodoxy is challenged and replaced.

Conclusion

As the process of globalization widens the gap between 'winners and
losers' a severe tension is emerging between the centres of wealth and
power that have so far gained from unfettered globalization and broad
sectors of the international community who are condemned to remain
marginalized and impoverished at the periphery of the global system.
These trends are unequivocally contributing to an intensification of
north–south tensions.

In this context the US quest for military technological solutions to
global insecurity reflects an inappropriate and potentially destabilizing
response to many security problems which have their roots in the deep-
seated inequities of the global economic and political system. If we

adhere to von Clausewitz's maxim that war is the continuation of politics by other means, then contemporary conflicts which are rooted in the deep inequalities produced by the global economic system are unlikely to be resolved by military technological solutions. On the contrary, the introduction and use of RMA and a growing reliance on ballistic missile defences and nuclear weapons are likely to make the global security environment more insecure and less stable.

We have entered a difficult phase of transition in which globalization has already had a profound impact on the reordering of the global strategic environment, but this has not dispersed political power to the point where traditional strategic assessments have lost their saliency. Thus we face a world in which classical balance of power assessments combine with elements of a different world. Traditional notions of security are being imposed on a world in which the boundaries between communities are blurred and traditional centres of power diluted. Moreover the methods used to ensure security in one arena are precisely those that undermine it in another.

If the international community is to address the current causes of violence a wholly different approach is required, one that addresses global inequities and recognizes the need for transformational forces that are based on a different value system than those that are at present being promoted through the international institutions.

Globalization, predicated upon the liberal values advocated by the Washington-based institutions, has contributed to the growing insecurities and uncertainties of the new world (dis)order. Economic growth as measured by GDP gains is clearly not a substitute for sustainable human develoment or global political stability, particularly where neoliberal growth strategies perpetuate an unequal distribution of wealth, social instability and conflict. The current absence of any mechanism for redistribution other than the market, raises questions about the compatibility of neoliberal doctrine with the international communities' broader demands for peace, security and basic human rights.

Notes

1. Key texts on globalization include E. Kofman and G. Youngs, *Globalisation: Theory and Practice*, London: Pinter, 1996; A. Giddens, *The Consequences of Modernity*, Cambridge: Polity; D. Held, *Political Theory Today*, Cambridge: Polity, 1991; M. Featherstone, *Global Culture: Nationalism, Globalisation and Modernity*, London: Sage, 1990; D. Harvey, *The Condition of Postmodernity*, Oxford: Blackwell, 1989.

2. R. Gilpin, 'The Economic Dimensions of International Security', in H. Bienen (ed.), *Power, Economics and Security: the United States and Japan in Focus*, Boulder: Westview Press, 1992.
3. A. Minc (1993) *Le Nouvean Moyen Age*, Paris: Gallimard.
4. United Nations Development Programme (1994), *The Human Development Report*, Oxford: Oxford University Press.

9

Labour in the Age of Globalization

Robin Cohen

Let us start with an account of globalization, altered only very slightly for my current purpose.

> The need for a constantly expanding market for their products chases *transnational corporations* over the whole surface of the globe. *They* must nestle everywhere, settle everywhere, establish connections everywhere.
>
> The *transnational corporations have* through *their* exploitation of the world-market given a cosmopolitan character to production and consumption in every country...All old-established industries have been destroyed or are daily being destroyed. They are dislodged by new industries, whose introduction becomes a life and death question for all *developed* nations, by industries that no longer work up indigenous raw material, but raw material drawn from the remotest zones; industries whose products are consumed, not only at home, but in every quarter of the globe. In place of the old wants, satisfied by the products of the country, we find new wants, requiring for their satisfaction the products of distant lands and climes. In place of the old local and national seclusion and self-sufficiency, we have intercourse in every direction, universal interdependence of nations. And as in material, so also in intellectual production...National one-sidedness and narrow-mindedness become more and more impossible...
>
> The *transnational corporations*, by the rapid development of all instruments of production, by the immensely facilitated means of communications, draw all, even the most *undeveloped*, nations into *one world*. The cheap prices of *their* commodities are the heavy artillery with which *they* batter down all Chinese walls, with which *they*

force the *underdeveloped countries'* intensely obstinate hatred to foreigners to capitulate. *They* compel all nations, on pain of extinction, to adopt the *capitalist* mode of production; *they* compel them to introduce what *they* call civilization in their midst, i.e. to become *modernized* themselves. In one word, *they* create a world after *their* own image. (Marx and Engels, 1967/1848: 83–4, amended in italics)

The quote is from the 153-year-old *Communist Manifesto*. I have made a few tactical changes (for 'the bourgeoisie' I've substituted 'transnational corporations'; for 'civilized' nations I've used 'developed'; and for 'barbarian', which in any case was used ironically, I've used the expression 'underdeveloped'). But we can instantly recognize that this is a pretty good account of the process we have come to call 'globalization'.

An obvious question immediately poses itself. If Marx and Engels were so prescient about the likely triumph of the free market and the impulses propelling the globalization of the capitalist mode of production, how come they were so wrong about the capacity of the organized working class to oppose or transcend this outcome? Some may protest that they have not *yet* been proved wrong, that in Mao's immortal words about the significance of the French revolution, 'It's too early to tell'. I will make a few comments that are partly in support of this proposition; however, I think it is impossible to avoid focusing on the story of failure, and a catalogue of disappointed hopes concerning the inability of labour meaningfully to oppose the power of capital.

A flyweight has been put into the same boxing ring as a heavyweight. The story of this unequal contest starts with a brief history.

The Internationals, 1864–1939

In the *Communist Manifesto*, Marx and Engels claimed that the working class had no country, and that it had nothing to lose but its chains. The manifesto concluded with the famous plea: 'Workingmen of All Countries Unite, You Have Nothing to Lose but Your Chains'. The same sexist language was displayed in the formation of the first international organization of workers inspired by the manifesto, the International Working Men's Association (IWMA), founded in 1864.

Though this was an achievement of some note, the Association was split between the followers of the leading socialists and anarchists of the time – Marx, Proudhon, Blanqui and Bakunin. Powerful English and French trade unionists dominated the body and it never spread much beyond Europe in the 8–10 years of its existence. Moreover, support for the organization in Britain was largely determined by the strikes of building workers over the 1859–61 period, when employers threatened to import cheap European labour to break the strikes of those years. This sort of defensive posture was to mark much of the support from sections of the national labour forces. Subsequent labour scholars and political activists grandly described the IWMA as the *First International*, but in truth it was a fairly paltry affair. It lasted just 12 years. Its core membership never exceeded 20 000 while its annual income never exceeded £100 (Boyd et al., 1987: ch. 1).

The *Second International*, which was a more vigorous affair, had an effective life from 1889–1914, when it fell apart under the impact of the nationalism of the First World War. The latter year was the decisive test for worker internationalism. Lenin, Luxemburg and Martov (in a resolution in 1907) had argued that workers should be persuaded not to join their national armies. They reasoned that the coming war was simply a reflection of the inter-imperialist and national rivalries of the European powers: this should be a moment where the decisive battle with capitalism took place. In the event, many of the affiliates of the Second International declared a pacifist position or felt unable to oppose their national governments. The workers themselves lined up in great numbers behind their king, emperor, kaiser or tsar. Many were slaughtered in the battles that followed. Soldiers remained loyal to their nation-states, despite the incompetence and lack of regard for human life of their commanders. In one memorable phrase, the British troops were described as 'lions led by donkeys'. This collapse into nationalism was to be the decisive moment in labour history – a crushing defeat from which the spirit of worker internationalism has never fully recovered.

Under the direction of the Soviets, a *Third International* was formed in 1919, which lasted 20 years to 1939. But the organization become a tool of Soviet foreign policy on the grounds that as only the Soviet Union had achieved a workers' state, all communist forces should defend it. So the labour movements in other countries under the control of the communists became subordinated to the national communist parties in each country. These in turn were subordinate to the Communist Party of the Soviet Union (CPSU), which for much of its existence was subordinate to the whims and direction of Joseph Stalin. Stalin regarded the Third International, also known as the Comintern, as a vehicle for his personal use and he often commanded local parties and unions to take up positions that served Soviet aims, but were not in the interest of the local revolutionaries.

Also formed in 1919 was the *Socialist International*, which organized those parties like the socialist and social democratic parties of Europe that explicitly adopted a 'parliamentary road to socialism'. The organization still survives and is active today, but it is more of a vehicle for discussions between party leaders than trade unionists. Currently it is being used as a forum to promote the idea of a 'third way'.

To complete the history of the Internationals it is worth mentioning that the *Fourth International* was formed during the 1930s as a response to the rising tide of Fascism and Nazism in Europe. Leon Trotsky, one of the founders of the Russian Revolution who went into exile, lent his support to the organization, and it remained a haven for dissident intellectuals, small splinter parties of the left, and for Trotsky's followers. Many of the small militant groups that organize on university campuses worldwide still owe their fealty to the Fourth International.

It is difficult to escape an adverse assessment of the Internationals. They remained rather bureaucratic and top-heavy or, in the case of the Comintern, became perverted for other ends. They were, however, effective in lining up support for anti-colonial and anti-Fascist movements. The creation of the International Brigades to support the Spanish Republicans in the Spanish Civil War owed a lot to the Internationals, while anti-imperialist campaigns in support of the struggles of the Vietnamese and Cuban revolutionaries were also notable. They also provided a rallying point for those who believed in Marx's slogan of proletarian internationalism. Nonetheless, an overall judgement must remain negative. Successes were episodic and fragmentary. The Internationals never constituted an effective force against the transnational corporations, or the nation-state system, let alone world capitalism. They were never seriously in a position to promote world revolution.

The trade union federations

After the Second World War there was, once again, an attempt to reconstitute labour internationalism, this time explicitly through the trade unions. A worldwide body, the Prague-based World Federation of Trade Unions (WFTU) was formed, but this was seen by the US unions to be too close to the Soviets. During the Cold War (1945–89), the Americans were obsessed with the idea that any international body with progressive ends could be penetrated by the Soviets and turned into a pro-Soviet tool. Led by the formidable George Meany, a powerful US trade union leader, the Americans pulled out of WFTU and formed the Brussels-based International Confederation of Free Trade Unions (ICFTU). In his parting shot, Meany rather coarsely suggested that the WFTU were a 'bunch of queers [gays] and commies'. Later, the British and non-communist French trade unions joined the ICFTU, increasingly leaving the WFTU as the rump organization mainly, if not exclusively, organizing unions in the communist countries.

The two big trade union federations slugged it out throughout the period of the Cold War, trying to win allies to their sides. Nominally, the WFTU still linked itself to the tradition of proletarian solidarity established by the Internationals, while the ICFTU proclaimed the virtues of 'non-political' trade unionism. However, as far as many Third World unions were concerned, they cared little about the ideological differences between the two sides and simply traded their loyalties in response to favours, overseas invitations and offers of financial support.

Other conventional forms of labour internationalism

The labour movement has also set up other kinds of complementary bodies to the Internationals and the trade union federations. Some bodies were set up on *religious* grounds, like the International Federation of Christian Trade Unions. Others, like the Organization of African Trade Union Unity, were set up on *regional* grounds. Since the mid-1960s, World Corporation Councils (WCCs) have been organized in a number of *companies* – so, for example, there are WCCs in General Motors, Ford, Philips, Michelin, Nestlé, Shell and Unilever. Finally, whereas the basis for organization of the WCCs was by company, another more vigorous strand of labour internationalism was organized by *sector or trade*, thus their designation as 'International Trade Secretariats' (ITSs) There are fourteen ITSs.

Labour in the global age

Has the old story of dreams, fragmented organizations and failure continued into the age of globalization? Certainly, Munck and Waterman (1998: 4) are blunt about the difficult straits in which the labour movement finds itself:

> The trade union movement internationally has been increasingly stymied or peripheralized by a series of interlocking crises. One is the on-going world economic crisis. Another is the uneven transition from an industrial to an information phase of capitalist development. A third is the deleterious effect on labour and unions of the economic

policies of neo-liberalism. A fourth is the collapse of Communism and Thirdworldism (radical nationalism), two major international projects with which major union tendencies have been allied. A fifth is the gradual decline of the reformist option traditionally associated with labour and social democratic parties. The last is globalization – economic, social and cultural – which seems to be undermining the very nation state to which labour's hopes have been pinned and to which it seems to be tied.

Their negative assessment was echoed by one of the union federations, the World Confederation of Labour. According to their Report on Trade Union Rights (www.cmt-wcl.org), notwithstanding country variations, globalization has led to:

• the dismantling of labour laws;
• labour market flexibility with many more workers in precarious situations;
• a rise in unemployment, generating social exclusion;
• an expansion of the free trade zones, shifting power to the transnational corporations;
• repression of the trade unions, including an erosion of the right to strike;
• the violation of a wide range of ILO conventions including safety at work, and minimum wages.

These negative assessments have nonetheless been accompanied by more optimistic visions of the future. Hope springs eternal to those still committed to the labour movement and the struggle for socialism.

Eight positive developments

On what are these hopes based? Can the labour movement recover or discover itself 'as a moral force for progress'. A number of writers (cf. Munck and Waterman, 1998: ch. 1) point to eight developments in support of this proposition:

New realism

In Europe and the USA there is recognition that 'a new realism' is needed. Old tactics, organizational modes and objectives are being changed as the politics of production gives way to a recognition that unionists share many objectives with other consumers. Unions, for example, co-operate in attempts to stop price-fixing and cartels. They are also important allies in struggles to prevent the further erosion of public services like health care, education and transport. These struggles are not only at the point of production, but at the points of reproduction and consumption.

Accepting flexibility

Unions have recognized that flexible specialization means that all labour forces are far more heterogeneous and that not all the new work arrangements are negative. Opening out more secure spaces for those with family commitments or those that seek rewards other than those accruing from a full-time job can be an important way of protecting workers in the new conditions they face.

Women workers

Women workers worldwide, but particularly those in the newly industrialized countries (NICs) and the export processing zones (EPZs) have pioneered forms of struggle that link workers to the community. Issues of child care, the provision of training for economic independence and the alteration of old patriarchal ways are as much part of the women's demands as improved wages.

Political interventions

Labour movements have found their feet in terms of their post-Cold War political interventions. The most notable case of worker involvement in a political transition is the *Solidarity* movement in Poland, which started in the Gdansk shipyards. Moreover, workers have played notable roles in the pro-democracy movements in the Philippines, Brazil, South Africa, Indonesia, South Korea and Nigeria. Unions in these countries have become vocal, vital and resilient parts of civil society.

Trade secretariats

The ITSs have launched a number of successful global campaigns in recent years. For example, the International Transport Workers' Federation protested against the practice of ship owners using Flags of Convenience (registering their ship in places like Liberia and Panama) which led to lax labour and safety regulations. With dockers acting in support, the protests resulted in a substantial number of new crewing agreements with ship owners that protected seafarers from all over the world.

Better communications

With the help of easier and cheaper communications union-to-union contacts across borders (called 'grassroots internationalism') have mushroomed. Unionists are rapidly establishing a global 'labournet'. This is intended to lead to 'on-line company councils', an international labour university, a global labour press and an early-warning network identifying places where violations in trade union rights are taking place. For Lee (1997), the spirit of Marx's International will be reborn on the Internet.

Grassroots initiatives

Unions have reached out to international contacts either on a union-to-union basis or using the good offices of the international trade secretariats. The Teamsters' Union of the USA have linked up with the Finnish union to oppose Huhtamaki, a Finnish food corporation, moving its business from Illinois. US workers in a tyre plant used their ITS (the International Federation of Chemical, Energy, Mine and General Workers' Unions) to oppose the anti-union conduct of their Japanese employers, Bridgestone. The US telecommunications company, Sprint, closed its plant in San Francisco after workers there said they wanted to join a union. Workers employed by the company in Spain, France and Germany brought pressure on Sprint to reverse the decision. Liverpool dockers protesting against privatization and casualization sent delegates to Bilbao in Spain and ports in Canada. One major US container company had to leave the port under threat of boycotting their ships by US longshoremen.

ICFTU

With the diversions of the Cold War in the past, the major surviving trade union federation, the ICFTU, has recruited many unions in the former Soviet bloc, approached unions in China and has made significant interventions to internationalize 'labour standards' and protect workers in those areas. The ICFTU has proposed that a 'social clause' be inserted in all trade agreements. The four key ICFTU proposals (www.icftu.org) provide a useful benchmark, arguing that: 'While international labour standards do not necessarily mean global minimum wages and working conditions, unions have to stop governments trying to gain competitive advantage through the repression, discrimination and exploitation of workers.' The ICFTU is now effectively the only show in town and nominally organizes 175 million workers.

Labour and the 'new' social movements

The international labour movement has explored innovative forms of action in recent years. Unions in Brazil, South Africa and the Philippines have sought to fuse traditional interventions at the point of employment or in the public sphere with the new social movements' interventions at the level of civil society – including joint actions with the women's, human rights, peace and environmental movements (Cohen and Rai, 2000). The result is a hybrid strategy described as 'social movement unionism'.

The expression 'social movement unionism' is used to suggest that the trade unions have not only to ally with the other social movements but also, Waterman (1998: 20–1) argues, to 'incorporate their demands' and 'respond to their new organization forms and practices'. He continues: 'This proposal recognizes that those who labour for, or under capitalism do not only exist for and identify with wage labour and as wage labourers. They are also urban residents, women, have ethnic or racial identities, need peace, a healthy environment, etc.'

This recognition of the complexity of a worker's identity under contemporary capitalism is a major breakthrough for the 'old' labour movement. It signifies an appreciation that there are more ways to skin the capitalist cat (or at least shorten one of its many lives) than acting solely at the point of production in the form of a strike or walkout. Alongside union power are such important tactics as consumer boycotts, the organizations of shareholders, political and media campaigns, and demands for health care, education, nursery provision or human rights. Unions increasingly have to recognize that the globality and mobility of capital and its capacity to free itself from territorial constraints mean that the old forms of action are not always effective.

Conventional labour protests: relocation

This is not to say that the days of more conventional labour protest are over. While this is largely true in the mature economies, even there we have to remember that sudden manifestations of militancy – for example in the transport industries in France in 1997 or at General Motors' plants in Michigan in 1998 – can still cause much disruption. While the mobility of capital has generally served to diminish the political clout of labour in Europe and North America, there has been a marked growth of labour activism in the NICs, in 'transitional societies' (those moving from official communism to capitalism) and in the periphery. These trends are given powerful empirical support in the Database of Labour Unrest compiled by scholars at the Fernand Braudel Center, Binghamton University, USA. Their data are based on a contents and statistical analysis of reports in the *New York Times* and *The Times* (London) from 1870–1990. One of the principal researchers, Silver (1995: 183), summarizes the results of her extensive research as follows:

> During the 1950s and 1960s – the decades of solid US hegemony – labour unrest declined world-wide... But, with the sharp intensification of inter-capitalist competition in the 1970s, as western Europe and Japan caught up with the US economic lead, old conflict containment strategies have ceased to function. Co-optation has become too expensive and has been replaced, in the core, by geographical relocation, restructuring, and union busting... In the periphery and semi-periphery, the result has been escalating conflict. The map of labour unrest waves for 1986–90 shows widespread conflict in the East and South. The core (with the exception of Scandinavia) remains untouched.

Case studies of labour protests in the NICs and transitional societies

To bring this account of displaced conflict into the final decade of the twentieth century, it is necessary to rely on journalistic accounts and internet postings on worker movements in the NICs and transitional societies. I will consider Indonesia in the first category and Russia in the second:

Indonesia

In May 1998 the long-ruling dictator of Indonesia, President Suharto, was forced to resign in response to the mounting Asian economic crisis, and demonstrations by students and workers. President Habibie, the new political leader, effected an agreement with the International Monetary Fund to stabilize the country's precarious finances, but strikes and protests continued. According to McInerney (1998), the protests took on a more and more working-class character after Habibie's accession to power. The apparent centre for the workers' movement is in the port of Surabaya, Indonesia's second-largest city, where dockers blocked shipping and demanded that their wages be doubled to US$1.80 a day.

McInerney (1998) further reports that 4000 other workers came out on strike on 22 June in a 'factory complex', while on the same day, 10 000 Kasogi shoe-factory workers demonstrated. The shoe workers tore down trees and blocked roads, while demanding wage rises. The Indonesia Prosperity Trade Union called a demonstration at the Surabaya regional parliament on 25 June 1998 when hundreds of demonstrators called for a 20 per cent workers' shareholding in every Indonesian company, the formation of a national labour organization and an end to the ban on forming unions. In response to this activity, McInerney (1998) contends: 'One thing is clear. The ouster of dictator Suharto in May was only the first page of an unfolding political and economic crisis, one in which the 90 million-strong working class has just begun to intervene politically.'

Russia

According to a statement released by the main international trade union federation, the ICFTU (www.icftu.org), 78 of Russia's 89 regions were involved in labour protests in the first five months of 1998. There were more than 12 000 strikes and stoppages of work at all enterprises, involving about two million people. Altogether about 14 million people took part in one or another form of protest like suspensions of work, strikes at enterprises, processions, meetings, picketing, processions and meetings. There have been occasional hostage-takings of business executives and even calls for the hiring of assassins.

What is the occasion for such activism? The answer is simple – the non-payment of wages. One Russian worker in four (more than 20 million people) is not paid regularly and delays can be as long as six or even twelve months. According to 1998 figures, Russia's wage debt amounts to US$10 billion. In Moscow, 400 enterprises have wage debts. Landsberg (1998) suggests that the government's response can be likened to that of the Roman emperor, Nero, who is said to have fiddled while Rome burned. In the middle of 1998, President Yeltsin appears to have adopted a similar stance in the face of a mountain of debt, social unrest and a collapsing currency. Yeltsin's claim (on 2 July 1998) that 'we have no crisis in Russia' was greeted with particular derision by coal miners camping outside the government building known as the 'White House'. One of the camping miners was 'Yegerov', a 26-year-old working in Vorkuta, a coal-mining outpost above the Arctic Circle. It is so far north, he said, that 'you can't even grow potatoes'. He got his last paycheque in September. Since then, he has lived off his mother's pension. Yegerov claimed that 'Russians are patient', but warned that

'When you roust a bear from his bed, he will smash everything in sight. Such is the case with Russians.'

Is there a revival of social democracy?

Despite the apparent capacity of neoliberalism to sweep all in front of it, in some countries – largely concentrated but not wholly concentrated in the Nordic countries and western Europe – there remains some considerable residue of the historic social democratic settlement between capital and labour. The expression 'social democracy' is often used in an inconsistent and vague way, but I use it here to signify a general commitment to social justice, to retaining or extending the social welfare system, to supporting communities and civil society over and above the individual free-market nexus. Let us give a few concrete examples.

In France, successive governments have substantially refused to dismantle the country's welfare, health and pension plans, while key politicians have denounced an unrestrained belief in the market as perfidious 'Anglo-Saxon economics'. A Socialist government under Lionel Jospin has been elected and welfare-related expenditure remains high.

In the UK and USA, there is much cynicism on the left regarding the political projects of Tony Blair and Bill Clinton. Yet those with just a little historical consciousness can see a substantial difference in both countries compared to the time when Margaret Thatcher and Ronald Reagan performed their transatlantic double act in praise of the invisible hand of the market.

Other places with social democratic parties in power in 1999 comprise Italy, Austria (now reversed), Greece, most of the Nordic/Scandinavian countries and, much more significantly, Germany.

In 1997, for the first time in 20 years, trade union membership is stabilizing. The highest trade union density (the proportion of workers organized) is in Sweden (85 per cent), but figures over 30 per cent are recorded for the Netherlands, UK and Germany. In the Netherlands the main trade union federation has made a special effort to secure members in traditionally unorganized sectors, like part-time workers. As a result it has gained 250 000 members in the last decade (*New Statesman*, 1997: 11, 12).

Throughout the 1980s – when neoliberalism was at its height – the poorest 10 per cent of people in Denmark experienced a real rise in income (while over the same period large declines were noticed in the USA). Similar observations emerge in the case of the Netherlands, where the welfare state appears to be still sufficiently robust to protect the poorest and newest residents.

While a number of Asian countries have suffered severely due to the economic crisis afflicting the region from 1997, it is notable that those with a higher level of social provision and political legitimacy (for example, Hong Kong and Singapore) have suffered less than those that have embraced unconstrained free market principles (for example Thailand and Indonesia).

We do not naïvely suggest that the left has made a major comeback, let alone that it is sweeping all before it. Rather, what these recent examples suggest is that there is more life in the old social democratic settlement than meets the eye. This is not usefully thought of as the 'Third Way' in some naïve ideological sense – a naïveté Giddens (1998) gets close to in his book, *The Third Way*. Self-interest is not far from the surface. On the one hand, the middle classes do not want to pay high taxes and they vote for parties that reduce them. On the other hand, these same indignant voters do not want their cars stolen or their houses robbed. They support free choice in education and health care, but they are nervous in case their savings and insurance cannot fully meet the bills. State provision is seen as a useful backup to *middle-class* choices, rather than simply a residual service for the poor, and recent immigrants. In the Nordic countries and in western Europe there are strong social movements and interest groups supporting the *public* provision of universities, railways, libraries, concert halls, parks and sports centres. In short, while the revived forms of social democracy are not supported in terms of religious or political principle, they are often instrumentally supported. Nonetheless, the poor and disadvantaged can to some degree be protected in this scenario.

Conclusion

In view of the triumph of free market ideology, is there any reason to turn our attention back to the labour movement and its struggles to improve the situation of working people?

Despite the failings of the old labour movement right from the beginning, there was some sense in which the interests of the working class corresponded to a more collective, universal interest. Though they failed, the Internationals and other organs of working-class power tried to organize black and white, young and old, male and female, and third world and first world workers. In the Marxist orthodoxy, the working class was regarded as 'the general representatives of humanity', rather than merely one interest group among many. In the 1970s and 1980s, the labour movement also began to learn from its own mistakes and adopt some of the campaigning techniques of the other global social movements. Shop-floor internationalism, acts of solidarity from the base up rather than from the leadership down, all began an important shift.

On closer examination, it seems that the obituaries for labour protest and its struggles for social justice have been posted prematurely. In the democracy movements of South Korea, Indonesia, Brazil and South Africa, as well as in many 'semi-peripheral' and newly industrializing countries, there is a strong revival of protests by working people. Even in such unlikely settings as post-communist Russia, independent and militant workers have fundamentally challenged the existing political regimes. The sudden financial collapse of many economies in Asia in 1997–8, periodic threats of recession, and unstable currency and stock markets have also stripped the chrome off the neoliberal bumper. Meanwhile, social democratic parties espousing non-state versions of socialism were returned to power in a number of European countries.

Again, in the wake of the collapse of communism in 1989, the burdensome legacy of the Cold War can now be jettisoned. The remaining large federation, the ICFTU, represents 175 million trade union members organized in 206 national trade union centres from 141 countries and territories. It is recruiting very successfully in the newly industrializing countries and has conducted impressive campaigns to support the payment of wages in Russia and the enforcement of international labour standards. The international labour movement is also well placed to profit from the surge in labour militancy in the NICs and transitional economies, where impressive protests and organizations have mushroomed.

Does all this suggest that the international labour movement and the struggle for social justice will be able to make a comeback? Few on the left now believe that the labour movement can alone act as a liberating force for humankind, as Marx had surmised. However, the movement will clearly have an important role acting on behalf of many workers and acting in association with other social movements to further particular campaigns. It is not so much a single revolutionary class, but nonetheless occasionally a valuable ally in the struggle for social justice, public services and democratic rights.

Acknowledgement

This chapter was drafted before I had a chance to examine the contribution on a similar subject by Munck (2000), one which I would heartily recommend to readers.

References

Boyd, Rosalind, Robin Cohen and Peter Gutkind (eds) (1987) *International Labour and the Third World: the Making of a New Working Class*, Aldershot: Avebury.
Cohen, Robin and Shirin M. Rai (eds) (2000) *Global Social Movements*, London: Athlone Press.
Giddens, Anthony (1998) *The Third Way: the Renewal of Social Democracy*, Cambridge: Polity Press.
Landsberg, Mitchell (1998) 'Russian Miners Protests Erupt'. Associated Press dispatch posted at www.icftu.org.
Lee, Eric (1997) *The Labour Movement and the Internet*, London: Pluto Press.
Marx, Karl and Friedrich Engels (1967/1848) *The Communist Manifesto*, Harmondsworth: Penguin.
McInerney, Andy (1998) 'Indonesia: Workers Around the World'. Dispatch posted at www.icftu.org.
Munck, Ronaldo (2000) 'Labour in the Global Era: Challenges and Prospects', in Robin Cohen and Shirin M. Rai (eds), pp. 83–100.
Munck, Ronaldo and Peter Waterman (eds) (1998) *Labour Worldwide in the Era of Globalisation: Alternative Union Models in the New World Order*, Basingstoke: Macmillan.
New Statesman (1997) *The 1998 Trade Union Guide*, London: the New Statesman in association with Neil Stewart Associates.
Silver, Beverly J. (1995) 'World-Scale Patterns of Labor-Capital Conflict: Labor Unrest, Long Waves, and Cycles of World Hegemony', *Review* (Fernand Braudel Center), 18 (1), pp. 155–92.
Waterman, Peter (1998) *Globalization, Social Movements and the New Internationalisms*, London: Mansell.
www.icftu.org
www.cmt-wcl.org

10
The Sustainability of Welfare States: Reshaping Social Protection[1]

Gosta Esping-Andersen

Introduction: a diagnosis of the ills of contemporary welfare states

Social protection systems mirror prevailing conceptions of social risks. During the postwar phase of welfare state construction in the rich countries, the principal risks were seen as concentrating among the aged and large child families. Social policy became biased in favour of pensions, health care and family allowances. The reigning assumption was that families and labour markets would, for most people most of the time, secure adequate welfare; that market and family 'failure' was limited. Families were stable and could be assumed to provide for their own caring needs via the full-time housewife, and via the resources that came from a stably employed male breadwinner. Even low-skilled workers enjoyed strong real income growth up until the mid-1970s, and this meant also expanding welfare state finances.

Postwar welfare models were, perhaps, premised on a similar understanding of the risk structure, but not on best practice. Besides the well-known differentiation between universalistic flat-rate protection, social insurance and targeted assistance, welfare states also diverged in terms of their basic assumptions about *potential market and family failure*. The Nordic countries exemplify the idea that private welfare is inherently inegalitarian and inadequate, and should therefore be supplanted by comprehensive public protection. The thrust towards public services to families since the 1960s was partly a campaign in favour of women's employment and equality, and partly an effort to minimize the unequal resources that stem from family background. The Anglo-Saxon nations' more residual and targeted approach to social protection mirrors their assumption that market failure problems are generally limited to specific risks, like single mothers, who have objective difficulty making ends meet in normal markets.[2] And the continental European systems (with Japan), largely premised on employment-based social insurance, are explicitly 'familialistic' in the sense that they assume that, once guaranteed incomes, families will and can absorb most welfare responsibilities. Likewise, most Anglo-Saxon systems have assumed that markets can meet most needs for most of the population.

There is a parallel differentiation in nations' approach to employment protection. The typical continental European approach has been to safeguard the individual worker's job via strict regulation of hiring and firing rules (what is usually termed 'rigidities'). Since families have been assumed to depend uniquely on their prime earner, his job security was clearly of paramount importance. Officially, rigid labour markets always have their offsetting flexibilities. In continental Europe, early retirement has been the chief instrument of labour force adjustment. The small, open economies, like those of Scandinavia and the Netherlands, opted for an alternative design, namely to insure workers via public welfare rather than job-guarantees and, mainly in Scandinavia, also via active labour market policies. The objective here was to harmonize the quest for 'equality' and security with the need for flexible labour force adaptation. Again, the Anglo-Saxon group is distinctive for its deregulated approach to wage setting and labour market clearing – especially since the early 1980s.

It is broadly agreed that all welfare state models today face a profound crisis. As commonly diagnosed, their growing unsustainability derives from three simultaneous *exogenous* shocks, all basically related to economic and societal transformation. The first, and possibly most widely cited, is the impact of economic internationalization. This includes three components, each of which has different effects. Financial globalization does not, *per se*, affect welfare state viability or its redistributive aims *if*, that is, its finances are in order and a reasonable level of savings can be assured.[3] Capital mobility may undercut employment in uncompetitive industries and may put pressures on governments to reduce taxation and labour costs and raise social dumping. The evidence on this is, however, rather mixed. Global trade and the globalization of technological change weakens the position of low-skilled workers who, with youth and women, are the main constituents of contemporary mass-unemployment.

For the welfare state, then, the main challenge that emanates from globalization is the need to maintain sound public finances, and to manage the increasingly precarious position of poorly educated workers. The view that ambitious welfare aims are incompatible with the new global order is not persuasive. Indeed, the principal reason why the

Nordic countries are welfare state leaders is that they were *always* open economies. Historically, the chain of causality ran the *opposite* way: small, open economies adopted strong welfare states with a 'productivist' edge as a means to enhance their capacity to compete, adjust rapidly to global forces beyond their control and, above all, to persuade their labour force to acquiesce (Cameron, 1984; Katzenstein, 1985).

The second welfare state shock comes from population ageing or, rather, declining fertility. Most prognoses suggest that the cost of retirement as a percentage of GDP will double by 2040 (OECD, 1988). The ratio of contributors to beneficiaries of pensions is rapidly deteriorating. The number of contribution years has shrunk, the number of beneficiary years expanded.[4] Italy is the first country to arrive at parity 1:1. Equally alarming is the growth of the highly care-intensive, ultra-aged (80+) population which is doubling every twenty to thirty years. The problem of ageing lies less in the number of old people, and more in low fertility, early retirement, delayed first-job entry, and low overall employment rates. It makes a huge difference for welfare states' financial prospects whether fertility rates are low (1.2 or 1.4, as in Italy, Spain, Germany, or Japan), or higher, at about 1.8–2.0 (as in Scandinavia, Ireland, and North America). It also makes a difference whether the typical retirement age is at 55–58, as in continental Europe, or 60–65, as in Scandinavia. What really counts is the activity rate. In the Nordic countries the ratio of contributors to pension recipients is around 2.5:1 even if the proportion aged is roughly similar to Italy. This is chiefly because employment-population rates are high (70–75 per cent): 10–20 percentage points above countries like France, Germany, or Italy. The real problem, then, is how to stimulate fertility and maximize employment.[5] The ageing problem in continental Europe is especially acute because of the preference for a reduction in labour force participation as a strategy to manage industrial decline.

The third shock comes from family change and the new economic role of women. Families are much less stable and women often face severe trade-offs between employment and family obligations. Given that women's educational attainment today matches (and surpasses) that of men, the opportunity cost of having children becomes very high (if care services are unavailable). The new, 'atypical' family forms (especially single parent families) are often highly vulnerable to poverty. In contrast, two-income households are a vastly superior hedge against child poverty. In all cases, the marginal cost to families of having children is rising. If not counteracted, the result is low fertility. There is little doubt that almost all Scandinavian women work *and* have children (the rate is 80 per cent among mothers with small children) because of ample day care provision. Two-earner households have become the norm, thus assuring fertility and low poverty. Here it is mainly labour market earnings that matter, but to get the labour market to work, heavy public subsidies for women are a precondition.[6]

The emerging 'post-industrial' structure of risk

Socio-economic change over the past decades has drastically changed the distribution of social risks. Poorly educated workers can no longer count on strong earnings and, together with young people and – to a large extent also – women, they face the acute trade-off between welfare and jobs. Family instability promotes often dramatic poverty risks among children even if today large child families are virtually extinct. As illustrated in Table 10.1, the incidence of risk has shifted towards young households.

The paradox today is that the bias towards the *ageing* of many welfare states continues to strengthen all the while that family instability, declining earnings, rising poverty, and unemployment shift the incidence of risk towards the *young*. Measured in terms of the distribution of social expenditure, the age-bias is especially extreme in countries such as Japan, the US and in most of continental Europe.[7] A shift in priorities towards young families is, in contrast, limited to a few welfare states, mainly the Nordic and the Antipodean ones. Indeed, due to very generous income support, but mainly to higher employment rates (and dual

Table 10.1 Trends in social risk structure, 1980s–1990s (percentages)

	Poverty trends child families	Youth not at work or school	Growth of no-work households	Trend in net income (young HH)	Youth/ adult unemployment ratio
Australia	18	7.6	−4.4	2.2	+12
Canada	17	2.2	−1.8	1.9	−2
US	20	1.2	−9.5	2.8	+80
Denmark	12	0.7	−10.9	1.8	−10
Sweden	–	3.2	−15.8	2.2	−42
France	22	2.8	−8.9	2.4	+30
Germany	13	1.5	−1.9	1.0	+20
Italy	30	4.6	−4.8	3.7	–
Netherlands	13	7.8	−5.9	2.0	+31

Source: Figures taken from Esping-Andersen (1999), originally from LIS and OECD.

income households), the Nordic countries are the only ones where poverty rates are declining, *notwithstanding* falling earnings and unemployment. The age-bias can also be seen from trends in income. While, on average, net incomes in young families has declined by 7.4 per cent over the past decades, it has risen by 2.1 per cent among pensioner households.

In parallel fashion, the tension between careers and family responsibilities, the rise of single-parent households, and longer life expectancy all contribute to an intense demand for social and caring services. Nonetheless, most welfare states (with the exception of Scandinavia and, partially, France and Belgium) are service-averse and very biased towards social transfers. The private market can be a substitute *only* if costs are moderate. For a median income family, the markets for child care and other social services are a realistic option in the US, but not in Europe. Low-income families are priced out of the welfare market *everywhere*. And this is serious, because it is above all here that additional female labour supply might lower poverty risks.[8]

In brief, with few exceptions we are witnessing a growing disjuncture between the emerging structure of need and the organization of the welfare state. In the discourse of globalization we have 'foodist' welfare states in 'postindustrial' societies.

Divergent adaptation scenarios

The shifting structure of needs and the exogenous shock-effects on the welfare state have been growing in intensity over the past two decades. Until recently, at least in Europe, the bulk of family and market failures were absorbed by welfare states, implying mounting public deficits and debt. In extreme cases, like Belgium, Italy and Greece, the cost of managing the new political economy has produced debt ratios in excess of 100 per cent of GDP.[9] The predominant response, so far, mainly reflects a logic of institutional path-dependency, not merely because institutions are sturdy, but also because the median voter (growing older every year) is dedicated to the retention of accustomed benefits. The median voter, and his/her representative organizations, have a stake in perpetuating the kind of welfare state that prevailed in the 1960s. His/her interests are focused on pensions and health care, much less on family benefits, maternity leave or youth activation programmes. Hence, the reigning profile of welfare state adjustment is being sustained on the least unpleasant diet of policy options.

We can distinguish welfare state models or, better, 'welfare regimes', by how they allocate social responsibilities between state, market and family (and, as a residual, non-profit 'third sector' institutions). In one group (essentially the liberal, Anglo-Saxon nations) the emphasis is on a residual, minimal state and 'as much market as is possible'. Although there has been some (in practice modest) privatization of the welfare state, the most notable trend is to increase targeting. A common feature among the liberal welfare states is the introduction of some form of negative-income-tax plan as a way to provide a minimum income floor for the poor and low-wage workers, while strengthening incentives among the better-off to purchase private welfare.[10] Yet, it is not clear at all whether 'the market' has responded adequately. Apart from the huge gap in American health coverage (43 million), there is a more ominous long-term erosion of what has, traditionally, been the main-stay of private social protection: employers' occupational plans.[11] These are declining in part because of the cost containment strategies of employers, in part because of the decline of trades unions (see Cohen's chapter here), and finally also for structural reasons (most new employ-ment is in services and smaller firms). Hence, in the United States, there is a clear drift from collective risk-pooling towards *individual* market solutions in pensions, health and in services.[12] In any case, whether marketed welfare follows the 'occupational' or the individualized model, it typically requires public subsidies – such as generous tax treatment – if it is meant to expand beyond the top quintile earners.

The second group includes the prototypical Scandinavian, universalis-tic welfare states whose stated aim has always been to marginalize the market in the provision of welfare. Since the 1960s there has also been a deliberate attempt to 'nationalize' the family, as Assar Lindbeck puts it; that is to collectivize families' traditional caring burdens. The Nordic welfare states have become very service heavy: 30–35 per cent of total social outlays go to servicing as opposed to 5–15 per cent on the European continent. The servicing emphasis is doubly important for labour market functioning. It allows for record high female employment (with fertility) and it creates – until recently – an expanding labour market, mainly for these very same women. Since around 1970, public services have ac-counted for 80 per cent of total net growth in jobs. The Nordic welfare states have also been more ready to adapt to the changing needs profile by redirecting resources and by expanding *public* programmes for young families: with parental leave and active labour market policies in particu-lar. If the liberal welfare regimes have undergone an individualization of welfare, the Nordic ones have clearly expanded the realm of collective provision. The little comparative evidence we have shows that the infor-mal, non-profit sector plays a very small role in Scandinavia (Salamon and Anheimer, 1996).[13] So does family-provided welfare services. One way to estimate this is to look at time-budget data. The average weekly 'unpaid domestic work time' of a Danish woman is 25 hours in contrast to about 35 hours in Germany and the UK, 45 hours in Italy, and a whopping 50 hours in Spain (Esping-Andersen, 1999). Yet, Danish women have more children than in any of the other nations! Scandinavia has clearly been most capable of adapting and redesigning the welfare state to address the emerging new structure of needs. It is, however, increasingly difficult to sustain them financially. Paying equal wages for low-productivity services means a creeping cost-disease. Subsidizing women's permanence in the labour market *and* their high fertility is extremely expensive. In a highly controversial study, Sumner Rosen estimates that the total cost of maintaining working mothers with small children in Sweden is 50 per cent higher than the value they produce (Rosen, 1997). Even if we doubt this estimate, there is little doubt that the costs of securing adequate fertility rates in today's society can be steep indeed.

The third group is composed of most continental European countries, characteristic for their employment-linked (and therefore heavily male) social insurance and for their reliance on family care (the Catholic subsidiarity principle). Private welfare plans are usually very marginal and so also, strangely enough, is 'third sector' welfare (with the notable exception of Germany, where a significant share of health care is run by non-profit associations). Despite the active attempts of the Church to assert its dominance in the field of care and social assistance, Italy scores the lowest in available international rankings of third-sector size.[14] There is a unique continental European model of welfare state adaptation that combines two basic elements: first, the utilization of pension plans (and other labour reduction policies) as *the* main instrument of managing industrial reconversion. The underlying strategy has been to safeguard the wages and job security of the core (male) workforce and to finance the cost of pensioning-off excess labour via the anticipated productivity dividend of a 'high-quality production strategy', to use Soskice's term. The second element is not so much 'adaptation' as continuing to delegate emerging new social problems to families. One manifestation of this familialism is the sustenance of the unemployed: in Italy, 81 per cent of the young unemployed (aged 20–29) continue to live with their parents (compared with 8 per cent in Denmark).[15] The net consequences of this combined adaptation model can be summarized as follows: an overloaded and unsustainable social insurance system; a 'low-fertility equilibrium'; and a reinforcement of the insider–outsider cleavage in the labour market. High labour costs and pervasive job protection for the insiders (adult males) causes unemployment among their children and wives. In relying on the sole male breadwinner income, families (and thus unions and the median voter) act rationally in resisting both labour market deregulation, more wage flexibility and any erosion of social insurance benefits. Familiarizing welfare responsibilities can be as costly as collectivizing them.

The search for a sustainable win-win strategy

From this very cursory overview it is evident that all welfare states have responded to the new economic and social challenges by 'muddling through', by building on traditional premises rather than by radically redesigning their welfare architecture.[16] Most welfare states, therefore, have moved from a positive-sum to a negative-sum trade-off. They are not only increasingly unsustainable but are arguably hindering an optimal institution combination of welfare and efficiency. The Nordic model, although clearly the most adaptable to the new political economy, has become fiscally unsustainable because it was premised on universal full employment and cannot cope with mass unemployment; and also because of the inbuilt 'Baumol cost-disease' effect (see footnote 8) that, in the long haul, afflicts the cost of providing an immense network of social services. The liberal model, despite its low social expenditures but because of deregulation, is increasingly hard put to address growing inequalities and poverty. A monumental increase of non-old age *post-transfer* poverty has occurred in *all* the liberal welfare states since the early 1980s, especially in families with children in the US and Britain. Rising poverty is concentrated in two (growing) strata: single parent households and among the less-skilled. Public benefits may be modest, but so are also expected earnings. The liberal model is therefore vulnerable to poverty entrapment, and tends to reproduce both poverty and a low-skilled 'post-industrial proletariat'. And, as we have noted, continental Europe faces probably a worst-scenario negative-sum relation between welfare, employment and fertility.

It is therefore hardly surprising that most today believe that a radical overhaul, an entirely new welfare principle, is urgently needed. If we follow the diagnosis of insecurities presented in the beginning of this paper, any realistic win-win strategy must satisfy three aims: create employment (especially for youth, women and the less skilled), raise fertility, and protect families with young children. In the last section, I argue that the prevailing, purportedly 'win-win', strategies that are currently entertained (and often even followed) are not capable of simultaneously optimizing the three aims.

Let us firstly examine the single most popular strategy: privatizing welfare and deregulating labour markets. Although the US remains the *only* truly convincing case where deregulation generates jobs and minimizes unemployment, it is still arguable that less job protection and more flexible wages is positive for employment; at least for youth and the low skilled. It is, however, not a win-win model because employment is traded off against heavy social costs of poverty and wage inequality. Moreover, Europeans may be trapped in long-term unemployment, but Americans tend to become trapped in poor jobs and poverty, and this has powerful inter-generational effects in terms of life chances (OECD, 1996; Esping-Andersen, 1999). Hence, the system is not superior as far as equity and equal opportunities is concerned. Privatizing welfare, moreover, does not necessarily result in improvements in allocative efficiency. The reasons emerge when we contrast two welfare state extremes: Sweden and the US. As shown in Table 10.2, we find

Table 10.2   Public and private social protection spending

	Sweden	United States
	As percentage of GDP	
Public social expenditure, 1990	33.1	14.6
Private education	0.1	2.5
Private health (1)	1.1	8.2
Private pensions (1)	1.8	3.0
Total	36.1	28.3
	As percentage of private household expenditure, 1990	
Private health, education and pensions	2.7	18.8
Day care (child families)	1.7	10.4
Total	4.4	29.2
Taxes	36.8	10.4
Total + Taxes	41.2	39.6

Sources: OECD, *National Accounts. Detailed Tables* (1994); US Bureau of Labour Statistics, *Consumer Expenditures in 1990*.
(1) Private health data for Sweden are for 1992; American data include 'other social welfare'. Private pensions for Sweden are estimated from employer pension benefits in the OECD national accounts. Swedish tax data are from *Statistisk Aarsbok, 1994. Table T 226*. US private pensions and health expenditure data are from *Social Security Bulletin, Annual Statistical Supplement*, 1992, Table 3A4.

convergence in terms of total resource use at both the macro and micro-accounting level. The American model is far from Pareto-efficient, however, when we consider the huge gaps in coverage and that health care absorbs almost twice as much of GDP as it does in Sweden.[17] A final and fundamental reason why privatization is problematic is that all but individual insurance is increasingly unrealistic in the emerging economic structure. Collective welfare plans could thrive in an environment of large firms and powerful unions, but in a service-dominated, down-scaled economic structure they are much more difficult to establish.

A second, increasingly popular, strategy involves some form of a guaranteed citizens' income. For fiscal reasons, and to avoid negative work incentives, this almost invariably takes the form of a negative income tax (like the family credit). In reality, a basic citizens' minimum is the favoured solution among two very dissimilar groups. One, mainly on the European left, sees it as the answer to the emerging 'workless society' and, in fact, it is frequently accompanied by proposals to reduce the working week. But its underlying 'lump-sum of labour' assumption is blatantly erroneous. The liberal version, now becoming institutionalized in many nations, follows a very different philosophy, namely one of giving income support *and* work incentives simultaneously to low-income families. It is a means of subsidizing low-wage workers, but also low-wage employers. It would therefore slow down growth in productivity, and may even reinforce a low-skill equilibrium problem if not accompanied by active education and training policies.

There has, in the past decade, evolved a growing interest in the 'third sector' as an alternative to public sector welfare provision. There are several potential advantages: unloading burdensome government finances, decentralizing welfare delivery, and introducing an element of competition. The third sector is an amalgam of many different forms of welfare production, such as voluntary associations, co-operatives and various non-profit organizations. Only one type of organization in the third sector is, in fact, devoted to social welfare production. Where this latter is significant (as in Germany and the US) this is mainly because of the presence of a large network of established non-profit corporations (such as the Blue Shield) or co-operative movements. Otherwise, third sector welfare is typically concentrated on the 'margins' where the welfare state often fails: aid to drug users or clandestine immigrants, for example. The role of voluntary workers can be significant but really viable third sector providers rely on paid personnel and this in turn implies reliance on user fees and public financial support. Hence, as a viable strategy of shifting responsibilities, it is unlikely to bring about substantial savings. Gains will mainly come from increased decentralization and perhaps a stronger element of competition, but a 'third sector' strategy does not help resolve the basic dilemmas as outlined in this chapter.

How, then, can we envisage a 'win-win' strategy? How can we combine 'equality' with employment growth *and* high fertility? At first glance, a Scandinavian welfare model would appear positive-sum in this respect. It has universalized the dual earner household (which sharply reduces poverty which raises families' consumption of services and thus generates jobs) and provides the services and financial incentives for working women to have children. This is of course very costly, but whether this is covered through the public budget or household expenses is essentially a problem of cost-shifting and of the effective pooling of social risks. The more we individualize the cost of children, the more likely we will find ourselves in a low-fertility equilibrium.

At second glance, however, the Nordic formula has an inbuilt Achilles' heel, namely a long-term barrier to job growth that stems from high wage costs and egalitarian earnings. If more earnings inequality is a precondition for labour intensive *private* services to grow, we are back to the fundamental trade-off between equality and jobs. But are we?

One way to think of a win-win strategy is to recall Schumpeter's famous analogy of the autobus: always full of people, but always of different people. Low wages, unpleasant work and even poverty are not necessarily dis-welfare if there is a guarantee against entrapment. If people are mobile and exit at the next bus-stop, low-end jobs will have no consequences for overall life chances. The welfare state as we know it assumed that the labour market would provide well-paid (but not necessarily enjoyable) jobs for all. It put its faith in simple human capital theory and delegated the responsibility for life chances to education and to the labour market. This assumption is anachronistic in a post-industrial labour market which is subject to very rapid technological change, and which can promise full employment only if we accept a mass of low-end (and low productivity) servicing jobs. Income maintenance policies may help dampen income inequalities by subsidizing low wage workers, but they do not help them to get off at the next bus-stop. As we all know, mobility today requires the possession of skills and the capacity to be trained. And, as we also know, there is a basic problem of market failure as far as skill formation is concerned.[18] If, as OECD (1996) shows, about 15–20 per cent of the US adult labour force is functionally illiterate, even among high school graduates, we clearly also have a problem of public sector failure.

A 'win-win' strategy for recasting the welfare state does suggest itself. Firstly, neither privatization nor familialization are Pareto-optimal. This implies that a comprehensive welfare *state* (with or without an extensive third sector) is unavoidable. Secondly, such a strategy must optimize, at once, fertility, and employment and minimize poverty risks. And it must do so in an economic environment that cannot guarantee well-paid jobs for all. Full employment implies more wage inequality. As we have seen, the maximization of employment and fertility is possible, albeit very costly. To a degree this can be offset by the enlarged tax-base, to a degree by cost-shifting strategies. On the one hand, as we have seen, two-earner households enjoy dramatically lower poverty risks (which implies savings in both a static and dynamic sense). On the other hand, it is evident that contemporary pension systems often represent a massive misallocation of resources. The '30 per cent excess' among Italian pensioners is, of course, a source of savings but it is also a perverse mechanism of income redistribution (and savings can be induced elsewhere). A real location of resources from old to young families is potentially 'win-win' because it satisfies the goal of fertility, maximum employment and lessened poverty risks if, that is, these resources are utilized to help families with children reconcile work and fertility. The basic point here is to maximize family welfare by maximizing employment. The basic problem is that it is inherently very costly. The key missing link in this strategy is the jobs-equality trade-off, a trade-off that will remain as long as we are wedded to a 'equality for all, here and now' notion of egalitarianism. As hinted above, this trade-off can be surmounted by a redefinition of what equality means, namely some kind of a guarantee against entrapment in low paid employment. We know that this necessitates a massive investment in education and skills, in making people 'trainable' in the first place.

We can certainly all outline blueprints for reform. The bottom-line issue is essentially political: how can political majorities be mobilized for a reform that may be *societally* Pareto-optimal, but not necessarily so at the individual or group level? Political parties, interest organizations, and corporative veto-blocks represent a median voter who is rapidly getting older and older, a median voter whose definition of welfare and social justice reflects the kind of welfare state that was built in the postwar decades. As we have witnessed in recent years in Italy, France, Germany and Spain, the social identity of the median voter and the system of representation of his/her interests favours a politics of perpetuation of the least unpleasant options.

However, as we have also witnessed, major reforms of social protection systems (such as scaling down pension entitlements, raising retirement age or reducing unemployment and sickness benefits) and of labour market deregulation (such as flexibilizing hiring and layoffs) can be made politically possible under two conditions: either where entrenched collective interests can be seriously weakened (as in Britain), or where governments and the social partners are capable of building durable consensual social pacts (as occurred with the German, Italian and Swedish pension reforms, or with the Italian and Spanish labour market reforms). The preconditions for a British-style strategy are hardly present in most European countries. The prospects for meaningful reforms therefore depend largely on a nation's infrastructure of collective representation.

Notes

1. Most of the data and assertions presented in this paper derive from Esping-Andersen (1999) and from Regini and Esping-Andersen (1998).
2. Departing from a universalist, flat-rate approach, Britain has gradually shifted towards more selectivity since the 1970s.
3. Despite what is commonly believed, there is no correlation between aggregate national savings rates and welfare state size.
4. A simple comparison of the standard male life course in the 1950s and today is illuminating. When, in the postwar years, modern pension systems were designed, the average male was typically employed from age 16–65, followed by about 7–8 years of retirement. Education and youth unemployment means that today's workers start their 'real' careers around 20–25; early retirement means that they retire at age 55–58. And male longevity has risen by 8 years. All in all, we have cut contribution years by 15 or 20 years and we have extended pension years by about the same.
5. Or, alternatively, finance future pension burdens through productivity growth.
6. In most countries for which we have comparable and reliable data, child poverty tends to be three or four times higher in one-earner families (own calculations from LIS databases). There is also substantial evidence from the United States that the heightened earnings polarization and the rise of low-paid employment has been offset by a growth in spouses' labour supply.
7. There is, in fact, a case to be made for acute misallocation of national resources. According to my own analyses of Italian household expenditure data, the average pensioner receives an income that is 30+ per cent higher than what he/she consumes. Since the aged often also control substantial wealth (like home ownership), their real income advantage may be much greater. The consequence may be a perverse system of secondary income distribution, whereby the young come to depend on transfers from their parents and grandparents. The relative welfare of the young will, of course, come to mirror the economic success of their forebears; in other words, the welfare state may be reinforcing class inheritance.
8. The problem here is akin to the Baumol (1967) cost-disease effect in services. If long-run productivity gains in services lag behind manufacturing while real

wage growth is parallel, labour-intensive services will gradually price themselves out of the market. This is precisely the situation in contemporary Europe (except for the Nordic countries where welfare services are furnished by the public sector).

9. Until some years ago, annual Italian public deficits hovered around 10 per cent per annum, a third of which was to cover pension fund shortfalls.

10. The embrace of negative income tax systems is also a deliberate attempt to minimize poverty traps, a problem acutely present in means-tested systems.

11. Occupational welfare coverage in the US was, in the 1970s about 70 per cent for health and 50 per cent for pensions. Today, the former has dropped to about 50 per cent; the latter to 30 per cent (excluding individual plans) (Social Security Bulletin, *Annual Supplement*, 1996).

12. For lack of adequate state, market and family social provision, one might assume that the non-profit sector acts as a substitute. True, comparative data show that voluntary, non-profit social protection is considerably larger in the US than in most European countries. Much of it is of the not-for-profit Blue Shield-Blue Cross type. Yet, even if relatively large, and abundantly tax-favoured, non-profit associations are not even remotely capable of filling the welfare void (Salamon and Anheier, 1996).

13. Note, however, that governments (especially in Sweden, but now also in Denmark) have begun actively to encourage 'competition' from (regulated) non-governmental service providers in general, and co-operatives in particular.

14. Moreover, voluntary associations in Italy are invariably concentrated in the north (where need is less) and are very marginal in the south. This, as I shall argue below, reflects an inherent weakness of a 'third-sector' welfare strategy: voluntary and co-operative welfare organizations rely on ample public funding and support, and also on a strong social capital infrastructure – something that tends to be lacking exactly where most needed (see also Putnam, 1993).

15. Parental dependency implies also delayed family formation and low fertility. Forty per cent of young unemployed Danes have children, compared to about 5 per cent in Italy (data from Bison and Esping-Andersen, 1998).

16. There are some partial exceptions to this: New Zealand, Australia and the UK have all attempted to redesign their social contract, mainly by privatizing and by heavier targeting of social benefits. As Pierson (1994) has shown, the practical results pale in comparison to the intended aims.

17. Household budget data for the US show that an average income household spends about 5–6 per cent on health insurance. This jumps to more than 15 per cent for households in the bottom deciles.

18. Recent data suggest that employer provided training is much lower in the United States than in either Europe or Japan (OECD, 1994).

References

Baumol, W. (1967) 'The Macroeconomics of Unbalanced Growth', *American Economic Review*, 57, pp. 415–26.

Bison, I. and Esping-Andersen, G. (1998) 'Unemployment and Income Packaging in Europe'. Report to the EPUSE Project of the European Commission.

Cameron, D. (1984) 'Social Democracy, Corporatism, Labour Quiescence and the Representation of Economic Interest', in J. Goldthorpe (ed.), *Order and Conflict in Contemporary Capitalism*, Oxford: Oxford University Press.

Esping-Andersen, G. (1999) *The Social Foundations of Postindustrial Economies*, Oxford: Oxford University Press.

Katzenstein, P. (1985) *Small States in World Markets*, Ithaca, NY: Cornell University Press.

OECD (1988) *Ageing Populations*, Paris: OECD.

OECD (1994) *The OECD Jobs Study*, Paris: OECD.

OECD (1996). *Employment Outlook*, Paris: OECD.

OECD (1996) *Literacy and the Economy*, Paris: OECD.

Pierson, P. (1994) *Dismantling the Welfare State?*, Cambridge: Cambridge University Press.

Putnam, R. (1993) *Making Democracy Work: Civic Traditions in Modern Italy*, Princeton: Princeton University Press.

Regini, M. and Esping-Andersen, G. (1998) *Why De-regulate? The Impact of Regulation on Labour Market Performance*, Report to the European Commission, DGXII.

Rosen, S. (1997) 'Public Employment and the Welfare State in Sweden', *Journal of Economic Literature*, 34, pp. 729–40.

Salamon, L. and Anheier, H. (1996) *The Emerging Non-Profit Sector*, Manchester: Manchester University Press.

Index of Names, Countries and Places, Companies, Organizations and Subjects

References in italics indicate figures or tables